(continued inside back cover)

ENGLISH

Floyd C. Watkins
EMORY UNIVERSITY

Edwin T. Martin
EMORY UNIVERSITY

PRACTICAL

HANDBOOK

Houghton Mifflin Company · Boston

The Riverside Press Cambridge

PREFACE

This *Practical English Handbook* aims at presenting the elements of language and composition in a way that is concise and clear without being oversimplified or superficial. It is designed for the student who needs classroom drill on fundamentals as well as for the better prepared student whose chief need is independent study of particular problems in grammar, diction, mechanics, rhetoric, and research technique.

The approach is practical and functional, and instructions are specific. Principles are stated explicitly in heavy type, and care has been taken to avoid blanket exhortations to "spell correctly" or "punctuate in accordance with standard usage." Explanations and exceptions are then given at greater length in "regular" type; and all these are generously illustrated, sometimes with the aid of arrows, boxes, and other graphic devices to make structures and relationships at once apparent.

Beyond a brief introductory review of the basic structure of the English sentence, the theory of grammar is not emphasized. Rather, the focus is on salient features of English grammar with which students have trouble, beginning with a few "first aid" sections on the most common errors.

In matters of diction and usage, this handbook follows the most recent college desk dictionaries. The approach thus recognizes linguistic findings without denying students the support of the limits imposed by accepted practice.

The organization and development of themes is presented in two ways. One shows how the student may develop short papers from miscellaneous notes and an informal working outline; the other, how he may develop a paper of any length by more formal methods of outlining. The discussions of the theme and the research paper first explain in detail the conception and development of a topic, and only then present abstract principles and specimens of the finished product. A special section explains how to adapt research techniques to "controlled research" materials and the use of a casebook or sourcebook. The models given for documentation are based on the forms for footnotes and bibliographies recommended in the *MLA Style Sheet*.

A section on straight thinking analyzes clarity and weaknesses of thought in plain language, without recourse to the difficult terminology of formal logic.

We have tried to make examples and exercises both provocative and realistic, to avoid empty forms and to give intrinsic meaning while at the same time illustrating principles. A number of the exercises are sequential, to increase interest and to give practice in dealing with materials more extensive than discrete sentences. Many exercises are taken from student themes, and others are adapted from the work of professional writers.

Throughout the writing of this book we have been indebted to our helpful and patient associates, particularly to Miss Ruth Walling, Mr. David E. Estes, Professor J. Carlton Nunan, Dean H. Prentice Miller, and Professor Ward Pafford. For valuable suggestions and criticisms made while the manuscript was in process, we are grateful to Professors Jack C. Barnes, University of Maryland; Carl Benson, Alabama Polytechnic Institute; John S. Bowman, Pennsylvania State University; Wilson O. Clough, University of Wyoming; David A. Conlin, Arizona State University; Walter C. Foreman, Oregon State College; James B. Haman, Georgia Institute of Technology; William C. Hummel, Kansas State University; Ralph B. Long, University of Texas; and Mrs. Nina Willis Walter, Los Angeles City College. And especially we are grateful for the encouragement of our long-suffering wives.

FLOYD C. WATKINS
EDWIN T. MARTIN

Emory University, Georgia

of Maryland; Carl Bennett, Abraham Ashworth, Jonathan John S. Bowman, Benjamin ... University ... Henry ... Hirsch ... and his ... associates in ... ...

TO THE STUDENT

How to Use This Book in Revising Themes

In your composition course you will be required to write many themes as a means of extending the range of your expression. But the writing of the theme is only part of your assignment. When your instructor returns your paper to you, he will have marked it for errors of grammar, spelling, and punctuation, and for faults of style and diction and weaknesses in construction. You should then *revise your paper to correct these errors.* One method of revising is shown on the following pages: the correction is neatly written above the error. If more thorough-going revision is necessary, your instructor will tell you how he wishes you to proceed.

The instructor may point out an error by writing in the margin of your paper the number of the appropriate section of this book (see page x). For example, if he writes "15a" beside one of your sentences, look up section 15a. The chart inside the cover of this book (or the table of contents, pages xiii–xxii), together with the guide numbers at the tops of the pages, will help you find the section quickly. You will discover that section 15a discusses dangling constructions. Read it carefully; be sure you understand what a dangling construction is, why your sentence is so marked, and how you can correct it.

Or the instructor may point out an error by using a correction symbol (see page xi). A list of these symbols is given inside the back cover. There you will find that "dg" means "dangling construction," discussed on pages 78–80.

By either method of correction you will be directed to the pages of this handbook that will help you identify your mistakes and show you how to correct them.

Becoming Aware

21c   Becoming Aware.

When I was three years old, my parents

15a   At three years of age, my parents and

my grandmother   grandfather

36   I lived with my Grandmother and Grand-

Southern

36   father in a small southern town. Rusty

divided

33   railroad tracks devided the town, with

stores on one side of the tracks and

large white houses

22c   large, white, houses on the other.

largest

22c   My grandparents owned the largest,

white house in town.   Its

2   white, house in town, the wide front

wide front porch

52b   porch of the house overlooked the

tracks and an immense green valley

were

11   beyond. On the porch was green wicker

chairs with soft cushions and green

x

Becoming Aware

Becoming Aware.

~~When I was three years old, my parents~~

<u>At three years of age,</u> ~~my parents~~ and

my grandmother   grandfather

I lived with my <u>G</u>randmother and <u>G</u>rand-

Southern

father in a small <u>s</u>outhern town. Rusty

divided

railroad tracks <u>devided</u> the town, with

stores on one side of the tracks and

large white houses

large_, white_, houses on the other.

largest

My grandparents owned the largest_,

white house in town.   Its

white_, <u>house</u> in town, the wide front

wide front porch

porch of the <u>house</u> overlooked the

tracks and an immense green valley

were

beyond. On the porch <u>was</u> green wicker

<u>chairs</u> with soft cushions and green

pct

dg

lc

cap

sp

pct

pct

cf

rep

agr v

xi

CONTENTS

PART TWO: *Conventions*

PART THREE: *Words*

GLOSSARY OF USAGE

INDEX

PART ONE

SENTENCE

STRUCTURE

AND GRAMMAR

The Sentence Pattern

In English, as in most languages, the continuous flow of thought is divided into groups of words called sentences. These groups are not arbitrary. Sentences follow a basic pattern and are composed of parts that fit together in well-established ways which are recognized and expected by all users of Standard English, the English of educated speakers and writers.[1] We begin to learn the basic pattern of the sentence almost as soon as we begin to talk; the more we read, think, speak, and write, the more we improve our skill at handling the many varieties of that pattern. For most daily uses, a good many refinements and complexities of the English sentence are seldom needed and rarely practiced. But college students are quickly faced with the need to convey thought and information complex enough to require the full range and variety of the sentence pattern. Those who are not sensitive to the fine points of good sentences or whose environment has not supplied them with good models will need some analysis of how a sentence is constructed and how its parts fit together. The following pages sketch such an analysis.

Subject, Verb, and Complement

Sentences may be brief and direct or long and involved, but they all follow the same basic pattern. The essence

[1]For a fuller definition and discussion of Standard English, see pages 196–204.

of this pattern is a relationship between two parts, called the **subject** and the **verb.** The subject is usually a noun or a pronoun, and the verb makes a statement about the subject.

NOUN SUBJECTS	VERBS	PRONOUN SUBJECTS	VERBS
Dust	settles.	I	believe.
Birds	were flying.	They	could have stayed.
Dawn	broke.	Everyone	had laughed.

The verb is often one word but may be a **phrase,** that is, two or more words functioning together: e.g., *were flying, had laughed, could have stayed.* These groupings are **verb phrases,** and *were, had,* and *could have* are **auxiliaries.**

Few sentences are as simple as these. Many require a third element, a **complement,** that is, a completer. Some verbs express an "action" (not necessarily a physical action) which is performed by the subject and which affects someone or something else called the **direct object.**

SUBJECT	VERB OF ACTION	DIRECT OBJECT
I	like	cake.
Bill	hit	me.
Soldiers	carry	guns.
Horses	eat	oats.
He	saw	red.

The direct object receives the action performed by the subject and named by the verb. In such sentences, the verb is said to be **transitive.** Without objects the first three sentences would be incomplete; the last two would be complete but different in meaning. In such sentences ("Horses eat" and "He saw") where there is no "carry-over" to a direct object, the verb is said to be **intransitive.**

A few verbs, including some very common ones such as *be* and *become*, do not express actions but link the subject to another word which names or describes it. This other word, usually a noun, a pronoun, or an adjective,[2] is called a **subjective complement.**

SUBJECT	LINKING VERB	SUBJECTIVE COMPLEMENT
Albion	is	England.
John	is	captain.
It	was	he.
The engine	was	red.
The pill	tasted	bitter.

These two kinds of complement, the direct object and the subjective complement, and the kinds of statement in which they occur are readily distinguished. **A verb of action** may or may not take a direct object; but when it does, the object is usually someone or something other than the subject. **A linking verb** always takes a subjective complement, and the subjective complement is the same thing as (or an aspect of) the subject.

Sometimes a verb of action has two complements:

She baked **me** a *cake*.

He gave **John** a *shiner*.

Here *cake* and *shiner* are the direct objects, the things baked and given. *Me* and *John* are called **indirect objects.** They may be thought of not as completing the action of the verb but as receiving the direct objects. If these sentences are rephrased ("She baked a cake *for* me" and "He gave a shiner *to* John"), *me* and *John* are objects of the

---

[2]Adjectives are discussed on pages 8–10.

prepositions *to* and *for*.[3] Note that the direct object and the indirect object do not refer to the same person or thing.

In another variant of the sentence pattern, two complements do refer to the same thing:

> The committee elected *John* **chairman**.
> The farmer painted the *barn* **red**.

Here *John* and *barn* are direct objects, and *chairman* and *red* are complements not of the verbs but of these objects. They are therefore called **objective complements.** The sentences could be rephrased to show the relationship between the object and its complement by a linking verb:

> John *was* chairman.
> The barn *was* red.

Note that an objective complement may be either a noun or an adjective. Note also that it follows the direct object, whereas an indirect object precedes the direct object.

In all sentences in which the subject performs the action, the verb is said to be in the **active voice.** When such a sentence has a direct object, it can be "turned around" so that the performer of the action is no longer the subject. The verb then becomes a verb phrase in which a form of *to be* (usually *is, are, was,* or *were*) precedes the main verbal word. Such a verb is said to be in the **passive voice.** Note what happens when some sentences are turned around in this fashion.

ACTIVE VOICE	PASSIVE VOICE
Soldiers *carry* guns.	Guns *are carried* by soldiers.
Horses *eat* oats.	Oats *are eaten* by horses.
He *gave* John a black eye.	John *was given* a black eye.
The committee *elected* John chairman.	John *was elected* chairman.

[3] For prepositions and prepositional phrases, see page 11.

In the first two sentences, the direct object becomes the subject, and the subject becomes the object of the preposition *by*. There is a slight shift in emphasis from the old subject to the new. In the third and fourth sentences the shift is more complicated. One complement has been "retained" after the verb, and the other complement has become the subject. The original subject has disappeared. The principal usefulness of the passive voice is in sentences like these last two, where the performer of the action is unimportant or unknown — or so well known that it need not be mentioned.

> These rocks *were formed* millions of years ago.
> In 1860 Lincoln *was elected* President with a plurality of only forty per cent of the popular vote.

Other important variations in the basic sentence pattern are those used in **commands** and in **questions.** In typical commands the subject, *you*, is not expressed. The remainder of the pattern may or may not contain a complement after the verb.

> *Keep* off the grass.
> *Drive* carefully.
> Please *shut* the door.

The verbs in such sentences are always in the active voice.

A sentence which asks a question usually follows this pattern: auxiliary verb — subject — main verbal word.

STATEMENT	They *stood* at the door without knocking.
QUESTION	*Did* they *stand* at the door without knocking?
STATEMENT	We *were invited* for dinner.
QUESTION	*Were* we *invited* for dinner?
STATEMENT	We *were tired*.
QUESTION	*Were* we *tired*?

Some sentences can be made into questions without this kind of inversion, simply by putting a question mark at the end or by a rising inflection of the voice:

> He went home.
> He went home?

Finally, many sentences can be made **exclamations** simply by punctuation or inflection:

> We were tired!
> Were we tired!
> He went home!

In other exclamatory statements the basic elements are in inverted order:

> How tired we were!

Modifiers

The basic pattern of the sentence, then, is subject — verb, or subject — verb — complement, though there are important variations and inversions. In most sentences, one or more of these elements are elaborated by one or more words which point out (*a, an, the, this, that*), enumerate (*one, some, a few*), intensify (*very, quite, exceedingly*), state specific qualities (*red, tall, slowly*), or make more explicit (*down, here*). A word or group of words which performs such a function is known as a **modifier.**

A modifier of a noun (or a pronoun) is called an **adjective** or an **adjectival modifier.**[4] A modifier of a verb (or an adjective or another kind of word) is called an **adverb** or an **adverbial modifier.**

---

[4]*A, an,* and *the* are often subclassified as "articles," *the* being the definite article, and *a* and *an* the indefinite articles.

ADJECTIVAL MODIFIERS	NOUN	VERB	ADVERBIAL MODIFIERS
This	engine	slowed	down.
A red	engine	slowed	down here.
An old	engine	slowed	down gradually.
The big powerful	engine	slowed	down gradually and cautiously.

The position of modifiers is important, and skill in placing them is extremely important in the writing of good sentences. Except when used as subjective complements, adjectives usually precede nouns. Adverbs are more mobile. They may follow or precede the verbs they modify.

> He sat *down here slowly* and *cautiously* to admire the big powerful engine.
>
> *Slowly* and *cautiously*, he sat *down here* to admire the big powerful engine.

Moreover, some adverbs can modify words of nearly all kinds, and their position markedly affects meaning.

> *Just* two men came to see us.
>
> Two men *just* came to see us.

> He *still* stutters.
>
> *Still*, he stutters.

In the following sentences the adjectival modifiers are *italicized* and the adverbs are in **boldface** type. Notice that modifiers also can have modifiers. Study the positions of these words and be sure you understand what each of them modifies.

The night was **exceedingly** *still*.

Early tonight *the* moon shone **quite brilliantly**.

Several hours later, it was **pitch** *dark*.

Very quickly, Simon stepped **aside**.

Questionable premises **seldom** yield **absolutely** *dependable* conclusions.

Because of the modifiers, these sentences can express more highly elaborated meanings than those considered earlier. The sentence pattern is now expanded to include:

subject + modifiers—verb + modifiers—complement + modifiers

We now have five word classes: nouns, pronouns, verbs, adjectives, and adverbs. According to the way they are used in sentences, many words can belong to more than one class. Thus *tonight* may be used as a noun and a subject:

Tonight is not to be forgotten.

Or it may be an adverb, as in

Tonight the moon will be full.

Phrases

Each of the functions noted so far can be performed not only by a single word but also by a group of words. These word groups are of two kinds: **phrases,** groups which do not contain a subject-verb relationship; and **clauses,** groups which do contain such a relationship.

As we have seen, the **verb phrase** is a group of two or more words acting together as a verb.

The invasion *was expected*.

They *had told* the truth.

He *has sent* the man away.

Except for verb phrases, the most common kind of phrase in English is the **prepositional phrase,** a group consisting of a connective word, the **preposition,** and a word or group of words (usually including a noun or a pronoun) known as the **object of the preposition.** The connections expressed by prepositions are of several kinds:

PLACE	TIME	OTHER RELATIONSHIPS (possession, accompaniment, comparison, etc.)
on the table	after dark	of wealth
in the air	between meals	with him
over the hill	during class	like lightning
beside himself	before church	about a dozen
under the tree	until then	for good measure

The object of a preposition frequently has one or more modifiers: "on *the library* table," "of *exceptional* wealth."

The preposition also may have modifiers: "*precisely* in the center."

Usually a prepositional phrase modifies a noun, a pronoun, or a verb, but it can modify an adjective or an adverb:

NOUN   The book *on the table* was mine.

VERB   The compliment was intended *for you.*

VERB, NOUN   Gnats hovered *in the air over the hill.*

ADJECTIVE   I was ready *for a change.*

ADVERB   They responded favorably, *in the main.*

A third type of phrase clusters about a **verbal.** A verbal is a word derived from a verb but not capable of acting by itself as the verb in its given sentence; that is, it is not a finite verb. These are sentences with finite verbs:

11

He *acts*.
They *received* him.

These are not sentences but verbal phrases:

him *acting*
him *to act*
receiving him
to receive him

The verbals are **infinitives, participles,** and **gerunds.** They have three forms:

INFINITIVE	-ING FORM (present participle or gerund)	PAST PARTICIPLE
to believe (present active)	believing	believed
to be believed (present passive)		
to have believed (perfect active)		
to have been believed (perfect passive)		
to run	running	run
to go	going	gone

Participles serve as adjectives, and gerunds as nouns. Thus the -*ing* form is called a participle when used as an adjective, and a gerund when used as a noun.

PARTICIPLE *Doubting* Thomas felt the wound.

Believing neither story, I could not reach a conclusion.

The patient slept, *resting* comfortably.

GERUND   *Doubling* seldom makes *deciding* easier.

Seeing is *believing.*

The infinitive is usually, but not always, preceded by *to:*

Show me the way *to go* home.

He helped me (*to*) *move* the furniture.

They let him *go.*

It serves as noun, adjective, or adverb.

NOUN (subject)   Simply *to sit* in the sun would please me best of all.

NOUN (complement)   I like *to read.*

ADJECTIVE   A time *to weep*, and a time *to laugh;* a time *to mourn*, and a time *to dance.*

ADVERB   I am ready *to go.*
                       He came *to stay.*

Although verbals are used as nouns or as modifiers, they retain much of their character as verbs and can themselves have subjects, complements, or modifiers. They may thus form phrases:

Believing the battle to be lost, the King's men surrendered.

This sentence opens with a participial phrase. The participle, *believing*, has the rest of the phrase as object, and *battle* is subject of the infinitive *to be lost*. The whole phrase modifies *the King's men*. A verbal phrase may be based on a participle, a gerund, or an infinitive.

PARTICIPLE   *Neighing* in fright, the horse shied at the
(modifier)
                    figure *looming* out of the mist.

GERUND (subject)   *Expecting* Arthur's return gave the Welsh stubborn courage.

GERUND (direct object)   We hated *begging* for our bread.

GERUND (object of preposition)   We were reduced to *begging* for mercy.

INFINITIVES (subject and complement)   *To be* courageous is *to be* confident.

INFINITIVE (modifier)   *To be* courageous, one must have confidence.

Note again that verbals retain part of their ability to function as verbs in that they can have subjects, complements, and modifiers of their own.

Clauses

The second kind of word group, the **clause,** differs from the phrase in that it contains a subject-verb relationship. Every sentence contains at least one clause. The following are clauses, but not all of them are sentences:

> The *Progressive Movement* **dominated** American politics from 1900 to 1912.
>
> And Progressive *leaders* **included** members of both major parties.
>
> *Who* **were** reformers eager to correct social evils.
>
> Because *they* **believed** in progress.
>
> That big *industry and* big *politics* **brought** corruption.

Each of these groups has a subject (in italics) and a verb (in boldface type). The first two can stand alone as sentences; they can also be described as **independent clauses.** The last three groups are **dependent** or **subordinate clauses;** they are introduced by connectives which signal their dependent rank and the nature of their relationship to something else.

To grasp the pattern of many complicated sentences, and to write such sentences well, it is necessary to understand the use of these and other connectives known as **conjunctions.** A small group of conjunctions link equal words, phrases, or clauses. These are the **coordinating conjunctions.** Of these the most widely used is *and*, which can link many different elements:

SUBJECTS	John *and* I wished we had never been born.
COMPLEMENTS	Our chief executive is President *and* Commander-in-Chief.
VERBS	Eat, drink, *and* be merry.
ADJECTIVES	Wet, cold, *and* miserable, the refugees straggled over the border.
ADVERBS	His head swam dizzily *and* sickeningly.
PREPOSITIONAL PHRASES	She looked on the desk, in the bookcase, *and* on the floor.
CLAUSES	The furniture was tattered, *and* the rugs were threadbare.

Other coordinating conjunctions are *but*, *or*, and *nor:*

Go if you like, *but* ask no help from me.

Hot *or* cold, day *or* night, the watch must be kept.

I was not asked, *nor* would I agree if I were.

Some coordinating conjunctions are used in pairs. These are known as **correlatives.** The chief of these are *either* . . .

or, *neither . . . nor*, *not . . . but* (or *not only . . . but also*), *both . . . and*.

> These spirits dwelt *both* on the hills *and* in the fields.
>
> *Not only* his classmates *but* (*but also*, or *but even*) his teachers sensed his scorn for his social inferiors.
>
> *Neither* snow, *nor* rain, *nor* heat, *nor* gloom of night stays these couriers from the swift completion of their appointed rounds.

Sentences containing two or more independent clauses joined by coordinating conjunctions are called **compound sentences.**

> Black clouds loomed on the horizon, *and* lightning flashed in the distance, *but* no rain came.
>
> The scientist doubts, the prophet believes, *and* the poet feels.
>
> *Not only* was primitive man in awe of the forces of nature, *but* he believed in the power of magic to placate them.

For, *yet*, and *so* can also serve as coordinators, though they have other uses. *For* is often a preposition, and *yet* and *so* are frequently adverbial. (They sat *for* hours. We had not *yet* come. It got *so* late that they left.) They may also be coordinators, as in the following sentences:

> They stayed, *for* we had not yet come.
>
> They stayed, *yet* they knew it had grown late.
>
> It grew late, *so* finally they left.

Two independent clauses can also be linked by another kind of connective, the **conjunctive adverb,** such as *however*, *moreover*, *therefore*, or *nevertheless*.

> The United Nations was established in a glow of hope; *however*, it soon became clear that no nation would give up any part of its sovereignty.
>
> The company declared an extra dividend in December; it did so, *moreover*, in the face of declining sales and rising costs.

In such sentences the clauses are separated by a semicolon, not a comma, suggesting a strong pause and a marked break. In some sentences either kind of connective can be used.

> The United Nations was established in a glow of hope, *but* it soon became clear that no nation would give up any part of its sovereignty. (Compare sentence on page 16.)

While every sentence has at least one independent clause, many also have one or more **dependent clauses.** A dependent clause functions as a noun, an adjective, or an adverb, and is nearly always introduced by a connective which signals its relation to the independent clause. This connective is a **subordinating conjunction.**

The following sentences contain **noun clauses** in a variety of functions, and hence of positions within the sentence:

SUBJECT	*That science can save us* is doubtful in the extreme.
SUBJECTIVE COMPLEMENT	The truth is *that we simply do not know.*
DIRECT OBJECT	He asked *when I would be at home.* I told him *what he should say.*
OBJECT OF PREPOSITION	I have nothing but praise for *whoever fired the shot.*

Most noun clauses are introduced by *that, whoever, whomever,* or *whatever;* a few by *who, why, what,* or *when.* Some have no expressed connective:

> I told him *I didn't know.* (Often *that* is omitted before a noun clause which is a complement.)

A second type of dependent clause is the **adjective clause,** which has for a connective one of the **relative pronouns,** *who, whose, whom, which,* or *that,* and sometimes the adverb *where,* meaning *at which* or *in which.* An adjective clause generally comes immediately after the word it modifies.

> I hate a girl *who sulks.*
> The man *whose bread you eat* should not be scorned.
> There goes one politician *whom I admire.*
> This is the house *that* (or *which*) *Jack built.*
> That is the house *where I was born.*

Sometimes the relative is not expressed.

> the man *I love*
> the girl *I left behind me*

An adjective clause is not mobile. Because the relative is a pronoun and refers to a single word, its reference can be confused if the clause is not carefully placed:

> The *book* was no longer on the table *which I had brought home from the library.*

This is why an adjective clause should usually appear directly after the word it modifies.

The third and perhaps most common type of dependent clause is the **adverbial clause.** Most adverbial clauses are introduced by **adverbial conjunctions** and so are easily identified. These conjunctions express a variety of relationships:

CONDITION	if, unless
TIME	when, while, as, after, before, since, (as soon) as, (as long) as
CAUSE	as, because, whereas, since
CONCESSION	though, although, granted that, while, whereas
PURPOSE	so that, in order that, that, so
PLACE	where
COMPARISON	as . . . as, so . . . as, as, as if

Although clauses introduced by these conjunctions are called adverbial, they do not always modify the verb in another clause but more often the clause as a whole. Partly for this reason, they are mobile whereas noun and adjective clauses are not:

> *If man is to survive*, we must avoid using atomic bombs.
> We must, *if man is to survive*, avoid using atomic bombs.
> We must avoid using atomic bombs *if man is to survive*.

The versatile conjunction *where* can introduce all three types of subordinate clauses:

NOUN CLAUSE   *Where he lives* remains a mystery.

ADJECTIVE CLAUSE   The town *where he lives* is secluded.

ADVERB CLAUSE   I want to live *where he lives*.

A sentence containing an independent clause and one or more dependent clauses is called a **complex sentence.** A sentence containing two or more independent clauses and one or more dependent clauses is called a **compound-complex sentence.**

The foregoing sketch of the English sentence pattern has concentrated on main outlines. There are many variations, but these should give little trouble to the student who understands the principles described above well enough to sense the structure in the sentences he reads. An awareness of structure will improve both his ability to read with comprehension and his control of the pattern as he uses it in the sentences he writes.

EXERCISE

In the following sentences, identify each word as noun, pronoun, verb, adjective, adverb, etc., and give its function in its sentence (subject, verb of action, linking verb, direct object, subjective complement, etc.). Also identify phrases and clauses and describe the function of each.

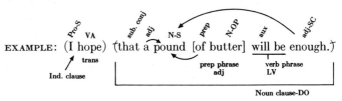

EXAMPLE: (I hope) {that a pound [of butter] will be enough.}

1. The postman handed me two letters.

2. He saw the shadow of the plane.

3. The ashtrays were empty.

4. Because he had always wanted to read the book, he bought it.

5. Mary attended the concert, but her husband stayed at home and slept.

6. He knew that the answer was correct.

7. It was he.

8. Having a theme to write, I spent the afternoon in the library.

9. He walked rapidly and arrived at his destination before it rained.

10. The turkey which he won in the raffle died before he left the fair.

11. An ornithologist is a student of birds.

12. That the motion will pass is doubtful.

13. Call me Ishmael.

14. Swimming is my favorite sport.

15. The friendly mechanic gave my car a checkup.

16. That either Philip or Tony had broken it was obvious.

17. They licked the platter clean.

18. Screaming with rage, the child was carried from the room.

19. The language of the law is exceedingly formal; however, this formality serves a purpose.

20. He who strives shall endure and prevail.

First Aid for
Sentences

To BE A SENTENCE, a group of words must satisfy two requirements: it must have a subject and a finite verb, and it must be capable of standing alone. To be an effective sentence, it must in addition show by its structure the relationships among the ideas it expresses; that is, it must make proper use of coordination and subordination. The following

---

When a student leaves home for the first time and enters college, he faces many new responsibilities.

Complete sentence

The arrangement of a schedule, the adjustment to new friends, the management of his budget.

Noun plus prepositional phrase, three times; no subject-verb structure

No parents calling him several times before he gets out of bed each morning.

Noun plus verbal plus dependent clause; no independent clause

Teachers who merely make assignments without reminding the student to study.

Noun plus "who" clause; no independent clause

That he should spend a certain amount of time on each unit of work.

Dependent "that" clause; should not stand alone

Because the freshman must become a man, live independently, and think for himself.

Clause made dependent by "Because"; should not stand alone

sections (1–6) discuss the most common sentence faults and point out how to avoid or correct them.

1/Sentence Fragment

A fragment is a part of a sentence written as a complete sentence. It can be a dependent clause, a phrase, or any other word group which violates the accepted sentence pattern. The principal objection to fragments is that they often reflect incomplete thinking and poor control of the sentence.

Compare the fragments on the left below with the completed sentences on the right. You will see that these fragments serve no purpose; they divide the thought at illogical points and they do not save words.

Complete sentence unchanged	When a student leaves home for the first time and enters college, he faces many new responsibilities:
Fragment made part of first sentence with colon	the arrangement of a schedule, the adjustment to new friends, the management of his budget.
Subject and verb added	*He cannot depend* on his parents to call him several times before he gets out of bed each morning.
"Who" omitted; "make" attached to "teachers"	Teachers merely make assignments without reminding the student to study
	and
Clause changed to phrase and made part of preceding sentence	to spend a certain amount of time on each unit of work.
"Because" omitted; clause stands alone	The freshman must become a man, live independently, and think for himself.

Incomplete sentences are of course common in conversation, for they save unnecessary repetition when the meaning is clear from the context.

CONVERSATION   "Do you study hard?"
                "Yes. Sometimes. Especially when the prof gives
                    long assignments."

                "Got a match?"
                "Here."
                "Thanks."

Fragments are therefore common in written dialogue where the aim is to reproduce the patterns of informal speech.

Sometimes fragments are used in more formal kinds of writing for special effect or emphasis.

FICTION   He stood naked and alone in darkness, far from the lost
           world of the streets and faces; he stood upon the ramparts
           of his soul, before the lost land of himself; heard inland
           murmurs of lost seas, the far interior music of the horns.
           The last voyage, the longest, the best.

                                    Thomas Wolfe, *Look Homeward, Angel*[1]

The incomplete sentence at the end of the passage contrasts effectively with the long, formally constructed sentence that precedes it.

EXPOSITION   It is one of the loveliest of stories. *So much irony; so
              much humour; so kind and understanding; and wrapped
              up in the most delicate poetic mood.*

                                    Sean O'Faolain, *The Short Story*[2]

This long and carefully constructed fragment lacks subject and verb ("It has" or "It contains"), but these are immediately clear from context. There is a vast difference between such clearly intentional constructions as those above

---

[1]Reprinted by permission of Charles Scribner's Sons, publishers.
[2]Reprinted by permission of the Devin-Adair Company, publishers.

and the pointless disregard of pattern in the fragments on page 24. Sentence fragments are generally considered unacceptable in college work, and students are advised to leave them to more experienced writers.

2/Comma Fault

The comma signals a slight pause and has many uses within clauses. Hence a comma is usually not a strong enough mark between independent clauses which are not joined by a coordinating conjunction. Use of a comma alone in such constructions is a comma fault, a failure to recognize the line between independent clauses.

There are four principal ways to express the relation between two independent clauses:

(1) Use a *period* and write two sentences.

(2) Use a *semicolon.*

(3) Use a *comma* and a *coordinating conjunction.*

(4) Make one of the clauses dependent.

COMMA FAULT   Human nature is seldom as simple as it appears in fiction, an author must simplify to give pattern to the lives of his characters.

CORRECTIONS   (1) Human nature is seldom as simple as it appears in fiction. An author must simplify to give pattern to the lives of his characters.

(2) Human nature is seldom as simple as it appears in fiction; an author must simplify to give pattern to the lives of his characters.

(3) Human nature is seldom as simple as it appears in fiction, *and* an author must simplify to give pattern to the lives of his characters.

(4) *Because* human nature is seldom as simple as it appears in fiction, an author must simplify to give pattern to the lives of his characters.

In any particular sentence, one or two of these solutions will be more appropriate than the others. Here (1), (2), and (4) are preferable to (3).

It is often possible to subordinate one of the clauses or reduce it to a phrase or even a single word. In (4), one of the independent clauses is made a dependent adverbial clause. The sentence might also be rewritten as follows:

ADVERBIAL CLAUSE   Human nature is *so* complex *that an author must simplify to give pattern to the lives of his characters.*

(or)

PHRASE   An author must simplify *the complexities of human nature* to give pattern to the lives of his characters.

A comma is usually not a strong enough mark between two independent clauses when the second is introduced by a conjunctive adverb, such as *however, moreover, therefore,* or *furthermore.* The methods of correction are similar to those outlined above.

In some sentences where the clauses are brief and closely related, a comma is sufficient. These are called "contact clauses":

> Our dog eats Growlo, his coat shines.
>
> Mary was my sister, I loved her very much.

3/Fused Sentence

Two independent clauses with no punctuation and no connective constitute a fused sentence. With no separation the clauses blur into each other. A fused sentence is usually more annoying to the reader than a comma fault, and more destructive to meaning.

FUSED   Human nature is seldom as simple as it appears in fiction
an author must simplify to give pattern to the lives of his
characters.

A fused sentence may be corrected in the same ways as
a comma fault. (See §2.)

EXERCISES

(1) *Point out the complete sentences in the following paragraphs.*
(2) *Point out the sentence fragments, comma faults, and fused sentences; copy the paragraph and correct these errors.*

A

When I was a boy, there was but one permanent ambition
among my comrades in our village on the west bank of the
Mississippi River. To be a steamboatman. We had transient
ambitions of other sorts, however they were only transient. When
a circus came and went, it left us all burning to become clowns,
the first Negro minstrel show that ever came to our section left
us all suffering to try that kind of life now and then we had a hope
that, if we lived and were good, God would permit us to be pirates.
These ambitions fading out, each in its turn. The ambition to be
a steamboatman always remaining.

Adapted from Mark Twain, *Life on the Mississippi*

B

The art of pleasing is a very necessary one to possess. But a very difficult one to acquire. It can hardly be reduced to rules your own good sense and observation will teach you more of it than I can. "Do as you would be done by" is the surest method that I know of pleasing. Observe carefully what pleases you in others, probably the same things in you will please others. If you are pleased with the complaisance and attention of others to your humours, your tastes, or your weaknesses. Depend upon it, the same complaisance and attention on your part to theirs will equally please them. Take the tone of the company that you are in do not pretend to give it, be serious, gay, or even trifling, as you find the present humour of the company, this is an attention due from every individual to the majority. Do not tell stories in company there is nothing more tedious and disagreeable, if by chance you know a very short story, and exceedingly applicable to the present subject of conversation, tell it in as few words as possible, even then, throw out that you do not love to tell stories. But that the shortness of it tempted you.

Adapted from Lord Chesterfield, *Letters to His Son*

4/Choppy Sentences

Short and choppy sentences not only become monotonous but fail to express thought relationships: cause, condition, concession, time sequence, purpose, and so on.

CHOPPY   He wanted a college education. He was a good student. His family was poor. The college gave him a scholarship.

Recognizing and expressing the relationships among these thoughts can yield one sentence like the following, in which three of the independent sentences have been reduced to phrases:

IMPROVED   The college gave him a scholarship because he needed money, wanted an education, and was an excellent student.

In the following sentences, notice how choppiness can be avoided by combining independent clauses and by using more dependent clauses:

CHOPPY	IMPROVED
That year the rains were heavy. They drowned out the crops.	That year the heavy rains drowned out the crops.
Jeff struck our last match. The wind was strong. It blew out our match.	The wind was so strong that it blew out our last match just as Jeff struck it.
Mary dropped listlessly into the hammock. She said that she was bored to death. Her grandmother was unsympathetic. She said that children of *her* generation were not bored. They were too busy to be bored.	Mary dropped listlessly into the hammock and said she was bored to death; but her grandmother, who was unsympathetic, replied that children of *her* generation were too busy to be bored.

Particularly in exposition, constant use of short and simple sentences sketches your thought but does not develop it, since most of the relationships between ideas are necessarily left unexpressed. The reader must then figure out these relationships without help and will almost certainly miss some of them.

EXERCISES

A

Make one sentence out of each of the groups below.

Main Street is a novel by Sinclair Lewis.
It was published in 1920.
It is a satire.
It condemns a typical small town, Gopher Prairie.
It attacks conventional, middle-class life throughout the country.

Carol Kennicott is the heroine.
She expresses Lewis's views.
She hopes to reform the town.
She is ultimately frustrated by the conventional and unresponsive citizenry.

Lewis satirizes the residents of Gopher Prairie.
He says that they are smug and self-satisfied.
In his opinion they are shallow hypocrites.
His primary indictment is that they are dull.
He says that they have made dullness their god.

B

Improve the following passage by combining choppy sentences into more fully developed ones.

Carol had walked for thirty-two minutes. She had completely covered the town. She had walked east and west, north and south. She stood at the corner of Main Street and Washington Avenue. She despaired.

Main Street had two-story brick shops. Its wooden residences were a story-and-a-half tall. From concrete walk to walk the street was a muddy expanse. Fords and lumber-wagons huddled on it. It was too small to absorb her. The broad, straight gashes of the streets were unenticing. They let in the grasping prairie on every side. She realized the vastness of the land. It was empty. A few blocks away stood a skeleton iron windmill. It was on a farm at the north end of Main Street. It was like the ribs of a dead cow. She thought of the coming of the Northern winter. The unprotected houses would crouch together. They would be in terror of storms. The storms would gallop out of that wild waste. They were small and weak. They were little brown houses.

They were shelters for sparrows. They were not homes for warm

laughing people.

Adapted from Sinclair Lewis, *Main Street*[3]

5/Excessive Coordination

Too many short clauses connected by *and, but, or, nor, yet, for, so,* and *and so* are monotonous and can be misleading. Too much coordination may hide other thought relationships and so distort meaning. English is rich in subordinating connectives, both prepositions and conjunctions, and a major skill in writing is the ability to use them.

STRINGY   This mountain is six thousand feet high, *and* it is only four miles from the airport, *and* the field is not a very large one, *but* no plane has ever crashed on it.

If the final clause is to be stressed, it can easily be made the independent clause in a complex sentence retaining one *and.*

IMPROVED   *Although* this mountain is six thousand feet high *and* only four miles from the small airport, no plane has ever crashed on it.

STRINGY   The Senator was a liberal, *and so* he was in favor of the welfare program, *and* the new tax bill seemed to him inadequate, *and so* he voted against it.

IMPROVED   Being a liberal and feeling that the new tax bill was inadequate to support the welfare program, the Senator voted against it.
        (The first two clauses have been subordinated and shortened; the participles *being* and *feeling* modify *the Senator.*)

---

[3]Adapted for this exercise by permission of the publishers, Harcourt, Brace and Company, Inc.

EXERCISE

Correct excessive coordination in the following by subordinating some of the ideas.

Yesterday I was sitting at the breakfast table, and I was talking to a young freshman. I have a vital interest in him; so I was talking to him about his next year's course. I suggested a subject, and told him I thought it would be good for him to take. "Is it easy?" was his first question, but I answered in the negative, and his interest waned. We must in time work in the world, and it has few easy roads. It has few "snap" courses. We shall be forced to do a great many hard things. If I were a freshman I should learn to do such things early.

Adapted from Thomas Arkle Clark,
"If I Were a Freshman Again"[4]

6/Improper Subordination

Sections 4 and 5 suggest ways to subordinate for variety and emphasis. Below are two pitfalls to avoid in deciding which thoughts should be subordinated.

---

[4]From *The American College Magazine*, July 1910.

6a/Placing the main thought in a dependent construction creates upside-down subordination.

In the following sentence, if the main thought is that a child was killed, that thought should be expressed in the main clause.

ACCURATE   *The child was killed* as he ran across the street.

DISTORTED   The child ran across the street *as he was killed.*

But if the important thought is the manner of the child's death, the sentence might read:

The child was running across the street when he was killed.

6b/A series of overlapping subordinate constructions, in which each depends on the last, can be monotonous and confusing.

A "stair-step sentence" of this kind often contains a number of constructions beginning with *who, which, that, for,* and *of.*

Othello is a play

which tells about a dark Moor

who loved the Venetian girl Desdemona

who was innocent of the sin of adultery

that he accused her of

after Iago had aroused his suspicions.

IMPROVED   The play *Othello* tells the story of a dark Moor's love
            for the innocent Venetian girl Desdemona and of his
            accusing her of adultery after Iago had aroused his
            suspicions.

The structure of this sentence may be plotted thus:

                                    of a dark Moor's love for the
                                  / innocent Venetian girl Desdemona
                                /
The play *Othello* tells the story   and
                                \
                                  of his accusing her of adultery
                                      /
                                    after Iago had aroused his
                                                    suspicions.

STILL BETTER   In the play, Othello accuses his beloved and in-
                nocent Desdemona of adultery because Iago has
                aroused his suspicion.

This sentence breaks into three simple parts.

PREPOSITIONAL PHRASE   In the play

INDEPENDENT CLAUSE   Othello accuses his beloved and innocent
                        Desdemona of adultery

ADVERBIAL CLAUSE   because Iago has aroused his suspicion.

The ability to write effective sentences depends very
largely on the ability to sense relationships and find neat
and simple ways of expressing them.

EXERCISE

Improve the subordination in the following passage.

For two years Mr. John Smith had been rather a nonentity on the City Improvement Committee though he arose one day and made a name for himself. He moved that the Committee publicly reprimand Mr. Frank Johnson, who had bought up the miserable houses in the worst slum area just before the city had finally appropriated the money which was intended for use in the slum-clearance project that was to be partly financed by funds that the Federal Government had promised for the improvement of the city. Mr. Smith again sat down after the furor grew louder and louder until the chairman had to pound upon the table and command order from each member of the Committee individually. Mr. Johnson spoke heatedly in defense of himself after he finally received the floor. The ensuing debate lasted long into the night and the decision hung in the balance, though Mr. Smith's motion was at last carried. Mr. Smith easily won his next election since he became known to the people as "Honest John."

Grammar:
The Forms of Words

LIKE SOME other languages, English once had an extensive system of endings and other changes in word form which showed the relationship of words to each other within sentences. In English most of these changes, called **inflections**, have long since disappeared. Some nouns, for instance, had one ending when used as a subject (Old English *seonu*, sinew) and another when used as an object (*seonwe*). Pronouns still have functional forms (*I, me; they, them*), and there are some distinct verb forms (*go, goes; ran, run; went, gone*). But these are only fragments of a once extensive system of changes in form to show grammatical relationships. Today, problems of change in the form of words cluster chiefly around four parts of speech: verbs, pronouns, adjectives, and adverbs.[1] The following sections (7–14) treat these changes.

7/Verb Forms

All forms of a verb are built upon the three **principal parts.** These are the present infinitive (without *to*), the

---

[1]Nouns are of course inflected for the plural and the possessive (*boy, boys, boy's, boys'*), but the problems arising from these form changes are matters of mechanics as much as of grammar and are therefore discussed under Spelling (§33e) and The Apostrophe (§35).

past tense form, and the past participle. The principal parts of the verb *to walk* are *walk, walked, walked.*

English verbs are regular or irregular. **Regular verbs** (such as *help, talk, nail, open, close*) form the past tense and the past participle by adding *-d* or *-ed* or sometimes *-t* (as in *burnt, dwelt*). **Irregular verbs** usually form the past tense and the past participle by a change in the root vowel: *drink, drank, drunk.* Consult a dictionary when in doubt; if only the infinitive form is given, the verb is regular. For an irregular verb like *think*, the dictionary also gives *thought*, the form of the past tense and the past participle, and *thinking*, the present participle. The principal parts are *think, thought, thought.* For a verb as irregular as *see*, the dictionary lists all three principal parts: *see, saw, seen.* The principal parts of troublesome verbs must simply be learned.

EXERCISE

Cover the two right columns in the list below and recite the principal parts of these verbs. Then check, and study those you missed.

PRINCIPAL PARTS OF SOME TROUBLESOME VERBS

INFINITIVE	PAST TENSE	PAST PARTICIPLE
awake	awoke, awaked	awoke, awaked
be	was	been
begin	began	begun
bid (to offer as a price or to make a bid in playing cards)	bid	bid
bid (to command, order)	bade, bid	bidden, bid
blow	blew	blown
burst	burst	burst
choose	chose	chosen

come	came	come
do	did	done
deal	dealt	dealt
dive	dived, dove	dived
	(colloquial)	
drag	dragged	dragged
draw	drew	drawn
drink	drank	drunk
drive	drove	driven
drown	drowned	drowned
fall	fell	fallen
freeze	froze	frozen
give	gave	given
grow	grew	grown
hang (to execute)	hanged	hanged
hang (to suspend)	hung	hung
know	knew	known
lead	led	led
lend	lent	lent
ring	rang	rung
run	ran	run
see	saw	seen
shine (to give light)	shone	shone
shine (to polish)	shined	shined
shrink	shrank, shrunk	shrunk, shrunken
sing	sang	sung
sink	sank, sunk	sunk
swim	swam	swum
swing	swung	swung
take	took	taken
write	wrote	written

In a few confusing pairs of verbs, it helps to remember that one is transitive (takes a direct object) and the other is intransitive (does not take a direct object):

TRANSITIVE	lay (to place)	laid	laid
INTRANSITIVE	lie (to recline)	lay	lain
TRANSITIVE	set (place in position)	set	set
INTRANSITIVE	sit (be seated)	sat	sat
TRANSITIVE	raise (lift)	raised	raised
INTRANSITIVE	rise (get up)	rose	risen

Lie (to tell a falsehood) is intransitive like *lie* (to recline), but has different principal parts: *lie, lied, lied.* There are two important intransitive uses of *set.* A hen *sets.* Concrete also *sets.* The intransitive verbs above have the root vowel *i* in the present tense: *lie, sit, rise.*

8/Tense and Sequence of Tenses

For each of the three time designations — present, past, and future — English verbs have three major tense forms: simple, progressive, and perfect.

	IRREGULAR	REGULAR
SIMPLE		
Present	I go	I walk
Past	I went	I walked
Future	I shall (or will) go	I shall (or will) walk
PROGRESSIVE[1]		
Present	I am going	I am walking
Past	I was going	I was walking
Future	I shall (or will) be going	I shall (or will) be walking
PERFECT		
Present	I have gone	I have walked
Past	I had gone	I had walked
Future	I shall (or will) have gone	I shall (or will) have walked

[1]Only the simple progressive forms are given here. There are in addition the forms with the auxiliary *do* (*I do go*, etc.), and the perfect forms (*I have been going, I had been going, I shall have been going*, etc.).

In general, the present, past, and future forms express present, past, and future times respectively, but there are exceptions. Compare the following:

I *eat* lunch. (Simple present — with the force of repeated or habitual action.)

I *am eating* lunch. (Present progressive — present action.)

I *leave* for New York tomorrow. (Present tense — future action.)

I *am leaving* in fifteen minutes. (Present progressive — future action.)

As the last two examples above illustrate, the time expressed by the tense form is often qualified or altered by an adverb or adverbial phrase.

The three perfect tenses indicate time or action completed before another time or action and are used in well-defined sequences: present perfect with present, past perfect with past, future perfect with future.

Study the following illustrations:

PRESENT PERFECT — PRESENT

I *have bought* my ticket, and I **am waiting** for the bus.

I *have bought* my ticket **already.** (Note that the controlling time word need not be a verb.)

PAST PERFECT — PAST

I *had bought* my ticket, and I **was waiting** for the bus.

I *had bought* my ticket before **three o'clock.**

FUTURE PERFECT — FUTURE

I *shall have eaten* by the time we **go.** (The controlling word, *go*, is a present tense form but has future force.)

I *shall have eaten* by **one o'clock.**

The future perfect is formal and rare. Less formal and more usual is a simple future tense (instead of the future perfect) linked with another future action which may be indicated by a verb or an adverbial expression:

> I *shall eat* before you **go.** (Future before present with future force.)
>
> I *shall eat* before you **have** to go. (Future before present with future force.)
>
> I'*ll eat* before **one o'clock.** (Future before future time adverbially expressed — no second verb.)
>
> I'*ll have* lunch before **one.** (Future before future time adverbially expressed — no second verb.)

In general, other sequences of related verbs or expressions of time should also reflect their relationships in time.

TWO PAST ACTIONS

> The sailor *stood* on the shore and *threw* pebbles at the seagulls. (Not *throws*.)
>
> He *turned* away when he *saw* me watching him.

TWO PRESENT ACTIONS

> As the school year *draws* to a close, the students *are swept* into a whirl of activities.

FUTURE ACTIONS

> We *shall fight* on the beaches, we *shall fight* on the landing grounds, we *shall fight* in the fields and in the streets, we *shall fight* in the hills; we *shall* never *surrender.* (Winston Churchill)

But again there are exceptions. Statements of natural truth or scientific law are generally in the present tense regardless of the controlling verb. Compare:

> The ancient Greek scholars *believed* that the earth *was* motionless.
>
> In 1851, Foucault's pendulum *gave* convincing proof that the earth *rotates* on its axis.

Verbals are generally in the present tense when they express action which occurs at the same time as that of the controlling verb, even though the verb expresses past time.

> I wanted *to go.*
>
> NOT I wanted *to have gone.*
>
> I had expected *to meet* my friends at the game.
>
> NOT I had expected *to have met* my friends at the game.
>
> I would have preferred *to wait* until they came.
>
> NOT I would have preferred *to have waited* until they came.

An exception is the perfect participle, a formal way to express an action which precedes another action.

> *Having completed* the operation, the surgeon left at noon.
>
> BUT NOT *After having completed* the operation, the surgeon left at noon. (*After* is redundant — repetitious; the perfect participle expresses the idea by itself.)

EXERCISE

Choose the correct form of the verb in the following sentences.

1. After graduation, the students realized how much extracurricular activities (contributed, had contributed) to their education.

2. That old gun has been (laying, lying) on the bench since I (laid, lay) it there yesterday.

3. (Having slept, After having slept, Sleeping) all afternoon, I felt rested when the basketball game began at eight o'clock.

4. By next month I shall have (know, knew, known, knowed) him for four years.

5. He would have preferred (to wait, to have waited) until the next day.

6. I (mailed, have mailed) the letter ten minutes ago.

7. I intended to (lie, lay) down for an hour, but John came over to (sit, set) and chat for a while.

8. A heavy rain makes the river (rise, raise) rapidly; last week it (raised, rose, risen) to flood level.

9. Carefully (laid, lain) away was every letter which Algernon had ever written her.

10. He was heartbroken to learn that his friend (died, had died) only the day before.

11. Galileo demonstrated that a light body (falls, fell) as rapidly as a heavy one.

12. He (sat, set) the chair in the shade of the tree and (sat, set) down.

13. When the water boy (came, come) onto the field, the players all (drank, drunk) from the old tin dipper.

14. I was halfway home before I realized that I (forgot, had forgotten) my coat.

9/Voice

A transitive verb is in the active or the passive voice (see pages 6-7).

ACTIVE   Everybody *had* a good time.
PASSIVE A good time *was had* by all.

ACTIVE   Joe *ran* a good race.
PASSIVE A good race *was run* by Joe.

The active voice is more forceful than the passive in sentences like these, which retain both the subject and the direct object in the passive form.

The passive is useful when the performer of an action is unknown or irrelevant; when the emphasis is on the receiver, the verb, or even a modifier; or when, as in technical writing, a tone of objectivity is desirable. In the following passive sentences, the performers of the actions (subjects in active sentences) do not appear; the emphasis is intentionally placed on the ideas expressed by the italicized words.

The race *was run in record time.*

The match *was played brilliantly.*

Behind the Iron Curtain, democratic elections *are forbidden.*

The police *were totally baffled.*

Readings were taken at half-hour intervals during the first forty-eight hours.

It is wise to examine carefully all sentences with passive constructions in order to decide whether the passive helps to place emphasis where it should be or is merely weak and wordy.

10/Mood

Mood (or mode) is the use or form of a verb which indicates how an action is thought of — as fact, command, wish, or condition contrary to fact. In modern English there are three moods: the indicative, for ordinary statements and questions; the imperative, for commands; and the subjunctive, now used in only a few situations to indicate wish, command, or condition contrary to fact.

INDICATIVE   He *stays* with me.
             Does he *want* to go with you?

IMPERATIVE   *Stay* with me.
             Let us pray.

SUBJUNCTIVE I wish he *were* going with you.
             If this *be* true, I cannot agree.
             It is necessary that he *stay* absolutely quiet.

The imperative is like the indicative present-tense form without -*s*. The commonest subjunctive forms are *were* and *be* (in the verb *to be*). All others are like the present-tense form without -*s*.

10a/Use of the subjunctive is now restricted largely to a few constructions expressing wishes, commands and requests, and conditions that are improbable or contrary to fact.

The subjunctive is used to express wishes, commands, requests, and recommendations in *that* clauses after such verbs and verbal expressions as *would*, *wish*, *insist*, *urge*, *require*, *request*, *ask*, *order*, *demand*, *beg*, *is necessary*, and *is important*.

> The minister *requested that* each member of the congregation **remain** in his seat.
>
> It *is important that* the Steering Committee **be** notified at once of any new developments.
>
> I *move that* the meeting **be** adjourned.
>
> I *wish that* he **were** here.
>
> *Would that* he **were** here!

The subjunctive is used in clauses expressing conditions that are improbable or contrary to fact.

> *If* I **were** you, I would finish school before getting married.
>
> *If* a causeway **were** built, more tourists would come to the island.
>
> **Were** a causeway built, more tourists would come to the island.

But the indicative, not the subjunctive, is used in *if* clauses expressing ordinary conditions.

> If a causeway *is* built next year, more tourists will come to the island.
>
> If it *rains*, the picnic will be postponed.
>
> I'll go if he *goes*.

Subjunctive ideas are often expressed by modal auxiliaries such as *should*, *would*, *may*, and *might*.

If he **should receive** a traveling scholarship, he would go to Italy.

I *wish that* I **might go** too.

It is well to avoid a subjunctive construction if the same idea can be expressed more naturally or economically by rephrasing.

It is necessary *that* repairs on the church **be started** at once. (Subjunctive)

It is necessary to start repairs on the church at once. ⎫
Repairs on the church must be started ⎬ (Statement recast in at once. ⎭ indicative mood)

10b/The sequence of tenses and moods in sentences expressing conditions involves special problems.

The tense and mood of the verb in the *if* clause govern the verb in the clause which follows:

If I *am* wrong, I *will admit* my error.

If I *were* wrong, I *would admit* my error.

If I *had been* wrong, I *would have admitted* my error.

EXERCISE

Use the proper form of the verb to be *in each of the blanks below.*

1. Although he was sober, he walked as if he _____ drunk.

2. Just after the initiation an upperclassman came over, slapped me on the back, and asked me if I _____ feeling all right.

3. If the company roll _____ read in order of competence, your name would be called last.

4. I hope dinner _____ ready when I arrive.

5. It is necessary that dinner _____ ready when the guests arrive.

6. _____ this statement true, he would have to change his entire argument.

7. The driver was unable to tell whether his tail light _____ on or off.

8. If he _____ not sick, I would demand that he _____ at work on time every morning.

11/Agreement — Subject and Verb

A verb agrees with its subject in number and in person.

The only English verb still extensively inflected for person and number is *to be:*

	1st person	2d person	3d person
PRESENT			
Singular	I am	you are	he is
Plural	we are	you are	they are
PAST			
Singular	I was	you were	he was
Plural	we were	you were	they were
FUTURE			
Singular	I shall be	you will be	he will be
Plural	we shall be	you will be	they will be

To be is inflected in the same way when used as an auxiliary: he *was* seen, they *are* seen, we *shall be* seen. (The distinction between *shall* and *will* indicated above is now seldom observed in speech and less and less often even in writing. *Will* is increasingly used in all persons.)

Other verbs are inflected for person and number only in the third person singular present, though they are inflected for tense:

	1st	2d	3d	3d
PRESENT				
Singular	I run	you run	he runs	he walks
Plural	we run	you run	they run	they walk
PAST				
Singular	I ran	you ran	he ran	he walked
Plural	we ran	you ran	they ran	they walked
FUTURE				
Singular	I shall run	you will run	he will run	he will walk
Plural	we shall run	you will run	they will run	they will walk

The *-s* or *-es* ending of the third-person present-tense form of the *verb* is a sign of the *singular;* the *-s* or *-es* ending of a *noun* is a sign of the *plural*.

> The dog barks. The ax does cut.
> The dogs bark. The axes do cut.

Most lapses in agreement of subject and verb occur with compound subjects or when a noun between subject and verb has a different number from the subject.

11a/A compound subject with *and* takes a plural verb.

Two or more subjects connected by a coordinating conjunction are said to be compound.

> *Work and play* **are** good for every college student during vacations.

> *Baseball and swimming* **are** my favorite summer sports.

EXCEPTION: Compound subjects connected by *and* but expressing a singular idea usually take a singular verb.

> *The secretary and treasurer* of the corporation **plans** to spend his vacation in Europe. (One person holds both offices.)

> *The tumult and the shouting* **dies.** (Kipling)

11b/After a compound subject with *or, nor, either . . . or, neither . . . nor, not . . . but,* the verb agrees in number with the nearer part of the subject.

> Neither the *farmer* nor the *businessman* is pleased by higher taxes.
>
> Either the *marbles* or the *knife* is first prize.
>
> Either the *knife* or the *marbles* are first prize.

11c/After a compound subject with *or, nor,* etc., the verb agrees in person with the nearer part of the subject.

> Neither *you* nor *I* am affected by the new regulation.
>
> Either *you* or your *roommate* is affected by the new regulation.

Because such constructions are frequently awkward, it is usually wise to find another way of expressing the idea.

> We aren't affected by the new regulation.
>
> Either you are affected by the new regulation or your roommate is.

11d/Intervening phrases or clauses do not affect the number of a verb.

> The *engine* as well as the fuselage and the wings was destroyed in the crash.
>
> The *pilot* along with all his passengers was rescued from the sea by helicopter.

Connectives like *as well as* and *along with* are not coordinating conjunctions but prepositions and do not form compound subjects. Similar phrases that cause errors in agreement begin with *in addition to, together with, with,* and *including.*

11e/A collective noun takes a singular verb when referring to a group as a unit, a plural verb when the members of the group are thought of individually.

A collective noun names a class or group: *family, flock, jury, congregation,* etc. Meaning often determines number.

> The *family* is going on its vacation to Florida, Maine, and Colorado. (All go together.)

> The *family* **are** going on their vacations to Florida, Maine, and Colorado. (Separate vacations.)

11f/Some nouns plural in form but singular in meaning may take either a singular or a plural verb.

Other nouns such as *economics* and *news* have definitely become singular, whereas still others such as *trousers* and *scissors* are plural except when used after *pair.* When in doubt, consult a good dictionary.

> *Tactics* is the art of maneuvering military forces.

> Northern and Southern *tactics* toward the end of the Civil War **were** quite different.

> The *data* about the rocket ship is confidential.

> *Data* about the project **were** collected from various underground sources.

BUT: The *news* of the defeat is disappointing.

> *Economics* is often thought of as a science.

> His *trousers* **were** unpressed and frayed about the cuffs.

> An old *pair* of *trousers* is a prime essential for the do-it-yourself artist.

> The *scissors* she had **were** so dull they wouldn't cut butter.

> If a better *pair* of *scissors* is what you want, take these.

11g/Singular verbs usually follow indefinite pronouns such
as *each, either, neither, one, no one, everyone, someone,
anyone, nobody, everybody, somebody, anybody.*

> *Neither* of his themes **was** acceptable.

> *Everybody* **has** some trouble choosing a subject for an informal
> essay.

> Each *student* **has** picked a date for his oral report.

> *Each student and each instructor* **has** agreed to follow the
> procedures suggested by the honor council. (Notice here
> that compound subjects joined by *and* and preceded by
> *each* take a singular verb.)

11h/Some words, such as *none, some, part, all, half,* and other
fractions, take a singular or a plural verb, depending
on the meaning of the noun or pronoun which follows.

> *singular*
> *Some of the sugar* **was** spilled on the floor.

> *plural*
> *Some of the apples* **were** spilled on the floor.

> *singular*
> *Half of the class* **is** concentrating on the lecture.

> *plural*
> *Half of the students* **are** looking out the window.

None is sometimes considered singular (*not one*) and some
times plural (*not any* of a number):

> *None* of those accused **was** really responsible.
> *None* of those accused **were** really responsible.

In sentences beginning "The number of," the verb is
usually singular, since *number* is considered the subject:

The *number* of questions on the exam **was** twice as large as I expected.

But "A number of" seems to be considered the equivalent of the adjective *some*, and the following noun or pronoun controls the number of the verb:

A *number* of the *guests* **were** whispering together.

11i/In sentences beginning with *There* or *Here* followed by verb and subject, the verb may be singular or plural, depending on the subject.

There or *Here* is merely a device to let the subject follow the verb, a "space filler" or expletive.

There **was** a long *interval* between the first and the second Crusades.

There **were** sixteen *starlings* perched on the fence.

Here **is** a *thing* to remember.

Here **are** two *things* to remember.

In sentences beginning with *it*, however, the pronoun is the grammatical subject. Hence the verb is singular.

It **was** many years ago.

It **is** the boys who are to blame.

11j/A verb agrees with its subject, not with a subjective complement.

Television and *radio* **are** his main source of pleasure.

The *entertainment* which he enjoys most **is** television and radio.

11k/When a relative pronoun (*who, which, that*) is the subject of a verb, the verb agrees in person and number with the antecedent of the relative pronoun (see pp. 17–18).

An **antecedent** is the word to which a pronoun refers and which lends its meaning to the pronoun.

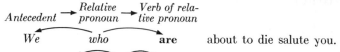

Antecedent → *Relative pronoun* → *Verb of relative pronoun*

We   *who*   **are**   about to die salute you.

The *costumes which* **were** worn in the ballet were dazzling.

I, who **am** old, must soon face death.

He was one *candidate who* **was** able to carry out his campaign pledges.

He was one of those *candidates who* **were** able to carry out their campaign pledges.

BUT: He was *the only one* of the candidates *who* **was** able to carry out his campaign pledges.

11l/A title is considered singular and requires a singular verb even if it contains plural words and plural ideas.

Men Working, by John Faulkner, **describes** Southern WPA workers during the depression.

"Prunes and Prisms" **was** a syndicated newspaper column on grammar and usage.

EXERCISE

Correct the errors in agreement in the following sentences. If a sentence contains no error, write C to indicate that it is correct.

1. The increase in the horsepower of modern automobile engines are amazing.

2. Two plans of action have been tried to some extent, but neither have proved to be very effective.

3. There are not as many convenient beauty parlors in this neighborhood as there was in the community where I formerly lived.

4. Ethics are the study of moral philosophy and standards of conduct.

5. Economy instead of looks are the major attraction of some small foreign cars.

6. The sparks which rise from the campfire into the dark night often stimulates the imagination.

7. Very seldom is profanity and insulting remarks heard at college dances.

8. The increasing number of scholarships in colleges are enabling more and more worthy students to get an education.

9. His commissions on sales and his salary amounts to more than ten thousand dollars a year.

10. It is probable that neither he nor you is going to get the advertised reward for making the best suggestion.

11. A football team form in a huddle to decide on its next play.

12. Knowing how to play several positions are the chief characteristic of a good utility man on a baseball team.

13. None of the pages was torn, but two thirds of the print were blurred.

14. According to Longfellow, every one of us are able to leave footprints on the sands of time.

15. D. H. Lawrence's *Sons and Lovers* are a landmark among the novels of our time.

12/Agreement and Reference of Pronouns

Most pronouns refer to a definite antecedent, either expressed or understood. Because in any particular sentence a pronoun takes its meaning from its antecedent, the reference of a pronoun should be clear. As an aid to clarity, a pronoun should agree with its antecedent in gender and number.

12a/A compound antecedent with *and* generally takes a plural pronoun.

> My *brother* and your *sister* strongly support **their** campus organizations.

> The *secretary* and the *treasurer* of the corporation made **their** reports.

> BUT: The *secretary and treasurer* of the corporation made **his** report.

Omitting *the* before the second noun signals that one person is both secretary and treasurer.

12b/After a compound antecedent with *or, nor, either . . . or, neither . . . nor, not only . . . but also,* a pronoun agrees with the nearer part of the antecedent.

Neither the *secretary of state* nor his *undersecretary* was in **his** seat at the council table.

Neither the *secretary of state* nor his *assistants* were inconsistent in **their** policy.

12c/A collective noun antecedent takes a singular pronoun when the members of the group are considered as a unit, a plural pronoun when they are thought of individually. (See §**11e.**)

A UNIT   The committee was charged to present *its* report no later than April 1.

INDIVIDUALS   The committee filed into the room and took *their* seats around the conference table, some of *them* obviously nervous.

12d/Such singular antecedents as *each, either, neither, one, no one, everyone, someone, anyone, nobody, everybody, somebody, anybody* usually call for singular pronouns.

Not *one* of the hunters felt that **he** had had a good day.

Everyone put **his** gun in the rack and went to **his** room to dress for dinner.

NOTE: Use *his*, not the needlessly explicit *his or her*, in a sentence like the following:

Each rider took *his* (not *his or her*) horse successfully over the hurdles.

12e/*Which* refers to animals and things. *Who* refers to persons, but may be used with animals and some things called by name. *That* refers to animals or things, and sometimes to persons.

The *boy* who was fishing in the dirty water was barefooted.

The *dog* which (or **that**) sat beside him looked listless.

In expressions like the following, *that* and *who* are interchangeable.

A child *that* (*who*) sucks his thumb

A woman *that* (*who*) giggles

The man *that* (*who*) sold papers on the corner

NOTE: *Whose* (the possessive form of *who*) is often used to avoid the awkward *of which*, even in referring to animals and things.

The *automobile* **whose** right front tire blew out crashed and burned.

12f/The antecedent of a pronoun should usually be a single word, or a word group, not an implied idea or several possible ideas.

This, that, which, and *it* offer easy temptation to confusing and misleading reference.

AMBIGUOUS   John lost his temper, and his boss reprimanded him. *That* was why he resigned.

CLEARER   John resigned because he lost his temper and his boss reprimanded him.

BETTER   John resigned because his boss reprimanded him for losing his temper.

OR   John lost his temper and resigned because his boss reprimanded him.

CONFUSED   Some ballads hundreds of years old are still enjoyed today. *This* is one of the differences between them and most modern hillbilly songs.

This may refer to the fact that some old ballads are still enjoyed, or that they are hundreds of years old; or it may refer to the unexpressed idea that their age indicates an enduring quality which many modern hillbilly songs do not have.

CLEAR   Some ballads hundreds of years old are still enjoyed today. It is not likely that modern hillbilly songs will have the same enduring value.

MISLEADING   Brian O'Donovan went to the synagogue, *which* shocked his family deeply. (What shocked them, the synagogue? Probably not.)

BETTER   When Brian O'Donovan went to the synagogue, he shocked his family deeply.

OR   By going to the synagogue, Brian O'Donovan shocked his family deeply.

Many fuzzy references result from starting a sentence without foreseeing problems that come up later.

NOTE: In informal writing especially, experienced writers sometimes let *this*, *which*, or *it* refer to the whole idea of an earlier clause or phrase when no obscurity is possible.

The employee heard that his boss had described him as incompetent. *This* made him resign.

12g/A pronoun should not ambiguously refer to several possible antecedents.

AMBIGUOUS   While *my father* and *my brother John* were fishing from the small boat, **he** fell in.

CLEAR   While *my father* and *my brother John* were fishing from the small boat, **my father** fell in.

EXERCISES

A

Correct errors in agreement and reference of pronouns in the following sentences. If a sentence contains no error, label it C.

1. Just as the father and his little boy walked up to the clown, he began to laugh.

2. The sideshows and the trapeze artists, which were the chief attractions of the circus, had been delayed by an accident.

3. In *The Call of the Wild* the dog Buck, who grew up in civilization, finally reverted to the primitive and lived with wolves.

4. When accused of a traffic violation by a police officer, you should not say anything to irritate him because it can't help the situation.

5. I can vouch for the authenticity of the following information because they are personal experiences.

6. Through military training, the youth of America acquire a great deal of knowledge. When he finishes his period of service, he has a more mature mind and is able to make quick decisions.

7. Each note was so clear that their effect on the audience was electrifying.

8. The audience did not express their full appreciation of the intricate steps of the ballerina.

9. The gardener and caretaker has not done their job well.

10. When I replaced the sword in the scabbard, I saw to my horror that it had been damaged.

11. He was angry with the police for two reasons: it had made a fool of him, and it had spoiled his fun.

12. Neither the boy nor his parents were aware of the great problems which their decision had caused.

13. Someone dropped their pencil on the floor, and it broke the silence.

14. All during my senior year in high school, I kept trying to decide among several good colleges, which made it hard for me to make a choice.

15. He had never seen a cow barn and never tried to milk one.

B

Point out and correct errors in agreement and reference in the following paragraph.

A small child's first trip to the dentist is a test of their courage. As he and his mother opens the door and takes their seats, a number of patients is already waiting his turn, and each of these are obviously nervous and frightened. Neither the dentist nor his assistant are to be seen from the waiting room, but sounds of drilling or groaning comes from down the corridor, which causes almost everyone to try to relieve their tension by glancing through the outdated magazines which they are holding. One of the patients who is waiting picks up a pair of gloves which has fallen to the floor. The smell of anesthetics pervade the room. But the child and his mother ignores their surroundings. Neither the pictures on the walls nor the view from the windows are interesting enough to take his mind off his fears. Occasionally he and his mother talk in hushed tones. At intervals the nurse enters and calls a patient's name. He or she rises and unhappily stalks down the corridor. At last the child's name is called.

13/Case

Another word-form distinction used in English to show relationship is case. **Case** is the form of a noun or pronoun which shows its use in its clause or sentence. English has remnants of three cases: subjective, possessive, and objective. Nouns are inflected for case only in the possessive (*father, father's*). An alternative way to show possession is with the "*of* phrase" (*the house, of the house*). Some pronouns, notably the personal pronouns and the relative pronoun *who*, are still fully inflected for three cases:

SUBJECTIVE (acting)	I, he, she, we, they, who
POSSESSIVE (possessing)	my (mine), your (yours), his, her (hers), its, our (ours), their (theirs), whose
OBJECTIVE (acted upon)	me, him, her, us, them, whom

To determine case, find out how a word is used in its own clause, whether it is a subject or subjective complement, a possessive, or an object.

13a/The subjective case is used for subjects and subjective complements, though in some informal situations, and in nonstandard English, this practice is not rigidly followed.

NONSTANDARD[1]   It looked like *him and I was* going to get the blame.

STANDARD   It looked as if *he and I were* going to get the blame.

NONSTANDARD   *Him and I* ain't been inside the library this term.

STANDARD   *He and I* have not been inside the library this term.

INFORMAL   The two guilty ones who went unpunished were *you and me.*

FORMAL   The two guilty ones who went unpunished were *you and I.*

It is I is punctiliously formal. *It's me* is informal standard English and almost universal in conversation. *It's us, it's him,* and *it's her* are also common informal usages.

13b/The object of a preposition is in the objective case.

FAULTY   The teacher had to choose *between* **you** and **I.**

RIGHT   The teacher had to choose *between* **you** and **me.**

Between is a preposition, and *you and me* is a compound object. People trying to be very proper often misguidedly use the subjective case in sentences of this kind.

---

[1]For definitions of Standard, Nonstandard, Formal, and Informal English, see §§41–42, pp. 196–204.

Be careful about the case of pronouns in constructions like the following:

FAULTY   A few *of* we girls learned how to cook when we went on a camping trip.

RIGHT   A few *of* us girls learned how to cook when we went on a camping trip.

If in doubt, test by dropping the noun: not *of we*, but *of us*.

13c/The subject or complement of an infinitive is in the objective case.

SUBJECT

I considered **him** *to be* the best swimmer in the pool.

Though she was suspected, they finally discovered the guilty

COMPLEMENT

person *to be* **him**.

13d/An appositive has the same case as the word it refers to.

An appositive is a substantive (a noun, or a word or group of words used in place of a noun) which follows and explains another substantive.

The *poet* **John Milton** was blind in his old age.

Case is no problem when both the appositive and the word it refers to are nouns, but it often causes trouble when the appositive is a pronoun. In the following sentences the pronoun appositives take different cases, depending on the case of the word they refer to.

SUBJECTIVE   Three *members* of the committee — **Bill, you,** and

I — were appointed by the chairman.

OBJECTIVE   The chairman appointed three *members* to the com-

mittee — **Bill, you,** and **me.**

3e/A pronoun after *than* or *as* in an elliptical clause (that is, a clause in which one or more words are "understood") takes the same case as it would if the clause were completely expressed.

No one else in the match was as versatile as *she.*

He admired no one else as much as *her.*

In the first sentence, *was* is understood after *she;* in the second, *he admired* is understood before *her.* They might be expanded to read:

No one else in the match was as versatile as *she was.*

He admired no one else as much as *he did her.* (Or *he admired her.*)

Do or *did* is often used to avoid repeating a verb used earlier, usually in the same sentence.

3f/A pronoun preceding a gerund is usually in the possessive case; a noun may be possessive or objective.

Representative uses of the possessive are the following:

My *driving* did not overjoy my father.

Mary's *singing* was not exactly suitable for opera.

Compare:

My *behavior* did not overjoy my father.

Mary's *voice* was not exactly suitable for opera.

When a phrase intervenes or when a noun preceding the gerund is plural, is abstract, or denotes an inanimate object, the noun is not likely to be in the possessive case.

There was a regulation against the **family** of a sailor *meeting* him at the dock. (Intervening phrase, *of a sailor*)

There is no rule against **men** *working* overtime. (Plural noun)

I object to **emotion** *overruling* judgment. (Abstract noun)

The crew did not mind the **ship** *staying* in port several days. (Noun denoting inanimate object)

When the verbal is a participle, not a gerund, the noun or pronoun preceding it is in the objective case.

I heard **him** *singing* loudly.

I hear **you** *calling* me.

13g/An of-phrase is used to indicate possession for most nouns denoting abstractions or inanimate objects.

INCONGRUOUS   The *building's* construction was begun when winter ended.

PREFERRED   The construction *of the building* was begun when winter ended.

There are well-established exceptions: e.g., *an hour's delay, for pity's sake, a month's rest, heart's desire, a moment's hesitation, a day's work.*

13h/A personal pronoun forms its possessive without an apostrophe; an indefinite pronoun requires an apostrophe.

PERSONAL PRONOUNS   *yours, its* (not *it's*, which means "it is"), *hers, his, ours, theirs*

INDEFINITE PRONOUNS   *everyone's, other's, nobody's, one's, anybody else's,* etc.

13i/The case of an interrogative or a relative pronoun is determined by its use in its own clause.

The interrogative pronouns are *who, whose, whom, what,*

which. The relative pronouns are *who, whose, whom, what, which, that,* and the forms with *-ever,* such as *whoever* and *whosoever.* Those which give difficulty through change in form are *who* and *whoever. Who* and *whoever* are subjective; *whom* and *whomever* are objective.

The case of these pronouns is clear in uncomplicated sentences.

Who *defeated* Richard III?

Winston Churchill, **whom** I *admire,* piloted England through her darkest hour.

But when something (usually another subordinate clause) intervenes between the pronoun and the rest of its own clause, its function is sometimes obscured:

Who do the history books say *defeated* Richard III?

Winston Churchill, **whom** it seems all the world *admired,* piloted England through her darkest hour.

The intervening expressions should not be allowed to draw the pronouns into a different case.

There are two simple ways of telling the case of the pronoun in such sentences:

(1) Mentally cancel the intervening words:

Who ~~do the history books say~~ defeated Richard III?

Winston Churchill, whom ~~it seems~~ all the world admired, piloted England through her darkest hour.

(2) Mentally rearrange the sentence in declarative order, that is, in the normal order of a statement: subject — verb — complement:

The history books do say who defeated Richard III.

. . . it seems all the world admired whom (him). . . .

In speech, *who* is the usual form for an object as well a
for a subject at the beginning of a sentence:

SUBJECT   **Who** *won* the race?

SUBJECT   **Who** do you think *won* the race?

OBJECT   **Who** were you talking *to* over there?

The case of a relative pronoun is determined by its us
in its own clause, not by that of its antecedent.

Here are three easy steps for checking this usage:

(1) Pick out the relative clause and draw a box around it

This is the boy **(who, whom)** the witness said started th
fight.

The police held the boy **(who, whom)** the plaintiff allege
John whipped.

(2) Cancel intervening expressions (*he says, it is reported*
etc.).

This is the boy **(who, whom)** ~~the witness said~~ started th
fight.

The police held the boy **(who, whom)** ~~the plaintiff allege~~
John whipped.

(3) Find the verb in the relative clause.

This is the boy | *subject* *verb* who ~~whom~~ started the fight.

This is the boy | *object* *subject* *verb* ~~who~~ whom John whipped.

NOTE: Do not confuse the function of the relative pronoun in its clause with the function of the clause as a whole.

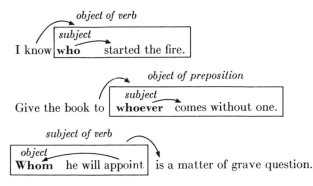

XERCISES

A

Select the accepted form in parentheses and label with one of the numbers below.

USES OF THE SUBJECTIVE CASE   USES OF THE OBJECTIVE CASE

S1. Subject of a verb
S2. Subjective complement
S3. Appositive to a word in the subjective case

01. Direct object of a verb or verbal
02. Indirect object of a verb or verbal
03. Object of a preposition
04. Appositive to a word in the objective case
05. Subject or complement of an infinitive

1. Members of the court-martial asked him (who, whom) he had marked absent at roll call.

2. He is the one (who, whom) it is thought shot down the plane.

3. I wonder (who, whom) it was.

4. He addressed the letter as follows: To (Whomever, Whoever) May Be Concerned.

5. At the party the host smiled most graciously at (whoever, whomever) he disliked most intensely.

6. In that club it does not matter (who, whom) the ladies are gossiping about as long as they are gossiping.

7. Ulysses slew the suitors (who, whom) he had found courting his wife.

8. Ulysses slew the suitors (who, whom) were courting his wife.

9. Out of the five English teachers (who, whom) taught me in high school, there is one (who, whom) I shall always remember.

10. (Who, Whom) did the inmate say that he was?

11. (Who, Whom) did Caesar say "Et tu" to?

12. My candidate is one politician (who, whom) I consider an honest man.

13. He was an honest man (who, whom) many people believe the Senator persecuted.

14. He is an honest man (who, whom) many people believe was persecuted by the Senator.

B

Select the acceptable form of the pronoun or noun in each of the following sentences.

1. (It's, Its) a pity that the team lost (it's, its) star end.

2. At that time Mr. Dillingham could not tell (who, whom) the winner of the election was.

3. It was a good (day's, days) work to repair the (house's roof, houses roof, roof of the house).

4. My father told both of (we, us) boys — John and (I, me) — to bring some more coal for the fire.

5. What kind of teacher did you expect (she, her) to be?

6. The English instructor objected to the (student, student's) working the exercises in class.

7. The chairman asked the first two speakers (she and I, her and I, she and me, her and me) to be brief.

8. The manager recommended (Bill and me, Bill and I) for a raise.

9. You must choose between (he and I, he and me, him and me, him and I).

10. He could always run the hundred-yard dash faster than (I, me).

4/ Adjectives and Adverbs

Adjectives modify nouns and pronouns; adverbs modify verbs, adjectives, other adverbs, prepositions, and conjunctions. (See pages 8–10.)

Most adverbs end in *-ly*, whereas only a few adjectives have this ending — e.g., *lovely, holy, manly, friendly*. Some adverbs have two forms, one with *-ly* and one without: *slow* and *slowly*, *loud* and *loudly*. Most adverbs are formed by adding *-ly* to adjectives: *warm, warmly; pretty, prettily*.

With some adverbs the presence or absence of *-ly* indicates a distinction in meaning. *High*, for example, is used in a physical sense. A drill team may "march fast and step high." *Highly* is used abstractly. Lincoln in the Gettysburg Address said, ". . . we here highly resolve that these dead shall not have died in vain. . . ." He could not have used *high* in this sentence. Similar pairs are *most* and *mostly*, *direct* and *directly*, *hard* and *hardly*.

Most of us habitually use the correct adjective and adverb forms in sentences like the following:

> He stood *close* to us.
>
> The barber gave him a *close* shave.
>
> He cut *close* to the marker on the turns.
>
> Study the text *closely*.
>
> He gave the clerk the *exact* change.
>
> He left *exactly* when the noon whistle blew.

Only long familiarity with the language enables us t
distinguish between certain forms. A frequent lapse is th
use of an adjective instead of an adverb to modify a verl
an adjective, or an adverb: e.g., *sure* for *surely*, *easy* for *easily*
good for *well*, *real* for *really*, *some* for *somewhat*, etc.

NOT   The *real* sincere student studies the rules *good*.

BUT   The *really* sincere student studies the rules *well*.

**14a/The comparative and superlative degrees are formec
by adding -er and -est to most short adjectives anc
some adverbs, and by placing more and most (or les:
and least) before long adjectives, participles, and mos
adverbs.**

ADJECTIVES		COMPARATIVE	SUPERLATIVE
	dear	dearer	dearest
	pretty	prettier	prettiest
	close	closer	closest
	slow	slower	slowest
	sincere	sincerer	sincerest
or	sincere	more sincere	most sincere
	pitiful	more pitiful	most pitiful
	grasping	more grasping	most grasping
ADVERBS	slow	slower	slowest
	slowly	more slowly	most slowly
	rapidly	more rapidly	most rapidly
	rapidly	less rapidly	least rapidly

Certain adjectives and adverbs have irregular compara
tive and superlative forms: *good, better, best; well, better, best*
little, less, least; bad, worse, worst; etc.

Some adjectives and adverbs are "absolute" and cannot
strictly speaking, be compared: e.g., *dead, perfect, complete*
unique. A thing cannot, logically, be more or less dead, etc

But there are exceptions as in phrases like "deader than a doornail."

14b/The comparative refers to two things; the superlative to more than two.

> *Both* cars are fast, but the small car is (the) faster.
>
> All *three* cars are fast, but the small car is (the) fastest.

14c/Usually a predicate adjective, not an adverb, follows a linking verb such as *is, seems, becomes, looks, appears, feels, sounds, smells, tastes.*

A predicate adjective describes the subject. An adverb modifies the verb.

> *He* feels **bad.** (He is ill or depressed. *Feels* is a link; it names a condition, not an action.)
>
> He *reads* **badly.** (*Reads* names an action; it is not a link.)
>
> The *tea* tasted **sweet.** (*Sweet* describes the tea, not the manner of tasting.)
>
> She *tasted* the tea **daintily.**
>
> She *sang* **sweetly.** (*Sweetly* tells how she sang.)

14d/Verbs like *keep, build, hold, dig, make,* and *think* can take a direct object plus a modifier, which may be an adjective or an adverb, depending on meaning.

> Keep your *clothes* **neat.** (Adjective — complement)
>
> *Keep* your clothes **neatly** in the closet. (Adverb — modifies verb)
>
> Make my *bed* **soft.**
>
> *Make* the bed **carefully.**

EXERCISE

Correct faulty adverbs and adjectives in the following paragraph.

Because it had been a difficult term at college, Blair was real happy when he completed the tiringest trip he had ever made and neared home safely and soundly. Walking home slow, he held his suitcase tight in his hand. He was thinking that it sure was a cold night and that he would enjoy a cup of real hot coffee. He felt badly because he hadn't done good on his examinations; and just before he had left school, his landlady had told him that if he came back he would have to keep his room cleanly and neatly for a change. Maybe a good long rest at home would make him feel well and think clear, he mused as he approached the front door. When he rang the doorbell, it sounded loudly. He opened the door slowly, smelled the coffee, and knew he was at home.

Grammar:
The Position of Words

BESIDES USING the proper forms of words, we must use words in their proper places in the sentence if we are to communicate clearly and effectively. The basic pattern of the English sentence (subject-verb, or subject-verb-complement) gives little trouble, for we have been habituated to it from earliest childhood when we first began putting words together. However, the modifying elements — words, phrases, and clauses — that are included within and added onto the basic sentence pattern do not have the same fixity of order or position as the subject-verb or subject-verb-complement relationship. These, therefore, are the elements with which problems of position are most likely to arise.

15/Modifiers

Poorly placed modifiers cause confusion, misunderstanding, and a good many howlers. Modifiers should not float loosely in sentences or seem to attach to the wrong word. Usually a modifying adjective precedes its noun, whereas an adverb may precede or follow the word it modifies. Prepositional phrases usually follow closely, but may precede; adjective clauses follow closely; and adverbial phrases and clauses have the greatest range of all in possible positions.

15a/Dangling constructions are those which refer to the wrong word or to none at all.

When a dangling construction relates to the wrong noun or pronoun, or when there is none present in the sentence for it to relate to, it may be confusing or unintentionally funny, and the joke is on the writer. Most danglers are verbal phrases, but a few are prepositional phrases or elliptical clauses.

DANGLING PARTICIPLE

Running along the street, my *nose* felt frozen. (A participle at the beginning of a sentence normally modifies the first noun or pronoun in the clause which follows. Here *running* seems to modify *nose* — as it could in a different context — and the proper agent, *I*, is not expressed.)

CORRECTION

Running along the street, *I* felt as if my nose were frozen. (The participle here refers properly to *I*.)

OR

As I ran along the street, my nose *felt* frozen. (The participial phrase has been changed to an adverbial clause, which now modifies *felt*. *I* is expressed in the subordinate clause.)

DANGLING GERUND

After **snooping** around the attic for several days before Christmas, a *cowboy*

suit was finally discovered. (A gerund early in a sentence normally attaches to the first noun or pronoun in the following clause. But *snooping* cannot refer to *suit*.)

CORRECTION	After **snooping** around the attic for several days before Christmas, *I* finally discovered a cowboy suit. (The gerund here quite reasonably refers to *I*. Notice that the sentence has been changed from passive to active. Beware the passive in such constructions.)
DANGLING INFINITIVE	**To get well,** an *operation* is necessary. (*To get well* refers to no word in this sentence.)
IMPROVED	**To get well,** *he* needs an operation. (*To get well* properly refers to the pronoun *he*, which has been added.)
DANGLING PREPOSITIONAL PHRASE	**In childhood** *Mother* read Shakespeare's comedies to me. (Mother's childhood?)
CORRECTION	**In my childhood** Mother *read* Shakespeare's comedies to me. (Inserting *my* prevents the faulty attachment.)
DANGLING ELLIPTICAL CLAUSE	**While still a child,** *Mother* read Shakespeare's comedies to me. (While who was a child? Mother?)
CORRECTION	**While I was still a child,** Mother *read* Shakespeare's comedies to me. (With its subject and verb expressed, the dependent clause does not seem to draw these elements from the main clause.)

Note that some phrases in which a verbal does not refer to anything in the rest of the sentence do not dangle:

> *Strictly speaking*, does this sentence contain a dangling construction?
>
> *To tell the truth*, it does not.

Neither of these sentences contains a word which says who is speaking or telling the truth. The phrases are sentence modifiers.

15b/Misplaced modifiers can be awkward, unintentionally funny, or actually misleading.

As we have seen, a modifying adjective generally precedes its noun; an adverb may precede or follow a verb, but it precedes an adjective. An adjective clause follows its noun or pronoun, but an adverbial clause may come at the beginning, in the middle, or at the end of a sentence. Most trouble comes with sentences that contain a number of modifiers, especially when several vie for the same position.

Since adverbial modifiers are most mobile, these offer the greatest chance for flexibility:

CONFUSING   Remove any silks that have stuck to the ear of corn *with a brush.*

CLEAR   *With a brush* remove any silks that have stuck to the ear of corn.

OR   Remove *with a brush* any silks that have stuck to the ear of corn.

Like the adverbial prepositional phrase just above, an adverbial clause can sometimes effectively occupy any of several positions in a sentence.

CONFUSING   I knew I would recognize my cousin even though I had never seen him because he had a wart on his nose when I stepped off the train.

Here three adverbial clauses follow the main clause, "I knew I would recognize my cousin." The modification of the first two adverbial clauses (beginning with "even though" and "because") is clear, but the *when* clause seems to modify the one just before it, as if my cousin had a wart on his nose when I stepped off the train, but probably not at other times. Note what happens in another arrangement:

> When I stepped off the train I knew I would recognize my cousin even though I had never seen him because he had a wart on his nose.

This change solves the first problem, but once more the final adverbial clause seems to modify the one before it. It is possible to change the construction of one adverbial clause; the other two can then come at the beginning and the end of the sentence:

> Even though I had never seen him, I knew I would recognize my cousin by the wart on his nose when I stepped off the train.

The sentence may also be written as follows:

> Even though I had never seen my cousin, I knew that when I stepped off the train I would recognize him by the wart on his nose.

An adjective clause will often seem to modify a noun which intervenes between it and the word it should modify.

> We rode a train to *Chicago* **which** carried many delegates to the convention.

It was the train, not the city, which carried the delegates.

> We rode *to Chicago* on a *train* **which** carried many delegates to the convention.

Almost any modifier which comes between an adjective clause and the word it modifies can cause awkwardness or misunderstanding:

> She worshipped her **brother** with all her *soul* **who** was five years older than she.

> **Alchemy** was the "science" of *transmuting lead into gold*, **which** was a common practice in the Middle Ages.

The first sentence is awkward but its intent is clear; the second is actually misleading. Here are better arrangements:

> With all her soul she worshipped her *brother* **who** was five years older than she.

> *Alchemy*, **which** was a common practice in the Middle Ages, was the "science" of transmuting lead into gold.

15c/A modifier placed between two words and capable of modifying either is said to "squint."

SQUINTING   The horse which was pawing *violently* kicked its owner.

Did the horse paw violently or kick its owner violently?

CLEAR   The horse which was *violently pawing* kicked its owner.

OR   The horse which was pawing *kicked* its owner *violently*.

SQUINTING   Because savage tribes believe in many gods *most of the time* their religious feelings are not very profound.

CLEAR   Because *most* savage tribes believe in many gods, their religious feelings are not very profound.

CLEAR   Because savage tribes believe in many gods, their religious feelings are not *usually* very profound.

EXERCISE

Correct the faulty modifiers in the following sentences.

1. While sawing the wood, my finger was cut off.

2. Grandmother was wearing her spectacles on her forehead, which she could not find.

3. The men who were beating on the door wildly began shooting their pistols.

4. After cackling loudly, I knew that the hen had laid an egg.

5. I sometimes comprehend things which others do not understand by using my imagination.

6. To keep from failing the course, the teacher advised me to study harder.

7. While having my teeth examined, the dentist told me that two wisdom teeth would have to be pulled.

8. To be absolutely certain, the answer must be checked.

9. The author urged his friends to buy his book by mail and by telephone.

10. The carpenter inspected the board before sawing for nails.

11. At the age of five my grandfather told me about his life as a soldier in the Confederate Army.

12. She said when the class was over she would meet him at Frank's Place.

13. Having been found guilty of drunken driving, the judge sentenced the young man to ninety days in jail.

14. The student waited for the teacher to give him his theme impatiently.

15. Where can I buy overalls for children that won't shrink?

16. Serve one of the melons for dessert at lunch; keep one of them for the picnic in the refrigerator.

16/Unnecessary Separation

Unnecessary separation of subject and verb, parts of a verb phrase, verb and object, or other closely related elements in a sentence pattern can be awkward or obscure.

AWKWARD   My brother, *having longed to go to Europe after he finished college and before he began teaching,* was greatly disappointed when he was refused a reservation in early June.

IMPROVED   *Because he had longed to go to Europe after he finished college and before he began teaching,* my brother was greatly disappointed when he was refused a reservation in early June.

AWKWARD   The dog had *for a period of several* days been hungry.

IMPROVED   The dog had been hungry *for a period of several days*.

LUDICROUS She is the man who owns the service station's wife.

ACCURATE   She is the wife of the man who owns the service station.

Separation by short modifiers and phrases is often idiomatic and seldom causes confusion. An adverb frequently precedes or follows a verb or comes between an auxiliary and a main verb:

> John *hardly ever* feels well.
> The Cabots speak *only* to God.
> It is *generally* known that bears love honey.
> We should *always* try to do our best.

An adverb seldom comes between a verb and its object:

NOT   John loves *exceedingly* Mary.

NOT   Jack loves *better than anybody else in the whole world* Jill.

In such situations the adverb tends to appear after the object or before the verb:

> John loves Mary *exceedingly*.
> John *never* loved Mary.
> Jack loves Jill *better than anybody else in the world*.

In a sentence with both indirect and direct object, the adverb tends to precede the verb; a modifier placed at the end of the sentence seems too far away.

> Joe *stealthily* gave me the hotfoot.

Some people look with disfavor upon a "split" infinitive, that is, an infinitive with a modifier between *to* and the verb form, as in *to loudly yell.* Hence if any other position for the modifier is natural and clear, it is wise to put it there. But sometimes it is almost necessary to split an infinitive to avoid stiffness or ambiguity.

UNNECESSARY He felt it *to absolutely be* impossible.

IMPROVED He felt it to be *absolutely* impossible.

JUSTIFIABLE It would be wise for the student *to clearly define* his reasons for entering college.

In the last sentence above, the adverb might be considered slightly awkward in any other position.

17/Parallelism

Sentence elements of equal grammatical rank should be expressed in parallel — i.e., similar — constructions. Parallel forms may be words, phrases, or clauses. When elements match in pairs or link in series, they should be in similar form.

17a/Elements connected by the coordinating conjunctions *and, but, or, nor* take similar grammatical forms.

Phrases equate with phrases, dependent clauses with dependent clauses, independent clauses with independent clauses, and so on.

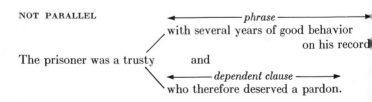

NOT PARALLEL

phrase
with several years of good behavior on his record

The prisoner was a trusty   and

dependent clause
who therefore deserved a pardon.

PARALLEL

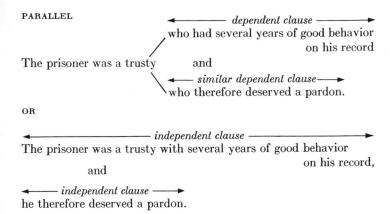

dependent clause
who had several years of good behavior
on his record

The prisoner was a trusty   and

similar dependent clause
who therefore deserved a pardon.

OR

independent clause
The prisoner was a trusty with several years of good behavior
on his record,

and

independent clause
he therefore deserved a pardon.

Infinitives equate with infinitives, participles with participles, gerunds with gerunds.

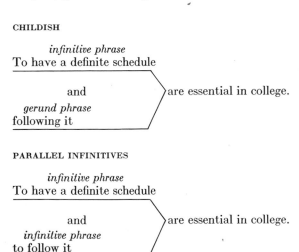

CHILDISH

infinitive phrase
To have a definite schedule

and   are essential in college.

gerund phrase
following it

PARALLEL INFINITIVES

infinitive phrase
To have a definite schedule

and   are essential in college.

infinitive phrase
to follow it

PARALLEL GERUNDS

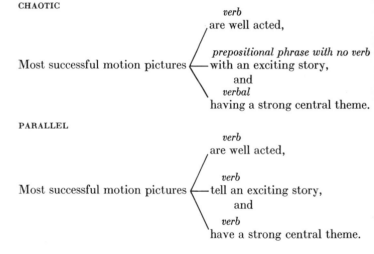

gerund phrase
Having a definite schedule

                and   ⟩ are essential in college.

gerund phrase
following it

Verbs equate with verbs.

CHAOTIC

                                        verb
                                        are well acted,

                                        prepositional phrase with no verb
Most successful motion pictures ⟵ with an exciting story,
                                        and
                                        verbal
                                        having a strong central theme.

PARALLEL

                                        verb
                                        are well acted,

                                        verb
Most successful motion pictures ⟵ tell an exciting story,
                                        and
                                        verb
                                        have a strong central theme.

17b/Parallelism requires that elements connected by the
correlative conjunctions (*either ... or, neither ... nor, not
... but, both ... and*) have similar grammatical form.

Lapses in parallel structure with correlative conjunctions
can be avoided by use of the same grammatical construction
after each correlative.

SLOPPY	I *not only* bought the dress *but also* the handbag.
NEATER	I bought *not only* the dress *but also* the handbag.
SLOPPY	*Either* I shall buy the evening dress this afternoon *or* tomorrow morning.
PARALLEL BUT WORDY	*Either* I shall buy the evening dress this afternoon *or* I shall buy it tomorrow morning.
PARALLEL BUT STRAINED	I shall *either* buy the evening dress this afternoon *or* buy it tomorrow morning.
PREFERRED	I shall buy the evening dress *either* this afternoon *or* tomorrow morning.

The preferred construction is the one which is most clear and natural and least repetitious.

EXERCISES

A

Correct the faults in parallelism in the following sentences. If a sentence is correct as it stands, label it C.

1. The problem of inadequate salaries for teachers not only exists in smaller communities but also in large cities.

2. You eat your breakfast, take your gun in your hand, your dog to your side, and start toward the fields.

3. The good speaker must possess sincerity, a good platform manner, and have the ability to express his thoughts exactly.

4. I began to feel as if I had been painting for hours and should never finish the job.

5. The best way to prepare for your examination is to go over your notes and reading your text again carefully.

6. A wife should never come to breakfast in her bathrobe and slippers and hair looking as if it had been combed with an egg beater.

7. This method of weeding the lawn will not only help you but your neighbors as well.

8. Alcohol slows the drinker's reactions to a minimum and causes him to delay in giving signals, to blow the horn, and come to a quick stop.

9. This article presents no facts favorable to either the Democrats or to the Republicans on this issue.

10. I can remember quite plainly what it is like to drink buttermilk fresh from the churn, to see a deer's track in the orchard, and to sit in the semidarkness of a light from the kerosene lamp and listen to the old folks talk.

11. The verdict was in my opinion unfair because the jury seemed obviously prejudiced and that the judge seemed antagonistic toward the lawyer for the defense.

B

Correct faulty parallelism in the following passage.

Men in great places are thrice servants: servants of the sovereign or state; fame's servants; and they serve business. Thus they have no freedom, neither in their persons, nor in action, nor in their times. It is a strange desire, to seek power and losing liberty; or seeking power over others and to lose power over a man's self. The rising unto place is not only laborious, but by pains men come to greater pains; it is sometimes base, and by indignities men come to dignities. The standing is slippery; and either the regress is a downfall, or at least an eclipse, which is a melancholy thing.

Adapted from Francis Bacon, "Of Great Place"

Grammar:
Completeness and Consistency

An EFFECTIVELY communicative sentence transmits the writer's full and exact meaning to the reader. To do this, it must be complete in grammatical structure and consistent in grammatical point of view. Any structural omissions or unnecessary structural shifts that might mislead, mystify, or annoy the reader are pitfalls that the careful writer will take pains to avoid.

18/Completeness

Every sentence should be clear; hence every sentence should be complete in structure, with every part either expressed or so unmistakably implied that there is no possibility of confusion or misunderstanding. In the struggle to put ideas into words, it is easy to omit or misuse words which are structural signs in the pattern of the sentence or to leave unexpressed some part of a thought which a reader will not be able to supply for himself. Constructions expressing comparisons and those involving "understood" prepositions and verbs are sometimes not completely enough expressed to be clear.

18a/In some sentences *so, such,* and *too* are intensives, roughly equivalent to *very.* When there is danger of misunderstanding, the idea should be completed or restated.

NOT CLEAR   The street was too narrow. (Too narrow for what?)
            Those coins were so rare. (So rare that what?)

CLEAR   The street was too narrow to admit an automobile.
            The street was extremely narrow.
            Those coins were so rare that the experts could not identify them.

However, to spell out all the implications of *so, such,* and *too* would often be pedantic and unnecessary.

CLEAR   I didn't dare pass the truck because the road was so narrow.
        I didn't go. I felt too sick.
        We stayed indoors because it was such a miserable day.
        I'm so young and you're so beautiful.
        Such nonsense!
        That's just too much.

18b/One preposition should not be "understood" when a different preposition is called for.

NOT   He was simultaneously *repelled* and *drawn* **toward** the city.

BUT   He was simultaneously *repelled* **by** and *drawn* **toward** the city.

BETTER He was simultaneously *repelled* **by** the city and *drawn* **toward** it.

OR   He was simultaneously *repelled* and *attracted* **by** the city.

18c/One verb form should not be "understood" when a different form is called for.

NOT   In the fire the silver coins were melted and the paper money burned. (Paper money *were* burned?)

BUT   In the fire the silver coins were melted and the paper money *was* burned.

NOT   I wanted to and would have gone to college if my father had let me. (Wanted to *gone*?)

POSSIBLE I wanted to *go* and would have *gone* to college if my father had let me.

BETTER   I wanted to *go* to college and *would have gone* if my father had let me.

NOT   I always have and always will be a person who enjoys arguments. (Always have *be*?)

POSSIBLE I always have *been* and always will *be* a person who enjoys arguments.

BETTER   I always *have been* a person who enjoys arguments and always *will be*.

Where the same form is called for in two constructions, it need not be repeated.

To err is human; to forgive, divine.

18d/For clearness in compound structures, it is sometimes necessary to repeat an article (*a, an, the*), an auxiliary verb, the sign of the infinitive (*to*), a possessive pronoun, or a relative pronoun.

My rich friend owns *a* red and chartreuse convertible. (He has one car, which is two-toned.)

My rich friend owns *a* red and *a* chartreuse convertible. (He has *two* cars.)

NOT *The* janitor and matron had left the dormitory.

BUT *The* janitor and *the* matron had left the dormitory.

My minister and guardian planned to advise me about this problem. (One person is referred to.)

My minister and *my* guardian planned to advise me about this problem. (Two persons are referred to.)

NOT He declared that he had tried *to* stop the saw and cut off his fingers. (The *to* carries over to *cut* and suggests a false meaning.)

BUT He declared that he had tried to stop the saw and *had* cut off his fingers. (*Had* forestalls *to* and asserts the intended parallelism.)

NOT She opened the door, *which* sagged on its hinges and squeaked as she entered.

BUT She opened the door, which sagged on its hinges and *which* squeaked as she entered.

OR She opened the sagging door, which squeaked as she entered.

18e/Omission of *that* sometimes obscures meaning.

OBSCURE The efficiency expert found one who can increase his efficiency in this way does not tire.

CLEAR The efficiency expert found *that* one who can increase his efficiency in this way does not tire.

19/Comparisons

A comparison should be logical and complete. Only similar terms should be compared. In the following sentences, dissimilar terms are compared:

My first semester in college was like most freshmen.

Leading a sober life is much better than beer joints and dance halls.

The crisscrossed comparisons in these sentences can be diagrammed thus:

The first needs something to equate with *semester;* the second, something to equate with *leading.*

My first *semester* in college was like *that of* most freshmen.

Leading a sober life is better than *frequenting* beer joints and dance halls.

The word *other* is often needed in a comparison:

ILLOGICAL   *Sanctuary* has been more popular than any of Faulkner's novels.

(This sentence incorrectly implies that *Sanctuary* is not a novel by Faulkner.)

RIGHT   *Sanctuary* has been more popular than any of Faulkner's *other* novels.

OR   *Sanctuary* has been the most popular of Faulkner's novels.

In "tandem" comparisons (*as tall as or taller than*, etc.), usage frequently demands that the first element be completed but not the second:

INCOMPLETE   Mrs. Grader was as strict, if not stricter, than my present chaperon. (*As strict* requires *as*, not *than*. Two constructions are telescoped.)

BETTER   Mrs. Grader was *as* strict *as* my present chaperon, if not stricter. (*Than she is* is understood.)

INCOMPLETE	Yellowstone National Park is one of the most beautiful if not the most beautiful park in the United States. (After *one of the most beautiful*, the plural *parks* is required.)
BETTER	Yellowstone National Park is one of the most beautiful parks in the United States, if not the most beautiful.
AMBIGUOUS	I like Mary more than Jane. (More than I like Jane, or more than Jane likes Mary?)
CLEAR	I like Mary more than I do Jane.
OR	I like Mary more than Jane does.
INCOMPLETE	Stanley is a better boxer.
CLEAR	Stanley is a better boxer than his brother.
OR	Stanley is a better boxer than wrestler.
INCOMPLETE	Stanley is the best boxer.
CLEAR	Stanley is the best boxer in the Golden Gloves Tournament.
FEEBLE	*The Red Badge of Courage* is different.
CLEAR	*The Red Badge of Courage* is different from other war novels of its time.
OR	*The Red Badge of Courage* is unusual.

EXERCISES

A

In each of the following sentences, repeat a word if necessary to clarify meaning.

1. His dog and favorite hunting companion were waiting for him at the back door just before sunrise.

2. Mr. Czerwinski said that his grandfather had migrated to Paris and London, the birthplace of his grandmother, had finally become their home.

3. His wife had planned to hide the package and present it to her husband on Christmas morning.

4. Mrs. Duncan told us that Susie had gone over to visit Mimi and David had not yet returned from the tennis courts.

5. He had done his best to miss the car and hit the child instead.

B

Make each of the following sentences logically complete and clear. If a sentence is correct as it stands, label it C.

1. The umpire stated that he was aware and worried about the attitude of the crowd.

2. Henry VIII was one of the most tyrannical if not the most tyrannical king that ever lived.

3. Now that he is growing old, his hair is becoming grayer.

4. More than any of the early Presidents of the United States, Thomas Jefferson helped to define American democratic government.

5. He feels, although it now appears impossible, man may someday fly to Mars.

6. During the Civil War the North felt more antagonistic toward Great Britain than the South.

7. Randy resembles his father more than his brother Brad.

8. The grass in my pasture is greener.

9. Everything in Jake's room was in such a mess.

10. O. Henry's short story "The Gift of the Magi" has such a surprise ending.

11. This secret was known to both my brother and closest friend.

12. The hat Anna finally selected was cheaper and prettier.

13. The doctor wanted to and would have operated on the baby if the parents had not been too far away.

14. The President reacted more favorably to the bill than the Senator.

15. My classmates enjoy the writings of Erskine Caldwell more than Shakespeare.

16. A day at the races, Mr. Beatty argues, is generally less harrowing than a prize fight.

17. There will be as many accidents this Fourth of July and maybe even more than there were last year.

18. The parents had not known that their son's illness was so serious.

19. Edgar Rice Burroughs' stories about Tarzan were much more exciting to boys of the 1920's than Superman is to boys today.

20. I did not know this was the correct way to hold the racket until the coach showed me.

21. My employer always has and always will be insolent to his employees.

22. The laughter of a loon is more frightening than an owl.

23. When the fire alarm rang through the building, the students were so calm.

24. It seemed to me at this point a change came over me.

25. George Bernard Shaw is the greatest dramatist.

26. I would have entered the sewing contest, but the other girls were so skillful.

27. The Aleutian Islands are one of the windiest, if not the windiest, place in the world.

28. *Ah! Wilderness*, the only comedy which Eugene O'Neil wrote, is quite different.

29. He had had little knowledge and experience with the trigger mechanism of the bomb.

30. The librarian became excited when she discovered the English workbook and chemistry laboratory manual were missing from the reserve shelf.

31. He wished very much to and probably would have taken the sedative if the doctor had not forbidden it.

32. I soon returned home because the climate was not too healthful.

33. To many students, quantitative analysis is as difficult if not more difficult than calculus.

20/Consistency

A consistent grammatical point of view makes for easy reading. Unnecessary changes in tense, mood, voice, number, and person can be annoying or misleading.

20a/Many unnecessary shifts in tense are from past to present or from present to past.

A shift in tense should reflect a real change in time, not a careless change in the writer's viewpoint.

NEEDLESS SHIFT FROM PAST TO PRESENT

I *sat* rigidly upright in the back seat of the taxi, wishing the traffic light would turn green. It *was* already five minutes of one, and my train *was* to leave at one. At last the light *changed*, and we *inched* through the heavy traffic to the station. Hope **is** almost gone, but I **hurl** myself through the door and **dash** madly toward the platform. I **risk** a glance toward the station clock. The hands **point** to twelve! The railroad *was* on Standard Time, and I *was* on Daylight Time.

NEEDLESS SHIFT FROM PRESENT TO PAST

Jane Austen's Emma *is* full of well-meant schemes for arranging other people's lives. She *persuades* her little friend Harriet that Farmer Martin *is* not a socially acceptable suitor, and she *diverts* Harriet's affections to the Reverend Mr. Elton. When that plan *misfires*, she *is* ready with still another, which *ends* even more disastrously. From this and other experiences Emma **learned** that it **was** dangerous to meddle with the affairs of others, and she **was** honest enough to admit her faults. Harriet **was** at last united with the young farmer, and Emma **married** the man who **had been** her unsparing critic.

Needless shifts between the conditional and other verb forms should be avoided. Conditional forms usually have *should*, *would*, or *could*.

> The next war *could be lost* within forty-eight hours if one of the powers *can make* a surprise attack. (Use *could be lost . . . could make*, or *can be lost . . . can make*.)

20b/The most frequent kind of careless shift in person is from the third to the second person, and vice versa.

> In felling a tree, *a good woodsman* [**3rd person**] first cuts a deep notch near the bottom of the trunk and on the side toward which *he* [**3rd person**] wishes the tree to fall. Then *you* [**2nd person**] saw on the other side, directly opposite

the notch. (The second sentence should read *Then he saws . . . .* Or the first, *you first cut . . . toward which you wish . . . .*)

20c/Unnecessary shifts in mood are typical of nonstandard English.

It is necessary that the applicant *fill* [**subjunctive**] in this form and *mail* [**not** *mails*, **indicative**] it by April 15.

If wishes *were* horses, beggars *would* [**not** *will*] ride.

20d/Unnecessary shifts in voice are often equivalent to failure in parallel structure.

POOR   My mother *cooked* [**active**] the shrimp casserole for thirty minutes; then it *was allowed* [**passive**] to cool.

BETTER My mother *cooked* the shrimp casserole for thirty minutes; then she *allowed* it to cool.

20e/Unnecessary shifts from one relative pronoun to another in a parallel construction weaken the parallelism.

SHIFT   She went to the cupboard *that* leaned perilously forward and *which* always resisted every attempt to open it.

CONSISTENT She went to the cupboard *which* leaned perilously forward and *which* always resisted every attempt to open it. (Or, *that . . . that.*)

20f/A shift from indirect to direct discourse in the same construction should be avoided.

 ←————————Indirect————————→
MIXED   Jan says she wants to go to the farmer's market and
 ←—Direct—→
 will it be open?

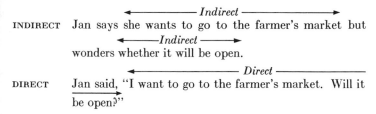

INDIRECT ← ———— *Indirect* ————— →
Jan says she wants to go to the farmer's market but ← ——*Indirect* —→ wonders whether it will be open.

DIRECT ← ————— *Direct* ————— →
Jan said, "I want to go to the farmer's market. Will it be open?"

Indirect discourse paraphrases the speaker's words; direct discourse quotes them exactly.

EXERCISE

Rewrite the following passage so that it maintains a consistent grammatical point of view.

Mother always told us that one who lives in a country town should know his neighbor, and you should try to love them as yourself. When the Swinsons moved to our town several years ago, they were at first loved by all of us. My brother became a good friend of their little boy Pete, who was the youngest child and that came to our house often to play. One day Pete tells us that he is going on a vacation and would we take care of his old bird dog Joe while he was gone. We agreed, and our troubles begin. Every night we were disturbed while Joe barked, and he also causes us trouble during the day. Joe tore up the clothes which were hung on the line and that were the best clothes we had, and the tomatoes in our garden were pulled off the vine by Joe. The row of corn was

pulled up by their roots. One day we found him sleeping in Aunt

Susan's petunias. Never take care of someone else's dog; you

should advise them to take them with them. Now we tell Mother

that no one should know his neighbor well. They impose on you.

PART TWO

CONVENTIONS

Punctuation

IN SPEAKING, we separate, group, and qualify words and sentences by means of pauses, intonations, gestures, and facial expressions. In writing, we must do without these aids and must depend on a set of symbols called **marks of punctuation.** These marks only partly reflect the signs of speech, so that it can be misleading to punctuate solely "by ear." A knowledge of the conventions of punctuation is therefore important, for punctuation marks, properly used, are essential to clear and easy reading. Consider the following:

What did you say asked Dolly twisting her handkerchief and screwing up her pretty face nothing to worry about dear quietly answered her mother what a fuss you do get into heavens now take the nice medicine

Without punctuation these sentences telescope confusingly, and it is not even possible to tell at first that two people are speaking. Now see how much clearer the passage becomes:

"What did you say?" asked Dolly, twisting her handkerchief and screwing up her pretty face.

"Nothing to worry about, dear," quietly answered her mother. "What a fuss you do get into! Heavens! Now take the nice medicine."

Many experienced writers punctuate almost by habit, but even they have to begin by learning to follow generally accepted practices. The chief of these are summarized in the following sections (**21–29**).

21/End Punctuation

End punctuation signals the end of a sentence, as a capital letter signals the beginning.

There are three end marks: the **period** (**.**), the **question mark** (**?**), and the **exclamation point** (**!**). Each also has special uses within a sentence.

21a/The **period** is used to end a sentence which makes a statement or expresses a wish or a command. Most sentences end with a period.

STATEMENT Professor Knight and Miss Johnson were married in the chapel on the campus.

     The best man asked the groom whether he had forgotten the ring. (This sentence is a statement even though it expresses an indirect question.)

WISH   I should like to be a million miles from here.

COMMAND Do not forget to pay the minister for performing the ceremony.

21b/Most abbreviations are followed by **periods.**

Use periods after such abbreviations as Mr., Dr., Pvt. Ave., B.C., A.M., Ph.D., e.g., ibid., and so forth.

In general, abbreviations of governmental and international agencies do not take periods: FCC, FBI, TVA, UN UNESCO, NATO, and so forth. Usage varies. When in doubt, consult your dictionary.

A comma or other mark of punctuation may follow the period after an abbreviation, but at the end of a sentence only one period is used.

After he earned his M.A., he began studying for his Ph.D. (*not* Ph.D..)

21c/The title of a theme (or book or periodical) does not take a **period** but may take a **question mark** or an **exclamation point.**

Shall We Dance?   *The Sound and the Fury*
Westward Ho!   *Ah! Wilderness*

21d/A **question mark** terminates an interrogative sentence, that is, a direct question. (See §**21a** for punctuation of an indirect question.)

Where were you at 12:30 on the night of December 10?

Did you file a report on the accident?

You filed a report on the accident? (A question in the form of a declarative sentence; see page 8.)

Question marks may follow separate questions within a single interrogative sentence.

Do you recall the time of the accident? the license numbers of the cars involved? the names of the drivers? of the witnesses?

21e/A **question mark** within parentheses is sometimes used to show that a date or a figure is doubtful.

Pythagoras, who died in 497 B.C.(?), was a mathematician and a philosopher.

Use of a question mark or an exclamation point within a sentence to indicate humor or sarcasm is a lame, unskillful device.

The comedy (?) was a miserable failure.

My roommate is so funny (!) he slays me.

21f/The **exclamation point** is used after a word, phrase or sentence to signal strong *exclamatory* feeling, but no just any intense emotion.

> Wait! I forgot my lunch!
> Stop the bus!

BUT NOT I don't think I ever felt more discouraged in my life

Never try to add feeling with an exclamation point when the exclamatory impact is not suggested by the wording of the sentence. Except in advertisements and comic strips modern writers are careful to use an exclamation point only when an expression is obviously exclamatory in tone.

Never use an exclamation point and a comma together

NOT "Help!," I cried.
"Help!", I cried.

BUT "Help!" I cried.

21g/Do not use two end punctuation marks together.

NOT What a fabulous day this has been!.
Just what do you think you will gain by that?.
Did you ask, "What time is it?"?

BUT What a fabulous day this has been!
Just what do you think you will gain by that?
Did you ask, "What time is it?"

In the following sentence, the second period is required because of the intervening parenthesis:

> He asked me how to punctuate interjections (*Oh, well, gosh* *etc.*).

E XE R C I S E

Correct errors in end punctuation in the following passage:

Dr Jeffrey E Tyndale, Sr, Ph D., JD., glanced at the sign which said "Fifth Ave" and wondered vaguely how he had lost his way? The siren sounded louder and louder!

"Stop," he heard someone shout! "You are headed wrong on a one-way street. Are you deaf, blind, drunk. Why didn't you stop when you heard the siren."

The handsome(?), frowning(!) policeman climbed off the motorcycle. "Well!", he said as he recognized the good doctor. "You were just driving forty in a fifteen-mile zone. I suppose this time you are chasing a spy for the C.I.C.."

"I'm awfully sorry!," said Professor Tyndale. "My new book *Why Were You Arrested.* was on my mind, and I wasn't thinking about my driving."

22/The Comma

The **comma,** the most common of the internal punctuation marks, is used within sentences partly to reflect pauses in speech, partly to mark off separate elements. It is chiefly used (1) to separate equal elements, such as independent clauses and items in a series, and (2) to set off modifiers or parenthetical words, phrases, and clauses. Elements which are set off within a sentence take a comma both *before* and *after.*

NOT   This novel, a best seller has no real literary merit.

BUT   This novel, a best seller, has no real literary merit.

22a/A comma is used to separate independent clauses joined by a coordinating conjunction.

NOT   The druggist prepared the prescription immediately for the girl seemed on the point of fainting.

BUT   The druggist prepared the prescription immediately, for the girl seemed on the point of fainting.

The weather was clear at Philadelphia, and the pilot requested permission to land there.

NOTE: The comma is sometimes omitted when the clauses are short and there is no danger of misreading.

The weather was clear and the pilot landed.

22b/A comma is used between members of a series, i.e., *three or more* similar items, whether words, phrases, or clauses.

In the attic we found old furniture, worn-out clothes, and several albums of pictures.

Some writers omit the final comma before *and* in a series.

In the attic we found old furniture, worn-out clothes and several albums of pictures.

But the comma must be used when *and* is omitted.

In the attic we found old furniture, worn-out clothes, several albums of pictures.

And it must be used when the final elements could be misread.

An old chest in the corner was filled with nails, hammers, a hacksaw and blades, and a brace and bit.

Series of phrases, dependent clauses, or independent clauses are also separated by commas.

PHRASES	We hunted for the letter in the album, in all the old trunks, and even under the rug.
DEPENDENT CLAUSES	Finally we decided that the letter had been burned, that someone else had already discovered it, or that it had never been written.
INDEPENDENT CLAUSES	We left the attic, Father locked the door, and Mother suggested that we never unlock it again.

In such series, the comma is not omitted before the final element.

EXERCISE

Insert commas wherever necessary in the following sentences.

1. I knew that she was smiling at me but somehow I could not force myself to look in her direction again.

2. The four books which he checked out of the library were *Of Time and the River Across the River and into the Trees Of Mice and Men* and *The Grapes of Wrath*.

3. The hamper was filled with cold cuts cheese crackers bread and butter mustard barbecue sauce and mixed pickles.

4. He picked up the book and the pencil fell to the floor.

5. The little boy liked all kinds of jellybeans but the ones with licorice flavor were his favorites.

6. The hunter should go into the blind load his gun sit perfectly still and wait patiently.

7. The instructor said that the class had not been doing very well in oral recitation that obviously everyone had failed to review his class notes properly and that he would be obliged to impose penalties.

8. For breakfast she served us bacon and eggs toast and jelly and hot coffee.

9. Careless driving includes speeding stopping suddenly making turns from the wrong lane of traffic going through red lights and so forth.

10. Driving was easy for a great part of the way was paved and traffic was light.

22c/A comma is used between coordinate adjectives not joined by *and*, but not between cumulative adjectives.

Note the difference:

COORDINATE

Madame de Stael was an attractive, gracious lady.

Ferocious, vigilant, loyal dogs were essential to safety in the Middle Ages.

CUMULATIVE

The tired old work horse finally topped the rise.

The witch turned out to be just a wizened little old woman.

Note that a comma is not used before the noun:

NOT   gracious, lady

       ferocious, dogs

BUT   gracious lady

       ferocious dogs

Coordinate adjectives modify the noun independently. Cumulative ones modify not only the noun, but the whole cluster of intervening adjectives. Two tests will be helpful.

TEST ONE   *And* is natural only between coordinate adjectives.

an attractive *and* gracious lady

ferocious *and* vigilant *and* loyal dogs

But not—

tired *and* old *and* work horse

wizened *and* little *and* old woman

TEST TWO   Coordinate adjectives are easily reversible.

a gracious, attractive lady

loyal, vigilant, ferocious dogs

But not—

work old tired horse

old little wizened woman

The distinction is not always clear-cut, however, and the sense of the cluster must be the deciding factor.

She was wearing a full-skirted, low-cut velvet gown.

(A velvet gown that was full-skirted and low-cut; not a gown that was full-skirted and low-cut and velvet.)

EXERCISE

Punctuate the following. When in doubt apply the tests described above.

1. the pretty little mountain village
2. a broad-shouldered sinister-looking man
3. a high-crowned lemon-yellow straw hat
4. a hot sultry depressing day
5. a little brick bungalow

6. a woebegone ghostly look
7. straight strawberry-blond hair
8. the present large freshman class
9. the first long base hit of the game
10. the gloomy forbidding night scene

22d/A comma generally sets off a long introductory subordinate phrase or clause.

LONG PHRASE   With this bitter part of the ordeal behind us, we felt more confident.

LONG CLAUSE   When this bitter part of the ordeal was behind us, we felt more confident.

When the introductory element is short (usually six words or less) and there is no danger of misreading, the comma is often omitted.

SHORT PHRASE   After this bitter ordeal we felt more confident.

SHORT CLAUSE   When this ordeal was over we felt more confident.

Regardless of their length, introductory participial, infinitive, and gerund phrases are generally set off by commas.

PARTICIPLE   Turning abruptly, she stalked from the room.

INFINITIVE   To verify or correct his hypothesis, the scientist performs an experiment.

GERUND   After surviving this ordeal, we felt relieved.

An element that would be set off by a comma at the beginning of the sentence usually does not require a comma if it comes at the end of the sentence.

BEGINNING   If you turn in your papers today, you need not come to class tomorrow.

END   You need not come to class tomorrow if you turn in your papers today.

XERCISE

Insert needed commas in the following sentences. If a sentence is correct as it stands, label it C.

1. As the ship left the harbor and entered the open sea the young scientist forgot his difficulties.

2. After checking the address once more the Reverend Joel Patrick dropped the letter in the slot.

3. By the time the telegram finally arrived Mary was no longer expecting it.

4. Since the library had not yet received a copy of *Atoms for Peace* I was obliged to order one from the publisher.

5. Still running at top speed he rounded the corner of the house and saw his father standing right in his path.

6. After properly grating the coconut you should sprinkle it on the cake.

7. Of all her many delightful qualities I like her quiet humor best.

8. To regulate the machinery he was first obliged to readjust the flywheel.

9. At midnight the bell tolled mournfully.

10. After Rima died Abel became a skeptic because God had not saved her from the wrath of the savages.

22e/Nonrestrictive appositives, phrases, and clauses are set off by commas; restrictive appositives, phrases, and clauses are not.

A restrictive modifier points out or identifies its noun or pronoun; remove the modifier, and the sentence radically changes in meaning or becomes nonsense. A nonrestrictive modifier describes and adds information but does not point out or identify; omit the modifier, and the sentence loses some meaning but does not change radically or become meaningless.

RESTRICTIVE Taxicabs *that are dirty* are illegal in some cities.

Water *which is murky in appearance* should always be boiled before drinking.

The priest *who died on the altar* was my uncle.

The man *in the gray flannel suit* typifies a vast group of Americans.

The play *Hamlet* has been a scholar's delight for over 300 years.

I did not do it *because my father told me to;* I did it *because I wanted to.*

In all these sentences, the italicized expressions identify the words they modify; to remove these modifiers is to change the meaning radically or to leave the sentence an empty shell. Contrast with the following:

NONRESTRICTIVE Taxicabs, *which are always expensive,* cost less in New York than elsewhere.

Oil, *which is lighter than water,* rises to the surface.

Father Preston, *who died on the altar,* was my uncle.

Red Walker, *in a gray flannel suit,* looked like a typical young American.

Shakespeare's last play, *The Tempest,* is optimistic and even sunny in mood.

We did not try to solve the problem, *because our teacher said it was too hard for us.*

In these sentences the italicized modifiers add information but they do not point out or identify. They do not tell which taxicabs, what kind of oil or water, which priest, and so on. They expand the meaning of the sentence, but are not essential to it.

NOTE: *That* never introduces a nonrestrictive clause.

Some modifiers can be read either as restrictive or as nonrestrictive, and the punctuation indicates which meaning is intended.

> The coin which gleamed in the sunlight was a Spanish doubloon. (There were several coins.)
>
> The coin, which gleamed in the sunlight, was a Spanish doubloon. (Only one coin.)

In speech, a nonrestrictive modifier may be preceded by a pronounced pause, whereas a restrictive modifier is not. Reading a questionable sentence aloud usually shows whether or not a modifier should be set off by commas.

EXERCISE

A

Answer the questions about each of the following pairs of sentences.

1. A. My sister Myrtle McBride came to visit me last week end.
   B. My sister, Mary Moore, came to visit me last week end.
      How many sisters has the writer of sentence *A*?
      How many sisters has the writer of sentence *B*?

2. A. James Thomson, who was the author of *The Seasons*, was a friend of Pope.
   B. The James Thomson who was the author of *The Seasons* was a friend of Pope.
      There were two English poets named James Thomson, one who wrote *The Seasons* in the eighteenth century and one who wrote *The City of Dreadful Night* in the nineteenth century. Why would sentence *A* be likely to appear in a biography of Pope? Why would sentence *B* be likely to appear in a history of English literature?

3. A. The boy, carrying a lady's purse, blushed with shame.
   B. The boy carrying a lady's purse blushed with shame.
      Explain both sentences.

4. A. With one shot I bagged the two turkeys which were feeding under the oak tree.
   B. With one shot I bagged the two turkeys, which were feeding under the oak tree.
      Explain both sentences.

5. A. The kitten which has a white ring around its tail is exceptionally frisky.
   B. The kitten, which has a white ring around its tail, is exceptionally frisky.
      Explain both sentences.

B

Insert necessary commas in the sentences below. If a sentence is correct as it stands, label it C.

1. Render unto Caesar the things which are Caesar's.

2. The English poet Milton composed his two most famous poems *Paradise Lost* and *Paradise Regained* when he was blind.

3. The quotation "Whatever is, is right" is from Alexander Pope's poem *Essay on Man*.

4. Dora is the most satisfactory maid who has ever worked for us.

5. I had a successful shopping trip, during which I bought a daring hat and a handbag to match. The hat which I got at Johnson's cost only $27.50, and the bag which I got at Thomason's cost only $10.98.

6. I read the book because it had been recommended to me by my roommate.

7. I did not promise to read the book because my parents had told me not to read it.

8. The water which comes from this mountain spring tastes better than that which we draw from the well at home.

9. All afternoon the band played "On, Old Ivy," and the crowd sang "On, Old Ivy." As I drove home after the game, these same words "On, Old Ivy" kept ringing in my ears.

10. Bluebeard's wife Fatima has become a symbol of feminine curiosity.

11. The people who found the lost child took him to their home where they fed him and put him to bed.

12. The cry "All aboard!" rang through the station just as I arrived.

13. When it was time to eat, we dressed and went down to the dining room which was very attractive.

14. The play *A Doll's House* which was written by the Norwegian dramatist Ibsen was very controversial when it was first produced.

15. The smallest soldier marching in the color guard is the one who has earned the Congressional Medal of Honor.

22f/**Sentence modifiers and sentence elements out of normal word order are usually set off by commas.**

Sentence modifiers like *on the other hand, for example, in fact, in the first place, I believe, in his opinion, unfortunately,* and *certainly* are set off by commas.

His mother, I believe, taught school before her marriage.

In my opinion, Wells's early novels stand the test of time better than his later ones.

The transitional conjunctions *therefore, moreover, then, consequently, nevertheless,* and so on are set off by commas when special emphasis is desired.

The secretary checked the figures once more; the mistake was therefore discovered.

OR   The secretary checked the figures once more; the mistake was, therefore, discovered.

Notice that *however* as a transitional conjunction should be set off by commas when necessary to distinguish it from the adverb *however*, meaning "no matter how much."

ADVERB   However beautiful she is, she cannot win this contest.

TRANSITIONAL   However, beautiful as she is, she cannot win this
CONJUNCTION   contest.

                          Beautiful as she is, however, she cannot win this contest.

When part of a sentence is out of its normal word order, it is set off by commas if necessary for clearness or emphasis.

Aged and infirm, the Emperor ruled through his loyal ministers.

OR   The Emperor, aged and infirm, ruled through his loyal ministers.

BUT The aged and infirm Emperor ruled through his loyal ministers.

He was determined, although he was unnerved by his fright, to spend some weeks in the house alone. (The adverb clause here interrupts the movement of the sentence.)

22g/Commas are used to set off such elements as dates, places, addresses, degrees, and titles.

DATES   Sunday, May 31, is the date of commencement this year.

August 1945 marked the end of our fighting with Japan but December 31, 1946, was proclaimed as the official day of victory. (When the day of the month is not given, the year may or may not be set off by commas.

When the day is given, the year should be set off; when the year comes within the sentence, as above, the second comma must not be omitted.)

I entered college on 21 September 1945. (This military style of writing dates requires no comma.)

The Korean War began in the year 1950. (No comma is used here because 1950 is a restrictive appositive. See §22e and §23j.)

PLACES   The name of Cairo, Illinois, is pronounced differently from that of Cairo, Egypt.

ADDRESSES

I suggest that you send your manuscript to the editor of *The Atlantic Monthly*, 8 Arlington Street, Boston 16, Massachusetts.

DEGREES AND TITLES

Bill Snipes, Ph. D., is our county historian.

Charles Morton, Jr., Chairman of the Board, was unable to attend. (A degree or a title is set off by commas. In alphabetical listings the abbreviations for *junior* and *senior* should come after the whole name: John Smith, Jr., but Smith, John, Jr.)

EXERCISE

Insert necessary commas in the passage below. Do not clutter the passage with needless commas.

However often Susan Miller read the short novel which she had written she found a paragraph that needed changing. Consequently she asked her best friend Steve Adams the noted columnist to read it and make suggestions. After six months Steve returned the manuscript yellow and stained by this time and suggested that it was excellent and that she should therefore send it to his literary agent James Walling 39 Sexton Place Philadelphia 39 Pennsylvania. Susan always cautious still felt however that the manuscript needed further revision. She read and revised it and typed it several more times and finally on February 13 1959 she mailed it to the agent. Immediately he placed it with the Universal Publishing Company. The editor accepted it with only two conditions: namely that she use a masculine pseudonym such as Ralph Sullivan Jr. and that she choose an exciting title. *Murder De Luxe* he suggested would be a good choice. The acceptance of this story in the year 1959 began the literary career of Ralph Sullivan Jr.

22h/Commas are frequently used to point a contrast, to give emphasis, and to set off short interrogative elements.

> She was beautiful, but devoid of personality.
> The pilot had been forced to use an auxiliary landing field, not the city airport.
> The landing strip was unpaved, and muddy, and unlighted. (Commas should not be used here unless you wish to give special emphasis to each adjective.)
> The field was safe enough, wasn't it?

22i/A comma is used to set off mild interjections and words like *yes* and *no*.

> Oh, I guess I'll go if you insist.
> Well, I did not think it was possible.
> No, it proved to be quite simple.

22j/Commas are used to set off words in direct address and to follow the salutation of a personal letter.

> Mary, have you heard the latest story about Mrs. Towers?
> Dear John,
>> It has been some time since I've heard from you. . . .

22k/Commas are used to set off expressions like *he said*, *he remarked*, and *he replied* used with quoted matter.

> She said, "I am planning to give up Latin at the beginning of next term."
> "I am planning to give up Latin," she remarked, "at the beginning of next term.
> "It's all Greek to me," she replied.

22l/Commas are used to set off an absolute phrase.

An absolute phrase consists of a noun followed by a modifier. It modifies the sentence as a whole, not any single element in it.

> ←*Absolute phrase*→
> Our journey over, we made camp for the night.

> ←————— *Absolute phrase* —————→
> The fighter having returned to his corner, the referee began the count.

22m/A comma is used to mark an omission or to prevent ambiguity or misreading.

> To err is human; to forgive, divine. (The comma here marks the omission of the word *is*.)

Notice how commas prevent misreading in the following sentences:

> After washing and grooming, the pup looked like a new dog.
> When violently angry, elephants trumpet.
> Beyond, the open fields sloped gently to the sea.

EXERCISES

A

Add necessary commas to the following sentences.

1. Pedro escaped to the New World with his friend Garcia and his father and mother went to Italy.

2. Once he had begun it did not take him long to read the book.

3. The children were noisy; the parents disgusted; the guests amused.

4. After all the states get help from the federal government in building highways.

5. As the motorcade rolled by the crowd cheered.

6. Although inexperienced workers may apply.

7. Inside the house cats were romping and playing.

8. He turned suddenly to John Brown not having arrived yet and began a story of how the fight started.

9. After saying that he left the room.

10. Since then he was paid we owe him nothing.

B

Add necessary commas to the following passage.

"I'm not afraid of you!" exclaimed Catherine who could not hear the latter part of his speech. She stepped close up her black eyes flashing with passion and resolution. "Give me that key! I will have it!" she said. "I wouldn't eat or drink here if I were starving."

Heathcliff had the key in his hand that remained on the table. He looked up seized with a sort of surprise at her boldness or possibly reminded by her voice and glance of the person from whom she inherited it. She snatched at the instrument and half succeeded in getting it out of his loosened fingers but her action recalled him to the present; he recovered it speedily.

"Now Catherine Linton" he said "stand off or I shall knock you down and that will make Mrs. Dean mad."

Regardless of this warning she captured his closed hand and its contents again. "We *will* go!" she repeated exerting her utmost efforts to cause the iron muscles to relax; and finding that her nails made no impression she applied her teeth pretty sharply. Heathcliff glanced at me a glance that kept me from interfering a moment. Catherine was too intent on his fingers to notice his face. He opened them suddenly and resigned the object of dispute; but ere she had well secured it he seized her with the liberated hand; and pulling her on his knee he administered with the other a shower of terrific slaps on the side of the head each sufficient to have fulfilled his threat had she been able to fall.

At this diabolical violence I rushed on him furiously. "You villain!" I began to cry "You villain!" A touch on the chest silenced me: I am stout and soon put out of breath; and what with that and the rage I staggered dizzily back and felt ready to suffocate or to burst a blood vessel. The scene was over in two minutes. Catherine released put her two hands to her temples and she looked just as if she were not sure whether her ears were off or on. She trembled like a reed poor thing and leaned against the table perfectly bewildered.

Adapted from Emily Brontë, *Wuthering Heights*

23/Unnecessary Commas

Modern practice does not demand a comma at every possible pause within a sentence. Most readers and writers today feel that it is better to use too little punctuation than too much.

23a/A comma should not be used between a subject and its verb or between a verb or verbal and its complement unless there are intervening elements which should be set off.

NOT
: The guard with the drooping mustache, snapped to attention.

: The colonel said, that he had never seen such discipline.

: Some students in the class, admitted, that they had not read, "Kubla Khan."

COMMAS WITH INTERVENING ELEMENTS
: Harry, when he had completed his assignment, began to read "The Rime of the Ancient Mariner."

: The guard, whose mustache drooped ridiculously, snapped to attention.

23b/A comma is not used in compound constructions consisting of two parts (subjects, verbs, complements, or predicates) except for contrast or emphasis.

UNNECESSARY
: *John,* and *James* **stood,** and **talked** with *Joan,* and *Jane.*

: He *left* the scene of the accident, and *tried* to forget that it had happened.

For the use of commas for contrast or emphasis, see §22h.

23c/A comma is not used before a coordinating conjunction joining two equal dependent clauses except for contrast or emphasis.

UNNECESSARY   The contractor testified that the house was completed, and that the work had been done properly.

For the use of the comma to separate independent clauses, see §22a.

23d/A comma is not used between an adjective and the word it modifies.

In such constructions a comma is most likely to slip in after the last adjective in a series.

FAULTY   Kay is a naive, innocent, mischievous, child.

23e/A comma is not used before *than* in a comparison or between compound conjunctions like *as . . . as, so . . . as, so . . . that*.

AVOID   John Holland was more delighted with life on the Continent, than he had thought he could be.

Mr. Holland was so pleased by his son's success in college, that he gave him a trip to Europe.

23f/A comma is not used after *like, such as,* and similar expressions introducing an enumeration.

A phrase introduced by *such as* is set off by commas only if it is nonrestrictive. The comma comes before *such as*, not after.

COMMA HERE
↓

Professor Tyndale knows ancient Germanic languages, such

NOT HERE
↓
as Gothic and Old Norse.

23g/ Modern practice does not favor a comma with a question mark, an exclamation point, or a dash. These marks stand by themselves.

AVOID   "Look!"꙳ Minna exclaimed; "the letter came."

"Did you get the job?"꙳ her roommate asked.

"I'll tell you꙳ — well, never mind."

23h/ A comma may be used after a parenthesis, but not before it.

NOT   When he had finished reading *The Pilgrim's Progress*꙳ (the most popular allegory in the language) he turned next to *The House of the Seven Gables*.

BUT   When he had finished reading *The Pilgrim's Progress* (the most popular allegory in the language)꙳ he turned next to *The House of the Seven Gables*.

23i/ A comma is not usual after a short essential introductory adverbial clause or phrase.

NOT PREFERRED   During his English class꙳ he tried to solve the problem in calculus.

NOT PREFERRED   After he had slept꙳ he felt more confident.

For the use of the comma after a long introductory clause or phrase, see **§22d**.

23j/ Restrictive clauses, phrases, or appositives are not set off by commas.

NOT   People꙳ who live in glass houses꙳ should not throw stones.

NOT PRE-FERRED   I have just finished reading the short story꙳ "The Murders in the Rue Morgue." (Commas are sometimes used in this kind of construction, but not usually.)

Refer also to **§22e**.

23k/A comma is not used between adjectives which are not
    coordinate.

FAULTY   The tired, old, work horse

            His new, Sunday suit

            A feeble, little, old man

Refer also to **§22c.**

EXERCISES

A

Remove unnecessary commas from the following paragraph.

Boys read *Huckleberry Finn* as an adventure story, and fail to
realize, that Mark Twain was making a vicious attack on society.
Many characters in this book, such as, the King and the Duke, the
Grangerfords, and Colonel Sherburn, exemplify man's depravity.
The unsophisticated, simple, boy, Huck, and the ignorant, almost
uncivilized, Negro, Jim, are the best two characters in the novel,
and the spokesmen of the author. But, even Huck sometimes
exemplifies Twain's pessimism, and illustrates man's lack of sym-
pathy for man. In Chapter 32, Huck tells Mrs. Phelps about an
accident on a river boat, and she exclaims, "Good gracious!, anybody hurt?" "No'm!", he replies. "Killed a nigger." Although
children think this serious, American novel is entirely humorous and
adventurous, and as adults never remember the scathing attack on
society and institutions, Mark Twain was so bitter when he wrote
Huckleberry Finn and his later works, that several studies have
been made of his pessimism.

B

Remove unnecessary commas from the following paragraph.

It was not so much his great height, that marked him [Ethan
Frome], for the "natives," were easily singled out by their lank
longitude from the stockier, foreign, breed: it was the careless,

powerful look, he had, in spite of a lameness, checking each step like the jerk of a chain. There was something, bleak and unapproachable in his face, and he was so stiffened and grizzled, that I took him for an old man, and was surprised to hear, that he was not more, than fifty-two. I had this from Harmon Gow, who had driven the stage from Bettsbridge to Starkfield in pre-trolley days, and [who] knew the chronicle of all the families, [who lived] on his line. . . .

Every one in Starkfield knew him, and gave him a greeting, tempered to his own, grave, mien; but his taciturnity, was respected, and it was only on rare occasions, that one of the older men of the place, detained him for a word. When this happened, he would listen quietly, his blue eyes on the speaker's face, and answer in so low a tone, that his words never reached me; then, he would climb stiffly into his buggy, gather up the reins in his left hand, and drive slowly away, in the direction of his farm.

Adapted from Edith Wharton, *Ethan Frome*[1]

24/The Semicolon

The **semicolon,** a stronger separator than the comma, is used between coordinate elements, especially closely related independent clauses which balance or contrast with each other.

Failure to use a semicolon may result in a comma fault or a fused sentence. See §2 and §3.

24a/A semicolon is generally used between two independent clauses not connected by a coordinating conjunction (*and, but, or, nor, for, so, yet*).

A semicolon is used when the second independent clause is introduced by a conjunctive adverb (*however, therefore,*

---

[1]Adapted for this exercise by permission of the publishers, Charles Scribner's Sons.

moreover, then, consequently) or by a sentence modifier (*in fact, in the first place, for example, on the other hand*).

WITH NO CONNECTIVE

For fifteen years the painting stood in the attic; even Mr. Kirk forgot it.

"It needed cleaning, and the frame was cracked," he explained later; "we just stored it away."

WITH A CONJUNCTIVE ADVERB

In 1955 a specialist from the museum arrived and asked to examine it; then all the family became excited.

WITH A SENTENCE MODIFIER

The painting was valuable; in fact, the museum offered five thousand dollars for it.

24b/A semicolon is often used between independent clauses to gain emphasis or to indicate strong contrast or balance, especially when the clauses are parallel in structure.

The teacher continued lecturing; but the class rose to go.

Autocratic power springs from the will of the ruler; but democratic power rises from the will of the people.

24c/A semicolon is used to mark off independent clauses which are complex in structure or which have internal punctuation.

In many compound sentences either a semicolon or a comma may be used.

COMMA OR   *Moby-Dick*, by Melville, is an adventure story; [*or* ,] SEMICOLON   and it is also one of the world's great philosophical novels.

SEMICOLON
PREFERRED
    Ishmael, the narrator, goes to sea, he says, "whenever it is a damp, drizzly November" in his soul; and Ahab, the captain of the ship, goes to sea because of his obsession to hunt and kill the great albino whale, Moby-Dick.

24d/A semicolon is used between items in a series which have internal punctuation.

    When Robert was fifteen he had three problems: Jean, his younger sister; Mary, who called him on the telephone incessantly; and Angela, who didn't.

24e/A semicolon is *not* used between elements which are not coordinate, such as an independent and a dependent clause or a clause and a phrase.

FAULTY
    After he had signaled to his friend twice; he gave up and left the library.

    Bertha always dreaded thunderstorms; remembering that time when lightning struck the big oak tree and set the barn on fire.

EXERCISE

Remove unnecessary semicolons and commas from the following sentences, and insert necessary ones. If a sentence is correct as it stands, label it C.

1. After Casey, the best hitter on the home team had struck out; hearts were sad in Mudville.

2. Since the dance was already almost over; Carol refused to stay longer and Joe then sullenly drove her home.

3. Read this sentence several times then punctuate it acceptably.

4. "If you will open the safe," he courteously said to the banker; "I will take the money."

5. "I am leaving now," he said politely, "you may open the door for me."

6. The dejected farmer thought about the crops he had produced during the driest year of the depression: corn, fifty bushels at fifty cents a bushel, peanuts, two tons at thirty dollars a ton, and cotton, two five-hundred-pound bales at five cents a pound. Then, he mused, times were hard, and it took a good farmer to make a living, but now with prices high and a good season coming every year, even a lazy farmer can do well.

7. He tried to stop smoking again; but again he could not.

8. The names of the winners were announced slowly and distinctly: Davis, third place, Matthews, second place, Erlman, first place. That was all; and Charlie rose to go.

9. The trainer watched for the horse to round the bend and come splashing down the muddy track, still he did not come.

10. Mr. Norman, assistant manager of the store, apologized, but Mrs. Newman, still disgruntled, was not appeased.

25/The Colon

The **colon** is a formal and emphatic mark of introduction. It also has certain conventional uses.

25a/A colon is used before quotations, statements, and series which are being introduced formally.

> Sock and Buskin announces the opening of the following plays: *King Lear*, May 10; *The Circle*, June 14; and *Death of a Salesman*, July 19.

> The attorney for the defense made a brief speech: "Gentlemen, you need no explanation of the case. The evidence has proved my client's innocence."

As shown just above, a quotation may be formally introduced without a verb of saying (*says*, *replies*, *remarks*, etc.). In very formal writing the colon may be used after such verbs, though a comma is more usual.

Then Othello said: "Keep up your bright swords, for the dew
will rust them."

OR   Then Othello said, ...

**25b/A colon may be used between two independent clauses
when the second explains or amplifies the first.**

Music is more than something mechanical: it is an expression
of deep feeling and ethical values.

The results of the hurricane were disastrous: the cottages were
completely swept from the beach, and even the shore line
was changed.

**25c/A colon may be used before formal appositives, includ-
ing those introduced by such expressions as *namely*,
e.g., and *that is*.**

Note that the colon comes before *namely* and similar
expressions, not after.

Our conduct, Dooley said, would have one result: dismissal.

He gave us only a warning: namely, that we should not practice
hazing again.

It was possible to reach a different conclusion: e.g., that our
offense had been trivial.

**25d/The colon has certain purely formal uses: between hours
and minutes to indicate time, after the salutation of a
formal letter, and (sometimes) between city and publisher in bibliographical entries.**

12:15 P.M.

Dear Dr. Tyndale:

Boston: Houghton Mifflin Company

**25e/A colon is not used after a linking verb, a preposition,
or an informal introduction.**

FAULTY   My three chief diversions are**:** bridge, billiards, and chess.
His partner accused him of**:** talking too much during the game and not remembering what had been played.

Colons serve no function in these sentences.

26/The Dash

The **dash** is used to indicate interruptions, to introduce summaries, and to set off parenthetical material.

26a/The dash indicates sudden interruptions, quick changes in thought, and breaks in construction.

There is no reason for — but perhaps I should discuss another topic now.
He replied, "I will consider the — No, I won't either."

26b/The dash is used for special and dramatic emphasis.

The dash is sometimes an informal equivalent for the colon:

Our conduct, Dooley said, would have only one result — dismissal.

Or it may give more stress than commas or parentheses to set off an element within a sentence:

His suit — a sickly green — was hardly appropriate to the occasion.
The old house — which, the boys assured me, was certainly haunted — stood in the gloom of towering pines.

26c/The dash is sometimes used before a summary of a preceding series.

Elephants, donkeys, and trapeze artists — all were performing at the same time.
Attic fans, window fans, air conditioners — nothing would cool that room.

26d/Dashes should be used sparingly.

Many immature writers use dashes indiscriminately instead of other marks of punctuation. Dull writing or childish sentences are not improved by a sprinkling of dashes.

27/Parentheses

Parentheses are used to enclose comment and explanation loosely connected to the structure of the sentence. They also enclose figures in a list or enumeration, and numerals used to avoid misreading when numbers are spelled out.

> The oil well (the company had drilled it only as an experiment) produced a thousand barrels a day.

> Although the company had not expected a significant yield from the new oil well (they had drilled it only as an experiment), it produced a thousand barrels a day. (Note that the comma comes *outside* the closing parenthesis; the parenthetical expression is part of or associated with the dependent clause.)

> John Nance Garner was Vice-President during Roosevelt's first term of office (1933–1937). (Note that the end punctuation of this sentence comes *outside* the closing parenthesis. When an entire sentence is enclosed in parentheses, however, the end punctuation is placed *inside* the closing parenthesis.)

> The oil company refused to buy the land (1) because the owner had no clear title to the property and (2) because it was too far from the company's other wells.

> I hereby agree to pay a sum of three thousand dollars ($3,000.00) on receipt of title.

Here are some useful rules of thumb:

Loosely connected parenthetical material is best enclosed in parentheses.

Closely connected parenthetical material is best set off by commas.

Material to be dramatically emphasized is best set off by dashes.

A formal appositive, list, or quotation at the end of a sentence is best introduced by a colon.

28/Brackets

Brackets are used to enclose material inserted within a quotation to explain or correct it, or to enclose a parenthesis within a parenthesis.

> "He [Mark Twain] was a newspaper reporter in Virginia City in 1862."

> "Mark Twaine [sic] is the pseudonym of Samuel Langhorne Clemens."

NOTE: *Sic*, Latin for "thus" or "so," bracketed within a quotation indicates that an error just preceding has been retained intentionally.

> The school he attended (Fernbank High School [the newest one in the county]) now has an enrollment too large for the plant.

EXERCISES

A

Insert colons, dashes, parentheses, and brackets where necessary in the following sentences. If a sentence is correct as it stands, label it C.

1. An objectionable roommate has several disagreeable characteristics punctuality, studiousness, and neatness.

2. She had but one thing to say to me "No!"

3. Professor Pennypacker began his lecture "He as usual the

Professor didn't say whom he was talking about used too many broken twigs in his stories."

4. Scattered about the room lay books, notebooks, loose sheets of paper, and two pairs of dirty shoes.

5. You should this is important notify him to come to the meeting at 920 A.M.

6. An athlete a true athlete must be more than a mere expert he must also pride himself on his sportsmanship, his spirit of competition, and his calmness.

7. I'm afraid that Tom won't get here he is now!

B

Add colons, dashes, parentheses, and brackets where necessary in the following passage.

The student's reading of the difficult poem was entirely unacceptable to Professor Pennypacker.

"Read the poem listen to me carefully read the poem again," the Professor grumbled. After the poor fellow had read through the poem once more it was extremely short, the Professor sighed.

"There's one thing you can't do read a poem," he remarked "It's impossible to teach you how in a moment. Tonight between six o'clock and 1200 midnight I want you to read some in three books 1 Guy Jones's *How to Read*, 2 Carl Taylor and Jane Edens's *Oral Expression*, and 3 Harvey Benjamin's *Reading for Pleasure* Jones, Taylor, Edens, and Benjamin these authors know the art of reading aloud. The way you read a poem is important it may cause you to love it or despise it."

Embarrassed, the student left the office with one determination to pick an easier poem next time.

29/Quotation Marks

Quotation marks are used to enclose the exact words of a speaker or writer and to set off some titles. Most American publishers use double quotation marks ("...") except for internal quotations, which they set off by single quotation marks ('...').

29a/Quotation marks are used to enclose direct quotations and dialogue.

DIRECT QUOTATION At a high point in the play, the Duke of Gloucester says, "As flies to wanton boys, are we to the gods. They kill us for their sport."

DIALOGUE "My grandmother," she said, "smokes a pipe."

"An imported brier?" he asked.

"No, an old corncob pipe with a cane stem." There was an uncomfortable lull in their conversation.

Note that in dialogue a new paragraph marks each change of speaker.

When a direct quotation is more than one paragraph long, quotation marks are used at the beginning of each paragraph but after only the last one.

In a famous short story, Ernest Hemingway uses short paragraphs to describe action:

"The old man stood up, slowly counted the saucers, took a leather coin purse from his pocket and paid for the drinks, leaving half a peseta tip.

"The waiter watched him go down the street, a very old man walking unsteadily but with dignity."

In typescript, quotations (other than dialogue) which are more than four lines long may be set in block form, that is, indented and single-spaced. Quotation marks are not used with blocked quotations. (See page 393.)

29b/Single quotation marks are used to enclose internal quotations, that is, quotations within quotations.

> Professor Jackson was a teetotaler, but he made this statement in his lecture on Hemingway: "In Hemingway's writing even an intoxicated octogenarian walks 'unsteadily but with dignity.'"

29c/Quotation marks are used to enclose titles of essays, articles, short stories, short poems, and chapters or other subdivisions of books or periodicals. Titles of paintings also are set off by quotation marks.

> "The Secret Life of Walter Mitty" is the story of a timid man who daydreams on a heroic scale.
>
> "The Raven" is Poe's most popular poem.
>
> Chapter IV of the book *Spots on the Cards* is entitled "The Jack of Diamonds." (For the use of italics to distinguish titles of books, see §32a.)
>
> A cheap reproduction of Van Gogh's "Sunflowers" hung on the wall above her desk.

29d/Do *not* use quotation marks to enclose indirect quotations, or to defend or emphasize slang, colloquialisms, or attempts at humor.

FAULTY Professor Ruggles asked "Whether anyone had failed to enjoy the story."

ACCEPTABLE Professor Ruggles asked whether anyone had failed to enjoy the story.

UNNECESSARY	The rumor was that Colonel Peters had once been a ""playboy.""
ACCEPTABLE	The rumor was that Colonel Peters had once been a playboy.

29e/There are rigid conventions for the placing of other punctuation with quotation marks.

In American usage, **periods** and **commas** are placed inside quotation marks.

> None of the students had read "The Raven."
>
> "Well," Professor Pennypacker sighed, "you should always study your lesson."

Semicolons and **colons** are always placed *outside* closing quotation marks.

> The customer wrote that he was "not yet ready to buy the first edition"; it was too expensive.
>
> Thomas Wolfe referred to three geographical areas as "Dark Helen": the South, New England, and Germany.

A **question mark** or an **exclamation point** is placed *inside* quotation marks only when the quotation itself is a direct question or an exclamation. Otherwise, these marks are placed *outside*.

> He asked, "Am I shot?" (Only the quotation is a question.)
>
> "Am I shot?" he asked. (Only the quotation is a question.)
>
> Did he ask, "Am I shot?" (The quotation and the entire sentence are questions.)
>
> Did he say, "I am shot"? (The entire sentence asks a question; the quotation makes a statement.)
>
> She tried to scream, "Shot!" (Only the quotation is an exclamation.)
>
> Curse the man who whispers, "No"! (The entire statement is an exclamation; the quotation is not.)

GENERAL EXERCISES

A

Supply quotation marks where necessary in the following sentences. If a sentence is correct as it stands, label it C.

1. She stated that she was delighted to accept his invitation.

2. By the time the speaker had finished, the audience felt that some things were rotten in places other than Denmark.

3. Did Ward say, It is Cindy's fault?

4. Is it Cindy's fault? Ward asked.

5. Cindy's! I exclaimed.

6. I exclaimed, Cindy's!

7. Ward asked, Is it Cindy's fault?

8. It will be bad weather tomorrow, our guide said, since the northeast wind has started blowing.

9. It will be bad weather tomorrow, our guide said; the northeast wind has started blowing.

10. Do you prefer, the professor asked, the passage beginning with Ah, love, let us be true or the one containing the words If Winter comes, can Spring be far behind?

11. Old Hickory is reported to have said, Damn the man who knows how to spell a word just one way.

B

Supply quotation marks as needed in the following passage, and indicate new paragraphs where necessary by inserting the sign ¶.

When Bartley Hubbard went to interview Silas Lapham for the *Solid Men of Boston* series, which he undertook to finish up in

The Events, after he replaced their original projector on that newspaper, Lapham received him in his private office by previous appointment. Walk right in! he called out to the journalist. He did not rise from the desk at which he was writing, and he rolled his large head in the direction of a vacant chair. Sit down! I'll be with you in just half a minute. Take your time, said Bartley. I'm in no hurry. There! Lapham pounded with his great hairy fist on the envelope he had been addressing. William! he called out. Will you mail this letter right away? He continued, Well, sir, so you want my life, death, and Christian sufferings, do you, young man? That's what I'm after, said Bartley. Your money or your life. I guess you wouldn't want my life without the money, said Lapham, as if he were willing to prolong these moments of preparation.

The most significant part of the interview was that in which Silas described how he had built his paint-manufacturing business.

I took hold of the paint and rushed it — all I could, said Lapham. But I found when I returned from the war that I had got back to another world. The day of small things was past, and I don't suppose it will ever come again in this country. My wife was at me all the time to take a partner — somebody with capital; but I couldn't seem to bear the idea. That paint was like my own blood to me. I used to say, Why didn't you take a partner yourself, Persis, while I was away? And she'd say, Well, if you hadn't come back, I should, Si. Always *did* like a joke about as well as any woman *I* ever saw. Well, I had to come to it. I took a partner.

Adapted from William Dean Howells, *The Rise of Silas Lapham*

C

Punctuate the following passage, adding capitals where necessary.

Many failures in college happen because freshmen think that college is a place in which to learn a trade or business having received high-school credit for typing shorthand automobile driving band and what not they are chagrined to learn that college is not like that Dean Whiteman of Yale says that students often complain about courses such as economics on the ground that these courses do not tell anyone how to run a business they just teach theories in much the same way every college of engineering has on its hands a number of freshmen who are misfits at the start because they are not working with their hands but are exposed to English history and psychology a college course in electricity is not for the embryo television-repair man who should go to trade school not college

Those who have this mistaken idea often drop out of the technical schools where mortality is high anyway in liberal-arts colleges students more often than not can adjust themselves to the idea of a liberal education but the adjustment is painful and often takes two or three years

Colleges aim not to produce what Dr J W Graham of Carnegie Tech calls the complete technician but instead a man whose education makes him able to fit a problem into its historical frame or as a professor of chemistry in a small liberal-arts college puts it in three or four years all one can learn is that there are unsolved problems for research

There are two real reasons for college education and the two are actually the same stated differently preparation for one of the professions and acquisition of an idea of culture together these two things mean the beginning of the development of the adult mind Woodrow Wilson once said the object of a university is intellect

Part of a circular given to each entering freshman at Columbia in 1953 reads as follows a liberal-arts education is one that aids the youth to grow into a mature well-rounded individual who knows how to think objectively to make the best use of his talents and to understand his responsibilities in a democratic society

A liberal-arts education means of course a general education in which the humanities literature language fine arts the social sciences history economics political science and the natural sciences chemistry biology physics are about equally balanced

Adapted from Robert U. Jameson, "How to Stay in College"[2]

D

Punctuate the following passage correctly. Add capitals. Indicate paragraphing in dialogue by inserting the sign ¶.

Puppy biscuit said Walter Mitty. . . . a woman who was passing laughed he said puppy biscuit she said to her companion that man said puppy biscuit to himself Walter Mitty hurried on he went into

[2]From *The Saturday Evening Post*, October 2, 1954. Adapted for this exercise by permission of Mr. Jameson.

an A & P not the first one he came to but a smaller one farther up the street I want some biscuit for small young dogs he said to the clerk any special brand sir the greatest pistol shot in the world thought a moment it says Puppies Bark for It on the box said Walter Mitty

His wife would be through at the hairdresser's in fifteen minutes Mitty saw in looking at his watch unless they had trouble drying it sometimes they had trouble drying it she didn't like to get to the hotel first she would want him to be there waiting for her as usual he found a big leather chair in the lobby facing a window and he put the overshoes and the puppy biscuit on the floor beside it he picked up an old copy of *Liberty* and sank down into the chair Can Germany Conquer the World Through the Air Walter Mitty looked at the pictures of bombing planes and of ruined streets

Adapted from James Thurber, "The Secret Life of Walter Mitty"[3]

---

[3] Adapted for this exercise from the short story by James Thurber, by permission of the author.

Manuscript Form and Mechanics

WHEN WE SPEAK of "form and mechanics," we refer to certain well-established practices that make the manuscript easy and agreeable to read. These practices have to do with matters of legibility, neatness, and adherence to conventional ways of handling italics, capitalization, hyphenated words, and other things that contribute to the smooth and unobtrusive communication of the written word. By following these accepted conventions, the writer shows his respect for his own work and his consideration for the persons who will read it.

30/Manuscript Form

The form and general appearance of a manuscript should be neat and attractive. Messy manuscripts, like slovenly and dirty clothes, create a bad impression. When you turn in a class paper, you should follow established practices and the requirements of your instructor.

30a/Use appropriate paper and ink.

Use white paper 8½ by 11 inches in size unless your instructor specifies otherwise. Ruled paper is preferred for handwritten papers and unruled paper for typescript.

If you write in longhand, use blue, black, or blue-black ink — not red, green, brown, or violet.

If you type, double-space, and use a ribbon whose imprint can easily be read.

30b/Place your writing neatly on the page.

If you are writing in longhand on ruled paper, center the title on the first line. If you use a typewriter, center the title about $1\frac{1}{2}$ inches from the top of the page. Leave extra space between the title and the text.

Leave ample and regular margins at the top and bottom of the page, and at least an inch on each side.

Indent the first line of each paragraph uniformly — about one inch in longhand and five spaces in typescript.

Number all pages except the first with an Arabic number in the upper right-hand corner: 2, *not* II. On the first page the number should be centered at the bottom of the page.

30c/Write or type on only one side of the sheet.

30d/Write neatly and legibly.

Do not draw your reader's attention from the content of your paper to messy, unreadable, or excessively fancy handwriting. Form each letter simply and distinctly.

Avoid ugly blotches or smears of ink.

Avoid erasures. Draw a straight line through material to be canceled, and place the correction neatly above the line:

I did not cry out ~~on purpose~~ voluntarily.

The Bluffton House ←— Center

Indent 5 spaces

←— Triple space

To me, Bluffton Farm is synonymous with summertime, and its

Double space

outstanding feature is our forty-year-old summer house. It sits

2 spaces after periods

back in a grove of pines and palmettos, looking like an ugly

duckling between the modern, two-story brick houses of my aunt

and uncle. It is built of heart-of-pine lumber, which has no

paint--and never has had. A once-red roof covers the long struc-

ture.

2 hyphens and no spaces for a dash

A rusted screen porch, which runs the full length of the

house, is notable by itself. It is furnished with Army surplus

cots covered with khaki cloth, and it has eight bright green rock-

ing chairs with deerskin bottoms. The cots are lined up like

prone bodies under the windows of the bedrooms, and the rocking

chairs seem to keep watch over the river in front of the house.

The porch is a marvelous place for wet swimmers to lounge, and

the dirt which clings to bathing suits cannot hurt the furniture.

In the middle of the porch floor is a crack about two inches wide.

Dirt and sand are swept into this crack, and a pile of dirt under

the house is evidence of many years of living and sweeping.

Behind the porch is the dining room, a very utilitarian

place about thirty feet long with a homemade table about twenty

feet long. Layers and layers of oilcloth cover the table, and

during family reunions I have seen twenty people sit down there

1

Page number for first page on bottom line

EXAMPLE OF CORRECT MANUSCRIPT FORM   **151**

If more than two or three such changes occur on a page, copy it over.

30e/Follow the form prescribed by your instructor for folding the paper and endorsing it with your name and class, the date, and other details required.

30f/Proofread your papers carefully.

You will want to guard against careless errors, for they are quickly noticed and are taken as a sign of haste, indifference, or even ignorance. Before submitting your paper, read it over two or three times, at least once aloud for sound. If possible, allow a period of time between readings. Writing is easier to judge when it "cools." Watch especially for misspellings and omissions made in revising or copying.

An example of correct typescript is shown on page 151.

31/Revision and Correction

All papers written out of class should be carefully revised and if necessary rewritten before they are turned in. In addition, many papers written for your composition class should be revised and corrected after they have been read and marked by your instructor.

When you revise and correct papers which have been graded and returned to you, be sure to follow the instructions given by your teacher. Procedures for revising vary greatly from college to college and even from class to class. The most common method is to write a brief correction neatly above the error. If you need to rewrite a long sentence or a paragraph, your instructor may request that you do so on an inserted page or on the back of a page of your manuscript. Follow instructions exactly. Conscientious correction and revision will help you to avoid similar errors in later papers, especially if you understand the changes you are asked to make. It may turn out to be the most rewarding work you will do in your composition course.

One method of revising a theme after it has been returned by the instructor is shown in the foreword to the student.

32/Italic Type and Underlining

Italics (*slanting type, like this*) are used in print to emphasize certain words and to set off some titles. In typescript or longhand, italics are indicated by underlining.

32a/Underline titles of books (except the Bible), periodicals, newspapers, motion pictures, musical compositions, plays, and other separately published works. Be precise: watch initial articles (*A, An, The*) and any punctuation.

BOOKS	Hemingway's The Old Man and the Sea and Willa Cather's O (not Oh) Pioneers!
PERIODICALS	The Atlantic Monthly and the American Quarterly
NEWSPAPERS	The New York Times (or, the New York Times)
PLAYS	Ah! Wilderness
MOTION PICTURES	The Birth of a Nation
MUSICAL COMPOSITIONS	Bizet's Carmen Beethoven's Mount of Olives

NOTE: In journalistic writing, quotation marks are frequently used instead of italics.

32b/Underline names of ships and trains.

the Queen Mary   the Silver Comet

32c/Underline foreign words used in an English context, except words which have become part of our language.

Consult your dictionary to determine whether a word is still considered foreign or has become Anglicized. See also §401.

Fried grasshoppers were the <u>pièce</u> de <u>résistance</u> of the meal.

      1899   1902   1902   1697   1880

BUT   The chauffeur garaged the limousine with verve and élan.
(The dates show when these words [all from French] came into English, according to the *Oxford English Dictionary*. Long accepted, they are not italicized.)

32d/Underline words, letters, and figures referred to as such.

The spy was not able to figure out what <u>in</u>, <u>5</u>, and <u>t</u> stood for in the coded message.

Don't forget to dot your <u>i</u>'s.

32e/Underlining for emphasis should be used carefully and infrequently.

Weak writing is seldom improved by mechanical means. Generally it is possible to gain emphasis by the choice and position of words, not by sprinkling a page with exclamatory underlinings or italics.

EXERCISE

Supply quotation marks (see §29) and italics where necessary in the following sentences. If a sentence is correct as it stands, label it C.

1. Almost all the questions about the book When? were based upon Chapter II, which was entitled Too Late Is Never.

2. I hope that our assignment for tomorrow is one of the short poems Ode to the West Wind or Dover Beach but not that novel The Octopus.

3. His a's often looked like o's, and the poor professor actually thought that he had written bottle-scored veteran instead of battle-scarred veteran.

4. The Quincy Times ran a blistering review of the motion picture The Queen of Hearts, which was taken from a wonderful short story, Last Call.

5. The word genuflection, which is derived from the Latin words genu, or knee, and flexio, or bending, means the act of bending the knee.

6. Flounder en papillote was the most exotic entree on the menu at the captain's table on the good ship Eldorado.

33/Spelling

Spelling is troublesome in English because many words are not spelled as they sound (*laughter*, *slaughter*); because some quite distinct pairs and triplets sound the same (*capital*, *capitol*; *to*, *too*, *two*; *there*, *their*); because many words are pronounced with the "neutral" vowel, "uh," which gives no clue to spelling (sens*i*ble, cap*a*ble, defi*a*nt, ind*e*pendent); and because many words are habitually mispronounced.

Poor spelling gives a bad impression. It is not necessarily a badge of ignorance, but so many people think it is that grades can be lowered and jobs given to someone else because of it. A college student who spells poorly is particularly liable to harsh judgment.

A first step to improved spelling is to keep a list of the words you misspell and consult that list every time you write a paper, a letter, or anything else. College students seldom have trouble with more than a handful of words, and it is no harder to learn these than to learn a handful of college songs and cheers.

A second step is to pronounce words carefully and exactly. Many misspellings are due to careless omission of syllables (*accident-ly* for *acciden-tal-ly*); careless addition of syllables (*disas-ter-ous* for *disas-trous*); changing of syllables (p*res*pi-ration for p*ers*piration). Listen to speakers who pronounce their words carefully, and when in doubt check the pronunciation in your dictionary. (See §40c.)

A valuable precaution is to look up all doubtful spellings when preparing the final draft of a paper, and to give the whole manuscript a final reading before turning it in.

There are no infallible guides to spelling in English, but the following are helpful. Knowing and using them will take you a long step toward better spelling.

33a/i-e or e-i?

> Use *I* before *E*
> Except after *C*
> Or when sounded as *A*
> As in *neighbor* and *weigh*.

I — E	E — I
believe, chief, field, grief, piece	After *C* receive, receipt, ceiling, deceit, conceive
	When sounded as *A* freight, vein, reign

	EXCEPTIONS TO MEMORIZE:
	    either, neither, leisure, seize, weird,
	    height

33b/Drop final silent **e**?

<table>
<tr><td align="center">DROP</td><td align="center">KEEP</td></tr>
<tr><td align="center">When suffix begins
with a vowel</td><td align="center">When suffix begins with
a consonant</td></tr>
<tr><td>curse......cursing</td><td>live.......lively</td></tr>
<tr><td>arrive.....arriving</td><td>nine.......ninety</td></tr>
<tr><td>come......coming</td><td>hope.....hopeful</td></tr>
<tr><td>pursue.....pursuing</td><td>love.......loveless</td></tr>
<tr><td>arrange....arranging</td><td>arrange....arrangement</td></tr>
<tr><td>dine.......dining</td><td></td></tr>
</table>

COMMON, TYPICAL EXCEPTIONS

couraGEous
chanGEable
peaCEable
notiCEable
dyEing (compare *dying*)
singEing (compare *singing*)
awful
ninth
truly
argument

33c/Change **y** to **i**?

<table>
<tr><td align="center">CHANGE</td><td align="center">DO NOT CHANGE</td></tr>
<tr><td align="center">When y is preceded by a consonant</td><td align="center">When y is preceded by a vowel</td></tr>
<tr><td>gully.....gullies</td><td>valley......valleys</td></tr>
<tr><td>try......tried</td><td>attorney....attorneys</td></tr>
<tr><td>fly.......flies</td><td>convey.....conveyed</td></tr>
<tr><td>apply....appliance, applied</td><td>pay........pays</td></tr>
<tr><td>party....parties</td><td>deploy......deploying</td></tr>
</table>

When adding -ing

try.........trying
fly.........flying
apply.......applying

33d/Double final consonant?

If the suffix begins with a consonant, do not double the final consonant of the base word: *man, manly.*

If the suffix begins with a vowel —

DOUBLE	DO NOT DOUBLE
When final consonant is preceded by single vowel	*When final consonant is preceded by two vowels*

Monosyllables

pen....penned

blot....blotted

hop...hopper

hot.....hotter

sit.....sitting

despair....despairing

greet......greeting

leer......leering

lead......leading

Polysyllables accented on last syllable	*Words ending with two consonants*

rebél....rebelled

defér....deferring

begín....beginning

omít.....omitting

occúr....occurring

jump......jumping

dent.......denting

rest........resting

work.......working

call........calling

attémpt....attempting

Polysyllables not accented on last syllable after addition of suffix

defér......déference

prefér......préference

bénefit.....bénefiting

devélop....devéloping

lábor......lábored

lábel......lábeled

33e/Add s or es?

ADD *S*	ADD *ES*

For plurals of most nouns   *When the plural has an extra*
syllable

girl . . . . . girls   church . . . . churches
book . . . . books   fox . . . . foxes
thrush . . . . thrushes

For nouns in o *preceded by*   *Usually, when a noun ends in* o
a vowel   *preceded by a consonant (consult*
your dictionary when in doubt)

radio . . . . . radios   potatoes
cameo . . . . cameos   Negroes

BUT   flamingos or flamingoes

EXERCISES   Filipinos

A

Form the plural of each of the following nouns.

bird	bamboo
brooch	brook
buffalo	calico
rodeo	coo
birch	blush
studio	sex

B

To each of the following words, add the indicated suffixes.

drop + er	abhor + ence
droop + ed	confer + ed
reap + er	confer + able
swim + er	confer + ence
sprawl + ing	confer + ment
concur + ing	conduct + or
concur + ence	elope + ing
abhor + ed	

C

Fill the blanks in the following words with i-e *or* e-i.

perc__ve	gr__vance
s__zure	w__ld
n__gh	v__l
conc__t	s__ge
ach__ve	d__gn

D

Cross out any superfluous e's *in the following words.*

ridiculeing	pronouncement
revengeing	nineteen
revengeful	useless
pronounceing	useing
pronounceable	duely

E

To each of the following words, add the indicated suffixes.

defy + ance	convoy + s
defy + ed	convoy + ing
obey + s	happy + er
ally + s	modify + ing
alley + s	modify + er

F

The following words are frequently misspelled. Study one column of these words per day. Then spell all the words in the column to a friend or a member of your family. Have him check each word you miss and then ask you to spell it again on another day. If you wish to be a good speller, you will learn to spell the words in this list correctly.

absence	accommodate	acquaintance
accept	accumulate	acquitted
accidentally	acknowledgment	advice

advise
affect
aggravate
all right
already
altogether
amateur
among
analysis
analyze
annual
apartment
apparatus
apparent
appearance
arctic
argument
arithmetic
ascend
athletic
a while (noun)
awhile (adverb)
attendance
balance
battalion
believe
benefited
boundaries
Britain
beginning
business
calendar
candidate
capital
capitol
cemetery
changeable

changing
choose
chose
commission
committee
comparative
coming
compelled
conceivable
conferred
conscience
conscientious
continuous
control
criticize
deferred
definite
description
desperate
dictionary
dining
disappearance
disappoint
disastrous
discipline
dissatisfied
dormitory
effect
eighth
eligible
eliminate
embarrass
eminent
encouraging
environment
equipped
especially

exaggerate
excellence
except
exhilarate
existence
experience
explanation
familiar
fascinate
February
fiery
foreign
formerly
forty
fourth
frantically
generally
government
grammar
grandeur
grievous
height
heroes
hindrance
hoping
humorous
hypocrite
hypocrisy
immediately
incidentally
incredible
independence
inevitable
intellectual
intelligence
interesting
irresistible

knowledge
laboratory
laid
led
lightning
loneliness
loose
lose
maintenance
maneuver
manufacture
mathematics
may be
maybe
miniature
mischievous
mysterious
necessary
Negroes
ninety
noticeable
occasionally
occurred
occurrence
omitted
opportunity
optimistic
parallel
paralyze
pastime
perform
permissible
perseverance
personnel
perspiration
physical
picnicking

possibility
practically
precede
precedence
preference
preferred
prejudice
preparation
principal
principle
privilege
professor
pronunciation
prophecy
prophesy
probably
quantity
quiet
quite
quizzes
recede
receive
recognize
recommend
reference
referred
repetition
restaurant
rhythm
ridiculous
sacrifice
sacrilegious
salary
schedule
secretary
seize
separate

sergeant
severely
shining
siege
similar
sophomore
specifically
specimen
stationary
stationery
statue
truly
their
there
too
to
succeed
successful
supersede
surprise
studying
temperamental
tendency
thorough
tragedy
tries
tyranny
unanimous
undoubtedly
until
usually
village
villain
weather
weird
whether
writing

34/The Hyphen and Syllabication

The **hyphen** (-) is used to divide words of more than one syllable at the end of a line and to join certain compound words (see **§40b**). Distinguish carefully between the hyphen and the dash. In longhand a dash should be about twice as long as a hyphen. In typescript a dash is made with two hyphens (--).

In dividing a word at the end of a line, hyphenate only between syllables, and place the hyphen only at the end of the first line, not at the beginning of the next one. Words of more than one syllable are generally divided between consonants (*lit-tle*, *wig-wam*). When in doubt about where a word should be divided, consult your dictionary.

Do not divide monosyllables even if they are fairly long (*thought*, *laugh*, *cheese*), and do not set off a single letter (*a-bout*, *might-y*). Prefixes and suffixes may be set off, though it is preferable not to carry over a two-letter suffix (*straight-ened*, not *straighten-ed*). Compounds are divided between their parts (*with-out*, *in-doors*).

34a/Use of the hyphen in compound words varies greatly.

Consult your dictionary to determine whether a compound is written as one word, a hyphenated word, or two words.

ONE WORD	HYPHENATED	TWO WORDS
selfish	all-American	governor general
export	ex-governor	water system
watermelon	governor-elect	white race
whitewash	self-satisfied	drop kick (noun)
backwoods	water-cooled	drum major
drugstore	white-hot	
	drop-kick (verb)	

34b/Many common expressions of two or more words are usually hyphenated when used as a single modifier before a noun but not in other positions.

HYPHEN	NO HYPHEN
He is a *well-known* executive.	The executive is *well known.*
It was a *never-to-be-forgotten* experience.	The experience was *never to be forgotten.*

A hyphen is not used when the first word of such a group is an adverb ending in *-ly*.

HYPHEN	NO HYPHEN
a *well-written* book	a *poorly written* book
a *half-finished* task	a *partly finished* task

34c/Spelled-out compound numbers from *twenty-one* through *ninety-nine* are hyphenated.

EXERCISES

A

Indicate whether each of the following words should be written solid, with a hyphen, or as two words. Then check your answers in your dictionary. (See §40b.)

eastbound	wellborn
eastsoutheast	welldoer
Easteregg	welloff
cowpea	weekday
cowpony	weekend
coworker	weakkneed

B

Indicate the points at which you might acceptably hyphenate the following words at the end of a line. Then check your answers in your dictionary. (See §40b.)

abridged	learned (verb)
accessible	learned (adjective)
amends	mediocre
collaborationist	previously
drought	through

35/The Apostrophe

The **apostrophe** (') indicates omission of one or more letters in a word or a contraction. It is a common sign of the possessive; *John's* represents an older form, *Johnes*. Problems in the use of the apostrophe are closely related to problems of case. (See §13.)

35a/Use **'s** to form the possessive of nouns not ending in *s*.

SINGULAR   child's, man's, deer's, lady's, mother-in-law's
PLURAL   children's, men's, deer's

35b/Use **'s** for the possessive of singular nouns ending in *s*.

Charles's, Watts's, Dickens's, waitress's, actress's

NOTE: When 's added to a singular noun ending in *s* causes an unpleasant sound, add only the apostrophe.

the actress' success, Dickens' stories

35c/Use the **'** without **s** for the possessive of plural nouns already ending in *s*.

waitresses', nieces', the Joneses', the Tullys'

35d/Use **'s** for the possessive of indefinite pronouns.

anybody's, everyone's, somebody else's, neither's

NOTE: Do not use the apostrophe for the possessive case of personal pronouns: *his, theirs, ours, its* (meaning *of it*). *It's* means *it is.*

35e/Use 's only with the last noun when two or more nouns express joint possession.

> Marge and Jack's bicycle (The two jointly own one bicycle.)
>
> Marge's and Jack's bicycles (Each owns his own bicycle.)

35f/The apostrophe is used to show omissions or contractions.

> the roaring '20's, o'clock, Jack-o'-lantern, we'll, don't, can't

35g/Use 's to form the plural of numbers, letters, and words referred to as words.

> three 7's, four *a*'s, six *the*'s

36/Capitals

In general, a **capital letter** suggests an individual or particular person, place, or thing; a small letter suggests any member of a group.

INDIVIDUALIZED
> Pittsburgh
> Mt. Rainier
> the Mississippi
> John P. Marquand

NOT INDIVIDUALIZED
> the city
> the great mountain
> the river
> a distinguished man and writer

CAPITALIZED   NOT CAPITALIZED

The first word of a sentence.

The pronoun I *and the interjection* O.

> How, O ye gods, can I bear this misfortune?

TITLES OF ESSAYS, BOOKS, ETC.

First, last, and important words	*Prepositions, conjunctions, articles*
Look Homeward, Angel The Ground We Stand On "Campus Politics"	Across the River and into the Trees "Out of High School and into College"

DIRECT QUOTATIONS

Words capitalized by the author	*Words not capitalized by the author*
Carlyle said, "Meanwhile we will hate Anarchy as Death, which it is. . . ."	Carlyle said that "we will hate Anarchy as Death, which it is. . . ."

DIALOGUE

The first word of a sentence in dialogue	*Expressions like* he said *and other words introducing the second part of a sentence*
He asked, "Was the accident very serious?"	"Yes," she replied, "it was fatal."

TITLES PRECEDING A NAME

President Kennedy
former President Eisenhower
Mr. Troover
Aunt Bess
Professor Pennypacker

CAPITALIZED	NOT CAPITALIZED

TITLES SUBSTITUTED FOR A NAME

President and other titles when a particular name may be substituted for the title. Words of family relationship not preceded by a possessive.	*Titles not used as names. Words of family relationship preceded by a possessive.*

The President is expected to veto the measure.	A college president has more duties than privileges.
I was summoned by the Dean of Men.	The old dean looked at me quizzically.
Lieutenant Yo pleaded not guilty; the Lieutenant was found guilty.	A lieutenant deserves a good living allowance.
Good morning, Doctor.	The doctor glanced at his watch.
Where is Mother?	my mother's favorite aunt

DEGREES AND TITLES AFTER A NAME

Abbreviations of degrees and titles of distinction	*Ordinary titles used descriptively*
Jeffrey E. Tyndale, Sr., Ph. D., J. D.	Jeffrey E. Tyndale, professor of law
George Washington, the first President	Bill Snipes, county surveyor
	Thomas H. England, president of the bank

PROPER NAMES

Names of persons, countries, cities, regions, and their derivatives	*Directions*
	He lives west of Denver.
Plato, Platonic, Platonism	The plane flew toward the southeast.
Canada, Canadian	
England, Englishman, English	*Proper nouns which have become common*
Venice, Venetian blind	
the South, Southern, Southerner	a set of china
	a bottle of cologne

CAPITALIZED	NOT CAPITALIZED
Organizations and institutions	*The word when it is not part of a name*
Berry College	a college, my college
Union High School	high school
the Citizen's Bank	He put his money in the bank.
the Democratic Party	The political party was democratic.
the Pi Beta Phi Sorority	She belongs to a sorority.
The Senior Class of Ivy College requests the honor of your presence . . .	a member of the senior class, a senior
Addresses and names of political divisions and places	*The same words as common nouns*
1072 Clifton Street, N. E.	the street
Forty-fourth Avenue	a broad avenue
Cherokee County	the county
Central Park	the park
the Mississippi River, the Missouri River	the Mississippi and Missouri rivers
the Louisville and Nashville Railroad, the Santa Fé Railroad	the Louisville and Nashville and Santa Fé railroads
Months, days of the week, holidays	*The seasons and numbered days of the month*
May, December	spring, winter
Friday, Sunday	the third of July
the Fourth of July	
Thanksgiving Day	
Movements, periods, events in history	*The name of a century unless it is thought of as a movement*
the Romantic Movement	the twentieth century
the Middle Ages	
the Civil War	

CAPITALIZED	NOT CAPITALIZED
B.C., A.D., *words designating the deity, names of religious denominations, sacred books*	*Pronouns referring to the deity may or may not be capitalized.*
in 273 B.C.	
the Messiah, our Maker, the Trinity	
Allah, Buddha	
Praise God from Whom all blessings flow.	Praise God from whom all blessings flow.
Catholic, Protestant, Presbyterian	
the Bible, Biblical, the Koran	
the Old Testament	
Names of specific courses	*Studies (other than languages) which are not specific courses*
Dean Parks suggested that I take English 101, Sociology 205, Chemistry 214, and Astronomy 225.	At the dean's suggestion I am now spending all my time on English, sociology, chemistry, and astronomy.

EXERCISE

Add necessary capitals to the following passage.

it was a cold afternoon in late autumn, and the yellow smoke hung low over memorial park as professor jeffrey e. tyndale hurriedly walked north two blocks until he arrived at 27 lullwater road, the home of his wealthy friend's sister. a rather heated argument with a student over the latter's paper on "the legal philosophy of the sage of monticello" had made the professor an hour late for his afternoon tea. "but perhaps it was worth it," he mused; "it simply would not do to let a graduate of our law school loose upon society thinking that the great southerner and third president of the united states, thomas jefferson, was founder of the present republican party! fortunately, the young man is only a junior; there will be time to enlighten him a bit before he graduates from ivy university. any course in law will probably help him; but when he takes my law 291 next year, i shall see to it that he has a better grasp of the legal and political thought in this country during the eighteenth and nineteenth centuries." he banged the knocker on the front door somewhat vehemently.

"come in, professor," said mrs. taylor in her habitually gracious manner. "you're somewhat later than usual. the group was just wondering what had delayed you on such a wintry day."

"the legal view from monticello, laura," smiled tyndale as he handed his hat and coat to the butler and smoothed down his thinning gray hair.

"always abstruse with your humor," said mrs. taylor. she smiled rather quizzically as the professor seated himself in his favorite chair and slightly adjusted his tiepin.

the conversation of the group was varied and lively. it touched rapidly upon such matters as the controversial railroad bill introduced in congress by the new senator, the proposal to place a power dam upon the cumberland river rather than upon another river in the southern part of the state, the advantages and disadvantages of the fraternity system in college, weaknesses in the public high school, the typical gentleman of the renaissance, sources of humor in *as you like it*, the indecision of prince hamlet and the part of the fool in *king lear*, the paintings of michelangelo, the pleasures of traveling.

professor tyndale held his delicate china cup and saucer in his left hand while he stirred the contents with a highly polished teaspoon. he was particularly aroused by the topic of traveling. "yes, i should love to sail about the world listening to the song of the mermaid," he said half whimsically. "sometimes i think it would be more delightful than the legal view from monticello."

37/Numbers

Numbers are commonly expressed in numerals in technical writing and spelled out in more formal and literary writing.

37a/Except in technical or statistical matter, round numbers which can be written in one or two words are usually spelled out. Figures are commonly used for numbers which cannot be so written.

WORDS	FIGURES
twenty-three	123
one thousand	$1\frac{13}{16}$
one thousand dollars	$1,001.00

EXCEPTION: Never use figures for a number at the beginning of a sentence.

37b/Figures are used for dates, street numbers, page references, percentages, and hours of the day used with A.M. or P.M.

The following forms are acceptable.

July 3, 1776 (*not* July 3rd, 1776)
the third of July or 3 July 1959 (the day preceding the month)
2 Park Street
Fifth Avenue
See page 50 of your textbook.
This book has only fifty pages.
The loan company charged 24 per cent interest.
The concert begins at 6 P.M. (or 6:00 P.M.)
The concert begins at six o'clock. (With *o'clock*, the number should be spelled out.)

37c/Figures are used for numbers in a series and for tabulations and statistics.

One polar bear weighed 200 pounds, another weighed 526, and the third 534.

One sold for $200, one for $275, and one for $325.

38/Contractions

Most **contractions** are out of place in formal writing.

INAPPROPRIATE   The President and Fellows of Rockhill College trust that *you'll* understand the spirit in which this, their annual report, is submitted.

In such writing, avoid *don't*, *I'll*, *you're*, *can't*, and other such contractions. Most student papers are less formal than a college president's report; even so, every contraction should be checked carefully for appropriateness to its context.

A few contractions are acceptable in all contexts. These are words that have an established formal spelling which is a contraction, such as *o'clock* and *jack-o'-lantern*.

39/Abbreviations

Abbreviations are short cuts. Some have proved so useful that they are accepted in all kinds of writing. Some are inappropriate in student papers and contexts of comparable formality.

The following abbreviations are acceptable in all contexts.

BEFORE A NAME	Mr., Mrs., Messrs., Mmes., Dr., St. or Ste. (for *Saint*, not *Street*), Mt., Rev. (but only with a first name: "the Rev. Ernest Jones," not "Rev. Jones")
AFTER A NAME	M.D. (and other degrees), Jr., Sr., Esq., D.C. (District of Columbia)
OTHERS	B.C. and A.D. (with dates expressed in numerals), A.M. and P.M. (with hours expressed in numerals)
FOOTNOTES AND BIBLIOGRAPHIES	cf., pp., ibid., op. cit., and others
TECHNICAL WRITING	cc., cm., gr., B.t.u., and others

EXERCISE

Write the numbers in the following passage correctly. For the purpose of this exercise, do not treat the figures as statistics.

When Doug first discovered his great-grandfather's 101-year-old diary, he irreverently hoped to find in its one hundred six pages stories of secret family passions and skeletons. Soon, however, he forgot this possibility and became an antiquarian. His ancestor, he discovered, had lived at 171½ 17th Street, now the site of the most modern office building in the city. Prices and family menus had changed as much as the residential sections of the city. The last 10 pages of the diary (from page 96 to page one hundred and six) had apparently been used as an account book. Once his great-grandfather had bought fifteen eggs for 18¢. $1.50 was the total cost of 10 pounds of sirloin steak. On April 3rd, eighteen hundred and fifty-six, a member of the family had bought eight and one-half pounds of bear meat, 16 pounds of flour, 3 gallons of sorghum syrup, and 6 pounds of coffee beans. In one entry Doug's great-grandfather had estimated that he spent for groceries ten per cent of the $17.50 which he drew as a week's salary when he quit on Saturday nights at seven P.M. Yet the entries indicated that the family had much excellent food. For the first time, Doug felt, he understood inflation.

PART THREE

WORDS

The Dictionary

A GOOD DICTIONARY is a treasure house of information about individual words, language in general, and many other subjects. Hence a reputable, up-to-date dictionary, designed *for college use*, should become part of your standard equipment, not only in your composition course but throughout college and after.

The dictionary you select for college use should be reasonably complete. Except for spellings and pronunciations, most "handy" or "pocket" dictionaries are likely to tell you little you do not already know. Most high-school dictionaries, while more useful, will also give you less complete information than you will usually need. Three modern **desk dictionaries** are particularly useful at the college level:

> *The American College Dictionary*, Random House, New York.
>
> *Webster's New Collegiate Dictionary*, G. & C. Merriam Co., Springfield, Mass.
>
> *Webster's New World Dictionary of the American Language*, The World Publishing Company, Cleveland.

Students who need information not found in one of these should consult an **unabridged dictionary.** Of these the principal ones are *Webster's New International Dictionary*, the *New Standard Dictionary*, the *Dictionary of American*

English, and the monumental *Oxford English Dictionary* The last (in twelve volumes plus supplement) is probably the most scholarly and voluminous dictionary ever pub lished. Its extensive examples of usage in all ages of the English language are particularly helpful in the study of the history of words.

To use a dictionary intelligently, one must first under stand that it is not an "authority" which intends to tell you what you "ought" to do. It is an "authority" only in that it records the current and past usage of educated speakers and writers, as nearly as its editors can determine Every good dictionary has a large staff of editors who are constantly observing and recording the ways in which word are used. They note the appearance of new words — thus *softball* and *beach wagon* were "new" entries when they were first recorded in an edition of a dictionary published in 1941 They list new uses of old words — thus *plastic* was firs given as a noun denoting various synthetic substances in that same dictionary in the same year. And they not great numbers of continuing usages as well as obsolete words that is, those no longer current, such as *dowsabel*. A dic tionary is not a prescription but a thermometer, and th more recent it is, the better a thermometer it is likely to be In minor matters dictionaries do not always agree. Thu one prefers *coöperate*, and another *co-operate*, and some lis *cooperate* while others do not.

Study the table of contents of your dictionary. Determin what its separate parts are and how it classifies the infor mation which it gives. In addition to the main body of th dictionary (the alphabetized entries of words), you will als find information on a variety of other subjects: commo signs and symbols, abbreviations, the pronunciation an meaning of given names, biographical and geographical in formation, rhymes, rules of spelling, grammar, and punctuation, printing and proofreading terms and marks, a listing of colleges and universities, a guide to effective letter writing, scholarly discussion of aspects of the language, weights and measures, and the forms of address.

Next, study carefully the specimen pages on pp. 182–185 as a general introduction to the use of a dictionary. These specimen pages have been made up by the dictionary-makers themselves. They provide examples of all the kinds of information that may be given in an entry. Then, if you will conscientiously work out the exercises given here, as they apply to your dictionary, you will have learned how to use a dictionary with speed, ease, and efficiency — a skill which will be invaluable to you for the rest of your life.

40/Using a Dictionary

Dictionaries follow somewhat different schemes in indicating preferred spellings, syllabication, accent, pronunciation, and so forth. Therefore, no blanket rules about the practices of different dictionaries can be given. Each dictionary in its prefatory pages explains its own particular system, and you should examine those pages carefully to familiarize yourself with what they contain. The following subsections indicate what information may be found in three widely used college dictionaries, give general directions about each topic, and refer to explanatory matter in each dictionary listed.

40a/Preferred and Variant Spellings

The first entry of a word usually gives the **preferred spelling.** Dictionaries indicate accepted **variant spellings**

Running Head

Vocabulary Entry

beau·ty (bū′tĭ), *n.*, *pl.* **-ties.** **1.** that quality of any object of sense or thought whereby it excites an admiring pleasure; qualification of a high order for delighting the eye or the aesthetic, intellectual, or moral sense. **2.** something beautiful, esp. a woman. **3.** a grace, charm, or pleasing excellence. [ME *beute*, t. OF: m. *beaute*, der. *beau*. See BEAU] **—Syn.** 1. loveliness, pulchritude.

Idiomatic Phrases

beck¹ (bĕk), *n.* **1.** a beckoning gesture. **2.** *Scot.* a bow or curtsy of greeting. **3. at one's beck and call,** ready to obey one immediately; subject to one's slightest wish **—***v.t., v.i.* **4.** to beckon. [short for BECKON]

Syllabication Dots

Pronunciation

be·di·zen (bĭ dī′zən, -dĭz′ən) *v.t.* to dress or adorn gaudily. [t. BE- + DIZEN] **—be·di′zen·ment,** *n.*

Example Contexts

be·fore (bĭ fōr′), *adv.* **1.** in front; in advance; ahead. **2.** in time preceding; previously. **3.** earlier or sooner: *begin at noon, not before.* **—***prep.* **4.** in front of; ahead of; in advance of: *before the house.* **5.** previously to; earlier than: *before the war.* **6.** ahead of; in the future of; awaiting: *the golden age is before us.* **7.** in preference to; rather than: *they would die before yielding.* **8.** in precedence of, as in order or rank: *we put freedom before ideas.* **9.** in the presence or sight of: *before an audience.* **10.** under the jurisdiction or consideration of: *before a magistrate.* **—***conj.* **11.** previously to the time when: *before I go.* **12.** sooner than; rather than: *I will die before I submit.* [ME *before(n)*, OE *beforan*, f. *be* by + *foran* before] **—Ant.** 1. behind. 2. afterward. 3. later.

Antonyms

Part of Speech and Inflected Forms

be·gin (bĭ gĭn′), *v.*, **began, begun, beginning.** **—***v.i.* **1.** to enter upon an action; take the first step; commence; start. **2.** to come into existence; arise; originate. **—***v.t.* **3.** to take the first step in; set about; start; commence. **4.** to originate; be the originator of. [ME *beginne(n)*, OE *beginnan*] **—be·gin′ner,** *n.*

Synonym Study

—Syn. 3. BEGIN, COMMENCE, INITIATE, START (when followed by noun or gerund) refer to setting into motion or progress something which continues for some time. BEGIN is the common term: *to begin knitting a sweater.* COMMENCE is a more formal word, often suggesting a more prolonged or elaborate beginning: *to commence proceedings in court.* INITIATE implies an active and often ingenious first act in a new field: *to initiate a new procedure.* START means to make a first move or to set out on a course of action: *to start paving a street.* **4.** institute, inaugurate, initiate. **—Ant. 1.** end.

Variant Principal Parts

be·jew·el (bĭ jōō′əl), *v.t.,* **-eled, -eling** or (*esp. Brit.*) **-elled, -elling** to adorn with or as with jewels.

Variant Spelling

be·la·bor (bĭ lā′bər), *v.t.* **1.** to beat vigorously; ply with heavy blows. **2.** to assail persistently, as with ridicule. **3.** *Obs.* to labor in. [Also, *Brit.*, **be·la′bour.**]

Hyphenated Entry

belles-let·tres (bĕl lĕt′r), *n.pl.* the finer or higher forms of literature; literature regarded as a fine art. [F] **—bel·let·rist** (bĕl lĕt′rĭst), *n.* **—bel·le·tris·tic** (bĕl′lĕ trĭs′tĭk), *adj.* **—Syn.** See literature.

Word Element

bene-, a word element meaning "well", as in *benediction.* [t. L, comb. form of *bene*, adv.]

Consecutive Definition Numbers

be·neath (bĭ nēth′, -nĕth′) *adv.* ① below; in a lower place, position, state, etc. ② underneath: *the heavens above and the earth beneath.* **—***prep.* ③ below; under: *beneath the same roof.* ④ further down than; underneath; lower in place than. ⑤ lower down on a slope than: *beneath the crest of a hill.* ⑥ inferior in position, power, etc., to: *a captain is beneath a major.* ⑦ unworthy of; below the level or dignity of: *beneath contempt.* [ME *benethe*, OE *beneothan*, f. *be* by + *neothan* below] **—Syn.** 3. See below. **—Ant.** 1. above.

Etymology

Usage Note

bent¹ (bĕnt), *adj.* **1.** curved; crooked: *a bent stick, bow, etc.* **2.** determined; set; resolved (fol. by *on*)] **—***n.* **3.** bent state or form. **4.** direction taken (usually figurative); inclination; leaning; bias: *a bent for painting.* **5.** capacity of endurance. **6.** *Civ. Eng.* a transverse frame of a bridge or a building, designed to support either vertical or horizontal loads. [pp. of BEND¹]

Synonym List

—Syn. 4. tendency, propensity, proclivity, predilection.

bent² (bĕnt), *n.* **1.** bent grass. **2.** a stalk of such grass. **3.** (formerly) any stiff grass or sedge. **4.** *Scot. and N. Eng.* a grassy tract, a moor, or a hillside. [ME; OE *beonet*, c. G *binse* rush]

Short Pronunciation Key

ăct, ăble, dâre, ärt; ĕbb, ēqual; ĭf, īce; hŏt, ōver, ch, chief; g, give; ng, ring; sh, shoe; th, thin;

b., blend of, blended; c., cognate with; d., dialect, dial. m., modification of; r., replacing; s., stem of; t., ta

bi-, a prefix meaning: **1.** twice, doubly, two, as in *bilateral*, *binocular*, *biweekly*. **2.** (in science) denoting in general two, as in *bicarbonate*. Also, **bin-**. [t. L, comb. form of *bis* twice, doubly, der. L *duo* two]

Bi, *Chem.* bismuth.

B.I., British India.

bi·son (bī′sən, -zən), *n., pl.* **-son.** *Zool.* a large North American bovine ruminant, *Bison bison* (**American bison,** or buffalo), with high, well-haired shoulders. [t. L, t. Gmc.; cf. G *wisent*]

American bison. *Bison bison*
(10 to 12 ft. long,
ab. 6 ft. high at the shoulder)

blood·mo·bile (blŭd′mə bēl′), *n.* a small truck with medical equipment for receiving blood donations.

Bos·ton (bôs′tən, bŏs′tən), *n.* **1.** the capital of Massachusetts, in the E part: the largest city and seaport in New England. 801,444; with suburbs, 2,354,507 (1950). **2.** (*l.c.*) a game of cards, played by four persons with two packs of cards. **3.** (*l.c.*) a social dance, a modification of the waltz. **—Bos·to·ni·an** (bôs tō′nĭ ən, bŏs tō′-), *adj., n.*

bot·tle[1] (bŏt′əl), *n., v.,* **-tled, -tling. —n. 1.** a portable vessel with a neck or mouth, now commonly made of glass, with which to hold liquids. **2.** the contents of a bottle; as much as a bottle contains: *a bottle of wine.* **3. the bottle,** intoxicating liquor. **4.** bottled milk for babies: *raised on the bottle.* **—v.t. 5.** to put into or seal in a bottle; esp. in England, to can or put up fruit or vegetables. **6. bottle up,** to shut in or restrain closely: *to bottle up one's feelings.* [ME *botel,* t. OF: m. *botele,* g. LL *butticula,* dim. of *buttis* BUTT⁴] **—bot′tle·like′,** *adj.* **—bot′tler,** *n.*

bot·tle[2] (bŏt′əl), *n. Brit. Dial.* a bundle, esp. of hay. [ME *botel,* t. OF, dim. of *botte* bundle]

bou·fant (bōō fän′), *adj. French.* puffed out; full, as sleeves or draperies. **—bou·fante** (bōō fäntʼ), *adj. fem.*

brain washing, systematic indoctrination that changes or undermines one's political convictions. **—brain-wash,** *v.*

brain wave, 1. (*pl.*) *Med.* electroencephalogram. **2.** *Colloq.* a sudden idea or inspiration.

brass (brás, bräs), *n.* **1.** a durable, malleable, and ductile yellow alloy, consisting essentially of copper and zinc. **2.** a utensil, ornament, or other article made of brass. **3.** *Mach.* a bearing, bush, or the like. **4.** *Music.* **a.** a musical instrument of the trumpet or horn families. **b.** such instruments collectively in a band or orchestra. **5.** *Brit.* a memorial tablet incised with an effigy, coat of arms or the like. **6.** metallic yellow; lemon, amber, or reddish yellow. **7.** *U.S. Slang.* **a.** high-ranking military officers. **b.** any important officials. **8.** *Colloq.* excessive assurance; impudence; effrontery. **9.** *Brit. Slang.* money. **—adj. 10.** of brass. **11.** using musical instruments made of brass. [ME *bras,* OE *bræs*] **—brassʼ·like′,** *adj.*

brig·and·age (brĭg′ən dĭj), *n.* the practice of brigands; plundering. Also, **brigʼand·ism.**

Bron·të (brŏn′tĭ), *n.* **1.** Anne, (*Acton Bell*) 1820–49, British novelist. **2.** her sister, **Charlotte,** (*Currer Bell*) 1816–55, British novelist. **3.** her sister, **Emily Jane,** (*Ellis Bell*) 1818–48, British novelist.

brown·ie (brou′nĭ), *n.* **1.** (in folklore) a little brown goblin, esp. one who helps secretly in household work. **2.** *U.S.* a small, highly shortened chocolate cake, often containing nuts. **3.** (*cap.*) a trademark for a type of inexpensive box camera. **4.** any inexpensive box camera. **5.** (*cap.*) a member of the junior division (ages 8–11) of the Girl Scouts or (*Brit.*) the Girl Guides. **—Syn. 1.** See *fairy.*

Brum·mell (brŭm′əl), *n.* See **Beau Brummell.**

brunch (brŭnch), *n.* a mid-morning meal that serves both as breakfast and lunch. [b. BREAKFAST and LUNCH]

---

oil, bŏŏk, ōōze, out; ŭp, ūse, ûrge; ə = a in alone; that; zh, vision. See the full key on inside cover.

der., derived from; f., formed from; g., going back to; from; ?, perhaps. See the full key on inside cover.

183

Labels in right margin:
Prefix
Abbreviation
Illustration
Caption
Geographical Entry
Run-on Entry
Homograph Numbers
Foreign Word Label
Two Word Entry
Subject Label
Geographic Label
Usage Label
Variant Form
Biographical Entry
Capitalization
Cross Reference
Short Etymology Key

	pawner

| Pronunciation. | |

pawn′er (pôn′ẽr), **pawn′or** (pôn′ẽr; pôn-ôr′), *n.* | *Law.* One w
pawns or pledges anything as security.

Centered Period for Syllabic Division

pawn′shop′ (pôn′shŏp′), *n.* A pawnbroker's shop.
paw·paw′ (*see* PAPAW), *n.* Var. of PAPAW.

Subject Label

pax (paks), *n.* [L.] **1.** Peace; — deified by the Romans. **2.** *R.C.*
A tablet bearing a figure or symbol of Christ, the Virgin Mary, c
saint, which in medieval times was kissed by the priest and the peo
before the Communion.

‖**pax vo·bis′cum** (vŏ·bĭs′kŭm). [L.] Peace (be) with you.

pax′wax′ (păks′wăks′), *n.* [For *faxwax*, fr. AS. *feax* hair + a w
akin to *weaxan* to grow.] In many mammals, the median ligamen
the back of the neck, composed of yellow elastic tissue and used in s
porting the head.

Principal Parts

pay (pā), *v. t.;* PAYED (pād); PAY′ING. [OF. *peier, poier,* fr.
picare to pitch, fr. *pix* pitch.] To smear or coat, as a vessel's bott
a seam, etc., with a waterproof composition, as of tallow, resin, e

pay (pā), *v. t.;* PAID (pād) or, *Obs.* exc. in sense 4, PAYED; PAY′I
[OF. *paier,* fr. L. *pacare* to pacify, appease, fr. *pax, pacis,* pea

Idiomatic Usage

1. To satisfy (one) for service rendered, property delivered, etc.;
munerate. **2.** To give (something due) in return, satisfaction, or
quital; also, to discharge indebtedness for; settle, as a bill. **3.**
make compensation or retaliation for. **4.** To give, offer, or ma
freely or as fitting; as, to *pay* court or a visit. **5.** To be profitable

Discriminated Synonyms

also, bring in as a return. **6.** To pass out, as a rope; — now with
or *away.* — *v. i.* **1.** To give a recompense; make payment. **2.**
be profitable; to be worth the expense, effort, or the like.

Syn. Pay, compensate, remunerate, satisfy, reimburse, indemnify,
pay, recompense, requite mean to give money or its equivalen
return for something. **Pay** implies the discharge of an obligation
curred; **compensate,** as here considered, a making up for services
dered or help given; **remunerate,** more clearly, a paying for services
dered; **satisfy,** paying a person that which is asked or required by
reimburse, a return of money that has been expended; **indemnify**
reimbursing for loss suffered through fire, accident, damage by war
the like; **repay,** a paying back in kind or amount; **recompense,** ofte
compensating for services rendered but, sometimes, for losses or
juries sustained; **requite,** a reciprocating or retaliation, often but
necessarily in kind.

Verb Phrase

pay off. **1.** To pay; specif., to pay in full and discharge. **2.** To
quite. **3.** To allow to run off, as a thread or cord. **4.** *Colloq.*
yield full return, either to one's advantage or disadvantage; also
attain full effectiveness. **5.** *Naut.* To turn (a vessel) to leeward
— *n.* **1.** Act of paying; payment. **2.** State or status of being p

Usage Label

pay′nim (pā′nĭm), *n.* [OF. *paienisme* heathendom, fr. LL. *pagan*
mus paganism.] [*Archaic.*] Pagans or pagan countries; also, a pag
an infidel, esp. a Mohammedan.

pay′off′ (pā′ôf′), *n.* [*Chiefly Colloq.*] **1.** Act or time of paying
ployees' wages. **2.** Repayment or accrual for settlement at the c
come of an enterprise; reward or retribution. **3.** Climax of an incid
or enterprise; specif., the denouement of a narrative. **4.** Decisive
or factor resolving a situation, bringing about a definitive conclus
as, the opinion of the Tax Court on taxability is the *payoff.* —
Colloq. Yielding results in the final test; rewarding or decisive.

Foreign Word

pay′roll′ (pā′rōl′), *n.* A paymaster's list of persons entitled to p
with the amounts due to each; also, the amount necessary, or
money, for distribution to those on such a list.

Capitalization

pay′sage′ (pā′ê·zàzh′), *n.* [F.] A landscape or a landscape pictu
PC (pē′sē′). [patrol craft.] *U. S. Navy.* A fast patrol craft equip
with submarine-detection devices, 3-inch gun, machine guns, anti
craft guns, and depth charges.

Word Story

pea (pē), *n.; pl.* PEAS (pēz) or PEASE (pēz) (see *Note* below). [
pise, pl. *pisan,* fr. LL. *pisa,* pl. *pisam,* fr. L. *pisum,* pl. *pisa,* fr. Gr.
pisos. The vowel may have been influenced by OF. *peis,* fr. L. *pis*
The final *s* was misunderstood in English as a plural ending.] **1.** A
plant of a family (Fabaceae, the pea family) of herbs, shrubs,
trees, the fruit of which is a true pod or legume. **2.** The rou
smooth or wrinkled, edible seed borne severally in dehiscent pods b
vine (*Pisum sativum*) of this family; also, the similar angular seed
related plant (*P. arvense*). **3.** Any of various leguminous plant
their seeds, resembling the common pea; as, the sweet *pea,* cow
etc. **4.** Something like a pea, as in size.

Plural Form

☞ The plural *peas* was formerly used to indicate a definite num
as contrasted with the collective plural *pease;* the tendency now i
use *peas* as plural in all senses.

peace (pēs), *n.* [OF. *pais, paiz* (F. *paix*), fr. L. *pax, pacis*]

Antonym

peace′ful (-fŏŏl; -f'l), *adj.* **1.** *Now Rare.* Pacific; peaceable. **2.** F
sessing, enjoying, or marked by, peace; tranquil; also, of or pert
peace. — **Syn.** See CALM. — **Ant. Turbulent.** — **peace′ful·ly,** *adv*
peace′ful·ness, *n.*

184

ce offering. A propitiatory gift; esp., *Bib.*, a ceremonial propitia-
y sacrifice.

ce officer. A civil officer whose duty it is to preserve the public
ace, as a sheriff, constable, or policeman.

ce pipe. The calumet.

ch (pēch), *v. t.* [ME. *apechen*, fr. AF.] *Obs.* To impeach; indict.
v. i. Obs. exc. Slang. To turn informer; to blab.

ch, *n.* [OF. *peche, pesche,* fr. LL. *persica,* fr. L. *Persicum* (sc.
alum) Persian apple, peach.] **1.** Any of a family (Amygdalaceae,
e peach family) of trees and shrubs distinguished by the single pistil
th united carpels and the druno or stone fruit. **2** The sweet,

Biblical Term →

cock blue. A color, bluish green-blue in hue, of medium saturation
d low brilliance. See COLOR. — **pea′cock′-blue′,** *adj.*

′fowl′ (pē′foul′), *n.* The peacock or peahen.

g (pēg), *n.* Also **peage** (pēg). Wampum.

green. A color, yellowish yellow-green in hue, of low saturation
d medium brilliance. See COLOR. — **pea′-green′,** *adj.*

′hen′ (pē′hen′), *n.* The female of the peacock.

jacket. [Prob. fr. D. *pij, pije,* coat of a coarse woolen stuff.] A
lor's thick loose woolen double-breasted coat.

Hyphened Word →

Noun Phrase in Alphabetic Place →

k (pēk), *v. i.* To grow thin and sickly.

k, *n.* [Var. of 1st PIKE.] **1.** The sharp or pointed end of any-
ng. **2.** [For earlier *pike,* fr. Sp. & Pg. *pico.*] Specif.: **a** *Now
cal.* A headland or promontory. **b** The top of a hill or mountain
ding in a point; one of the crests of a range; often, the whole moun-
n, esp. when isolated. **c** The projecting front part of a cap or the
e. **3.** The topmost point; summit; also, the highest point, as in a
aph; maximum. **4.** *Naut.* **a** The upper aftermost corner of a fore-
d-aft sail. **b** The narrow part of a vessel's bow or stern, or the part
the hold in it. **5.** A point formed by the hair on the forehead; —
felly in *widow's peak,* orig. such a point on a woman's forehead,
w often a similar point on a man's forehead. — **Syn.** See SUMMIT.
v. t. To cause to come to a peak; specif., *Naut.,* to raise to a position
rpendicular, or more nearly so, as a gaff.

Special Meaning →

Subject Label →

ked (pēkt; pēk′ĕd; -ĭd), *adj.* **1.** Pointed; having a peak. **2.**
ron. *usually* pēk′ĕd; -ĭd) [From PEAK to grow thin.] *Chiefly
lloq.* Thin; emaciated.

l (pēl), *n.* [Shortened fr. APPEAL.] **1.** *Bell Ringing.* **a** Loosely,
set of bells tuned to the tones of the major scale for change ringing.
A complete set of changes on a given number of bells; esp., the series
seven bells. **c** Any shorter performance than a full set of changes;
, a wedding *peal.* **2.** A loud sound, or a succession of loud sounds,
of bells or thunder. — *v. i.* To give out peals; resound. — *v. t.*
Obs. To assail or din, as with noise or loud sounds. **2.** To sound
rth in or as in a peal or peals; noise abroad.

an (pē′ăn). Var. of PAEAN.

Subject Label →

′nut′ (pē′nŭt′; -nŭt), *n.* A Brazilian herb (*Arachis hypogaea*) of
e pea family, of erect habit, whose peduncles bend after fertilization
d push the pods into the ground, where they ripen; also, the nutlike
ed of this plant. **peanut oil** is expressed from these seeds; **peanut
itter** is made from these seeds roasted, ground, and moistened.

r (pâr), *n.* [AS. *pere, peru,* fr. LL. *pera, pira,* fr. L. *pirum,* pl.
ra.] **a** The fleshy pome fruit of a tree (genus *Pyrus,* esp. *P. com-
unis*) of the apple family. **b** The tree bearing this fruit.

Variant Spelling →

rl (pûrl), *n.* [OF. *perle,* fr. ML. *perla, perula.*] **1.** A dense con-
etion, lustrous and varying in color, formed as an abnormal growth
thin the shell of some mollusks, and used as a gem. **2.** Something
sembling a pearl in shape, size, color, beauty, or value. **3. a**
other-of-pearl; nacre. **b** In full **pearl blue.** The color of mother-
-pearl, a nearly neutral gray (slightly bluish) of high brilliance. See
LOR. **4.** *Print.* A size of type (5 point). See TYPE. — *v. t.* **1.** To
orn with pearls. **2.** To form into small round grains, as barley.
To give to or suffuse with a pearly luster. — *v. i.* To fish or search
r pearls. — *adj.* **1.** Of, like, or set with pearls. **2.** Formed into
all round grains; as, **pearl barley; pearl tapioca.** — **pearl′er,** *n.*

rl. Var. of PURL.

rl′ash′ (pûrl′ăsh′), *n.* Purified potash. See POTASH, 1.

rl gray. The color of a fine pearl; a nearly neutral gray of high bril-
ance. See COLOR. — **pearl′-gray′** (-grā′; 2), *adj.*

rl′ite (pûrl′īt), *n.* [*pearl* + *-ite.*] **1.** *Metal.* The readily fusible
loy of carbon and iron, containing 0.85 per cent carbon. **2.** *Petrog.*
PERLITE. — **pearl-it′ic** (pûrl-ĭt′ĭk), *adj.*

Cross Reference →

rl′y (pûr′lĭ), *adj.;* PEARL′I·ER (-lĭ-ẽr); -I·EST. Of or like pearl or
other-of-pearl; adorned with or abounding in pearls.

rly nautilus. See NAUTILUS, 1.

r′main (pâr′mān), *n.* [OF. *permain,* : *ermain.*] An apple of one
several different varieties.

rt (pẽrt; pyẽrt), **peart′ly.** Dial. vars. of PERT, etc.

as′ant (pĕz′ănt; -′nt), *n.* [OF. *païsant, païsent,* fr. *païs, pays,*
nd, country, fr. LL. *pagensis,* fr. L. *pagus* country district. See

Etymology →

in different ways — usually with a comma or with the words *or* or *also*. To learn how your dictionary treats spellings, refer to the following pages:

> *Webster's New Collegiate Dictionary* (abbreviated NCD) — page xviii (paragraph 1)
>
> *American College Dictionary* (ACD) — page xxviii (paragraph VII)
>
> *Webster's New World Dictionary* (NWD) — page ix (paragraph I-A)

EXERCISE

Indicate the status of the following spellings (preferred, variant, or unaccepted) as recorded in your dictionary.

1. alright, all right, allright
2. development, developement, devellopment
3. envelop, envelope, invelop
4. fulfill, fulfil, fullfill, fullfil
5. jujutsu, jujitsiu, jiujutsu, jijitsu, jujitsu
6. through, thru, throo

40b/Syllabication and Compound Words

Dictionaries indicate the division of words into **syllables** by centered dots and accent marks (**car·na′tion**). **Compounds,** whether hyphenated or written separately or as one word, are shown in the accepted form or forms. See §34 for compounding and syllabication.

REFER TO: NCD — vii, xviii (1 and 2), xx (9 and 10); ACD — xxviii (I); NWD — ix (I-B).

EXERCISES

A

Indicate the syllabication of the following words.

> boogiewoogie
> committee
> factual
> semiphilosophical

B

Determine whether the following words are hyphenated, written solid as one word, or written as two words.

goodbye	nonconductor
homerun	postmark
homework	postoffice
inasmuchas	schoolboard
insofaras	schoolteacher

40c/Accent and Pronunciation

Accent and **pronunciation** are given in parentheses just after the boldface entry. Accents are indicated by a heavy accent mark (′) for the primary accent and a light mark for the secondary accent (′) — as in **de·vel′op·men′tal.**

In addition to marking accent, a dictionary also indicates consonant and vowel qualities by boldface or italic type and by marks or signs above, below, or through the letters (**diacritical marks**). None of the three college desk dictionaries we have listed uses diacritical marks for unvoiced *th* in words like *thin, three,* and *truth.* Methods of indicating voiced *th* in words like *then* vary: ~~then~~, t̷hat, *they.* Notice how your dictionary indicates the sound of such vowels as *a* in *alone, a* in *tale, e* in *here, i* in *ice, o* in *orb, u* in *nature.*

A key to the marks or symbols for these and other sounds is given at the bottom of the page or inside the front or back cover of your dictionary. Learn them; in many words they are more important than accent. Should *Devi* (Hindu goddess), for example, be pronounced *day·vee* or *dee·vi?* The diacritical marks will tell you. In other cases, if you correctly accent the main syllable (as the first syllable of **lam′en·ta·ble**), it is almost impossible to go wrong on the qualities of the sounds.

REFER TO: NCD — inside cover, vii–xvii, xviii (1), xviii (2).
ACD — xx, xxviii (II), inside front cover, bottom of every right-hand page.
NWD — inside front cover, bottom of every right-hand page, x–xii.

EXERCISES

A

For each of the following words, copy from your dictionary the re-spelling for pronunciation. Indicate changes in accent and pronunciation for words which function in different parts of speech.

contest, invalid, minute, perfume, present, refuse

B

Copy the respellings for pronunciation of six of the words in the following list. Be able to pronounce all the words in the list correctly.

abdomen	drought	mischievous
archetype	exemplary	precedence
cabala	Golgotha	sake (alcoholic beverage)
chantey	ignoble	Sault Sainte Marie
combatant	interesting	schism
comparable	irrelevant	sleazy
demesne	irremediable	syzygy
dictionary	Mackinac	vagary

40d/Etymologies

Etymologies, or the derivations of words, are given just before or just after the definitions. Knowing the etymologies of words can improve your vocabulary, your spelling, your grasp of meanings, your ability to interpret new words by relating them to familiar ones, and your sense of the historical development of the language. The dictionary tells you the language from which a word came into modern English (Greek, Latin, Old English, French, Middle English, and so forth), the word or words of origin, their meanings, and subsequent changes in meaning. *Curfew,* for example, is from Old French *cuevrefu* or *covrefeu,* from *covrir* (to cover) and *feu* (fire). *Feu* in turn came from the Latin *focus* (hearth). Curfew, in the Middle Ages, was the hour when fires had to be covered or extinguished.

REFER TO: NCD — xix (5); ACD — xxi–xxii, xxviii (VIII); NWD — xii (IV).

Dictionaries use many abbreviations in explaining etymologies. Each dictionary gives a key to the abbreviations it uses.

REFER TO: NCD — xxi–xxii; ACD — inside front cover, bottom of each left-hand page; NWD — inside front cover, xii (IV).

EXERCISE

Copy from your dictionary the etymologies of six of the following words. Spell out all abbreviations.

banana	croquet	July	squawk
biscuit	duke	khaki	tantalize
buxom	fiend	meander	tobacco
calaboose	friend	persimmon	tulip
carnival	gorilla	saxophone	ukulele
crimson	hussy	shibboleth	yodel

40e/Order of Definitions

Some dictionaries list **definitions** in historical order; others begin with the most common current definition and list the meanings in reverse historical order. Learn what principle your dictionary follows in establishing the order in which definitions are given. Note also how definitions are grouped by parts of speech and transitive-intransitive condition of verbs.

REFER TO: NCD — xix–xx (6); ACD — xxviii (VI);
            NWD — xii–xiii (V-A).

EXERCISE

Briefly describe the over-all historical pattern of change in the meanings of the following words. Style, *for example, originally meant* "an instrument used in writing." *Now it is either* "a quality which gives distinctive character to artistic expression" *or* "the status of being in vogue." *It has moved from concrete to abstract and from particular to general. Have the following words changed from a favorable to an unfavorable meaning, from general to particular, from concrete to abstract, or in any other way?*

awful, fond, girdle, gossip, nice

40f/Parts of Speech

Dictionaries indicate the **parts of speech** by abbreviations: *n.* for *noun,* *adj.* for *adjective,* etc. Some dictionaries number definitions throughout each entry regardless of changes in part of speech. Others renumber for each change in part of speech.

REFER TO: NCD — xviii–xix (3); ACD — xxviii (III);
            NWD, xiii (V-A).

EXERCISE

List the parts of speech in which each of the following words is used.

as	meet
fine	since
like	well

40g/Synonyms

Synonyms (words with similar meanings) are listed at the end of the entry. Making sharp distinctions between words of similar meaning will assist you in the precise expression of your thought. Watch carefully for cross references to lists of synonyms. Thus "—**Syn. 3.** See **humor,**" at the end of the entry for *indulge*, means that for the third meaning listed under *indulge*, synonyms will be found under the entry for *humor*.

REFER TO: NCD — xx (7); ACD — xxiii–xxiv, xxviii (X);
NWD — xiv (VI).

EXERCISE

Study the synonyms for the italicized words in the following passage and choose a more exact term for each. Write your choices.

Supervision in the summer camp was so *ascetic* that all the campers rebelled. My best friend played the piano at all hours although the director tried to *prohibit* her playing except for an hour during the evening. All of us openly questioned the *incentives* of the camp leaders after they closed the swimming pool. Many of the girls wrote letters home about the *vicissitudes* of life in the camp. But when parents came to *scrutinize* the *status* of the camp, the director *fibbed*, and the parents believed him. For all the campers it was a miserable vacation. We will not return next year unless reforms are *inaugurated*.

40h/Labels

Words may be given **usage labels** (*colloquial, slang*, etc.), **subject labels** (*medicine, grammar, chemistry*, etc.), and **geographic labels** (*United States, Western, British*, etc.). (For further explanation of these labels, see pages 203–214 in this handbook, and especially Exercise A on page 229.)

REFER TO: NCD — xix–xx (6b); ACD — xxiv–xxvi, xxviii (V and VIIc); NWD — xiii–xiv (V-B).

EXERCISE

What is the total number of usage, subject, and geographic labels that your dictionary attaches to the various meanings of each of the following words?

beat	sound
cone	space
man	strip

40i/Inflectional Forms

Your dictionary lists important **inflectional forms.** For nouns it lists irregular plurals (those not simply ending in *-s* or *-es*) thus: *man, men; cow, cows*, and the archaic *kine; goose, geese*, and *gooses* (plural for a tailor's iron); *pea, peas*, and archaic *pease*. It also lists the principal parts of irregular or unusual verbs — *dive, dived, dived* (and *dove* as U.S.

colloquial and British dialectal); and the comparative and superlative degrees of troublesome adjectives and adverbs — adjective, *lively, livelier, liveliest;* adverb, *well, better, best.*

REFER TO: NCD — xix (4); ACD — xxviii (IV);
NWD — xii (III).

EXERCISE

List all the inflectional forms given in your dictionary for two nouns, two verbs, and two adjectives chosen from the following list. Where differences in meaning and level of usage occur, make a note of them.

bad	dreadful	plump
bear	fly	quiz
benefit	gas	seraph
big	ill	sheep
boot	little	smite
church	metropolis	spell
cleave	mongoose	spoonful
daughter-in-law	Mrs.	travel

40j/Idioms

Idioms are phrases with special meanings different from the sum of the meanings of the words that make them up. Such phrases are given in boldface or italic type either among or after the definitions of a word. See §48.

Compare:

LITERAL	IDIOMATIC
run a race	*run* a business
run up a hill	*run up* a bill
run up to your girl	*run up to* town
run out of the house	*run out of* money
run out on the terrace	*run out on* your wife

REFER TO: NCD — xx (10); ACD — xxviii (VI);
NWD — ix (I-A), xii (V-A).

EXERCISE

List the idioms which your dictionary gives in connection with three of the following words.

back, go, lay, over, point, put, set

40k/Prefixes and Suffixes

Prefixes and **suffixes** are listed alphabetically along with the entries for complete words. *Con-, ex-, -able,* and *-ectomy* appear in proper position in the body of the dictionary.

REFER TO: NCD — xviii (1), xx (9); NWD — ix (I-A).

EXERCISE

Identify the prefixes and suffixes in four of the following words; then find the exact definition which your dictionary gives for each prefix and suffix as it is used in this particular word.

anteater	graciousness
antecedent	intramural
antiseptic	spinster
Germanophile	tonsillectomy

40l/Foreign Words

Dictionaries indicate **foreign words** (those not yet accepted as Anglicized) by parallel bars (‖), by labels (e.g., *Latin*), or by a double dagger (‡).

REFER TO: NCD — xviii (1); ACD — xxviii (I);
NWD — ix (I-D).

EXERCISE

Determine whether the following are considered foreign or Anglicized.

blitzkrieg	Kamerad	laissez faire
fiancé	khaki	menu
hara-kiri	kop	pièce de résistance

40m/Proper Names

Mythical, Biblical, literary, geographical, and biographical **proper names** may be listed in the body of your dictionary or in special appendixes. Notice especially whether your dictionary has a separate gazetteer (for geographical names) and a separate section of biographical names.

REFER TO: NCD — xviii (1), 1010, 1054;
             ACD — viii; NWD — ix (I-A), xiii (V-A).

EXERCISE

1. What is the population of the capital of Burma?
2. Who was Jason? Jocasta? Sisyphus? Powhatan? Ahab?
3. When is *Italic* not capitalized? *Arabic*? *Amazon*?
4. When is *center* capitalized?

Diction

DICTION IS CHOICE of words, and good diction is as important in writing as good grammar. Your courses in college and your reading will introduce you to a host of new terms, most of which you will learn without thinking of them as "diction"; rather, they will seem like "content," and will become part of your working vocabulary. This process of learning and coming to use new words will continue all your life, unless at some point you die on the intellectual vine.

But there is more to good diction than learning new terms. Learning when and how to use words and phrases, including those you already know, and how to choose the best ones for a particular purpose and occasion is important and often difficult. Learning to use words and phrases properly takes time, thought, observation, and patience. A good way to start is to become aware of the great spread of English from the most ignorant kind of usage to the most learned.

The Range of English

41/Standard and Nonstandard English

Broadly, there are two great ranges of English, Standard and Nonstandard. **Standard** is the language of the reasonably well educated — political leaders, writers, public speakers, educators, responsible business and professional men and women, and those who aspire to these and similar groups. **Nonstandard** is, in the main, the language of people in less favored walks of life, and hence generally of less extensive education — people who deal with things more than with thoughts.

The Standard and Nonstandard ranges of English overlap extensively. They have the same basic sentence pattern of subject-verb-complement, modifiers, and connectives; and they share large numbers of workaday words in all parts of speech. But Nonstandard frequently violates the conventions of grammar and usage, its vocabulary is limited, and its sentence patterns tend to be simple. Standard English, with its richer and more varied vocabulary and its greater skill in handling sentence patterns, is capable of a richer variety of expression, and there is never any doubt about which is which. Here are a few hallmarks.

	NONSTANDARD	STANDARD
Errors of agreement, tenses, and verb forms	I seen	I saw
	we done	we did
	he don't	he doesn't
	him and I done	he and I did
	him and me we went	he and I went
	could of	could have
	had of	had
Double negatives	ain't never	haven't ever, have never
	ain't got no	haven't any, have no
	never did nohow	never did
Stock questions	Right? Right!	Don't you think so?
		Absolutely.
		Agreed? Certainly.
	Know what I mean?	See why I felt depressed?
		Understand why I did it?
		Sure you see the reason?

Stock descriptions	a scream	funny, comic, amusing, hilarious, etc.
	terrific	exciting, amazing, original, terrifying, etc.
Few connectives	and, so, and so, but	and, so, and so, nevertheless, but, yet, notwithstanding, etc.

For the college student, and for anyone else who hopes to fill a responsible place in the world, Standard English has two advantages. It immediately marks him as sharing the language of the group to which he belongs and wants to belong. And it gives him far greater power in expressing his thoughts and communicating with others. Nonstandard English is often vigorous, colorful, and amusing. But there are whole areas of thought and meaning which it cannot express. A sample will show the difference.

NONSTANDARD   Him and me we was just a settin' there not doin' nothin' when all of a sudden up comes this guy and takes a poke at Joe. Was I mad! I coulda brained him with a feather if I'da had one handy.

STANDARD   Joe and I were sitting quietly on the steps, absorbing the August sun and the shimmering beauty of the tall white Colorado aspen, when suddenly out of nowhere appeared a man we hardly had time to see before he rocketed across the lawn and took a vicious poke at Joe. I was so mad I could have brained him, but the whole thing happened so quickly, and was so inexplicable, that I couldn't move a muscle.

42/Varieties of Standard English

Within Standard English are all degrees from the very formal and impersonal to the very informal, conversational and personal. For convenience we may say that there are two main areas, Formal and Informal. Most college writing assignments demand a reasonable degree of formality.

42a/Formal English

Formal English is the language of committee reports, official documents, instructions, most textbooks, scholarly and scientific writing, and some other kinds of serious non-fictional prose. Here is an example of the impersonal "committee" kind of writing:

It is strongly urged that all members of the association who by Tuesday, September 30, have not yet done so, should at their earliest convenience present their credentials to the commissioners of elections. Balloting may under no circumstances be attempted until this requirement has been met in full.

Formal English is impersonal; it uses *I* and *you* sparingly. It avoids colloquial (that is, conversational) English and slang expressions; its vocabulary is learned, elevated, or remote from talk, and it uses many long words. Its sentences are often long and fairly complex in structure. All these things contribute to its *tone*, that is, the tone of formality.

The following passage is formal, though it is free of the dry, colorless "committee" style of the passage cited just above:

As the university tradition came to America, it was based on four ultimate sources of strength: the cultivation of learning for its own sake, the educational stream that makes possible the professions, the general educational stream of the liberal arts, and, lastly, the never-failing river of student life carrying all the power that comes from the gregarious impulses of human beings.

James Bryant Conant, *Education in a Divided World*[1]

---

[1] Reprinted by permission of the Harvard University Press, publishers.

First notice the diction: *university tradition . . . ultimate . . . cultivation . . . professions . . . gregarious impulses.* These words are not from the language of daily chitchat, and they set the tone. Note also that the diction is all of a piece, all serious, though not solemn. Finally, notice the sentence structure: an introductory statement followed by four parallel phrases.

In the following passage, also formal, note the contrast between the adage quoted at the beginning and the formality of the discussion which follows it:

> "Actions speak louder than words" may be an excellent maxim from the pragmatic point of view but betrays little insight into the nature of speech. The language habits of people are by no means irrelevant as unconscious indicators of the more important traits of their personalities, and the folk is psychologically wiser than the adage in paying a great deal of attention willingly or not to the psychological significance of a man's language.
>
> Edward Sapir, "Language"[2]

The diction here is even more learned than that in the selection above, and again the sentences are very carefully constructed.

Good Formal English does not require so learned a vocabulary as Sapir's, but it is always correct, polite, and relatively impersonal.

42b/Informal English

Although a good deal of modern writing is Formal, and the student will need to practice and master Formal English for use in college and after, much is also **Informal**

[2]From *The Encyclopedia of the Social Sciences*, IX, 160. Reprinted by permission of The Macmillan Company, publishers.

English. The Informal is more relaxed, more personal, and often less elevated in tone. Nearly thirty years ago the English critic Bonamy Dobrée described the basic aim of much modern informal writing as follows:

What I think is going on at the present day is a return to speech rhythms. . . . Does it not seem, then, that the modern prose-writer, in returning to the rhythms of everyday speech, is trying to be more honest with himself than if he used, as is too wreckingly easy, the forms and terms already published as the expression of other people's minds? . . . It is the realization of this, a realization possibly new in our day, which impels authors to try to write as they speak in ordinary life on ordinary physical matters, for it is only in this way that one can achieve fidelity to one's self. . . .[3]

These sentences are not strikingly informal, though they contain one notable informal touch, the phrase "What I think is going on." But they accurately describe a trend. Informal English echoes not only the rhythms of speech, but to some extent also its sentence patterns and vocabulary.

The following is distinctly informal:

What greater violence can be done to the poet's experience than to drag it into an early morning classroom and to go after it as an item on its way to a Final Examination?

John Ciardi, *How Does a Poem Mean?*[4]

Note the more conversational choice of words, especially in *drag . . . go after it . . . an item . . .* and *on its way*. More formal (and, in this case, less interesting) equivalents would be *take*, *analyze it*, *a topic*, *later to be considered*. Read the sentence with these substitutions, and note the loss in color, energy, humor, and interest.

---

[3]From *Modern Prose Style* (Oxford: Clarendon Press, 1935), pp. 216–218.
[4]Boston: Houghton Mifflin Company, 1959.

The following is still more informal, especially in the first paragraph:

> You read a thesis set forth as a fact in the newspapers a certain number of times and you begin to think you have figured it out for yourself or at least had it at first hand from what the press would call an authoritative source.
>
> A book has a less treacherous effect. Even its least wary reader is strongly conscious that there is a *man* at the other end of the process, telling him something. . . .
>
> A. J. Liebling, "Professor Kills Santa Claus"[5]

The use of *you, figured it out for yourself*, and *a man at the other end* is distinctly conversational in tone. So is the sentence structure: *You read . . . and you begin . . . or at least.* Yet the passage is clearly writing, not speech.

While Ciardi and Liebling create a tone of informality by the conversational words and phrases cited above, both also use more formal expressions: *What greater violence . . . the poet's experience* (Ciardi), and *a thesis set forth as a fact . . . a less treacherous effect . . . its least wary reader . . . strongly conscious* (Liebling).

In other words, Informal English is by no means limited to the vocabulary of speech; it uses formal and even learned expressions wherever necessary to express meaning fully. As written, it is a mixed style, compounded of elements which strongly suggest the language of speech and others which strongly suggest the language of writing.

This very mixture makes Informal English difficult to handle. To be effective the mixture has to blend smoothly, and it is all too easy to combine elements which do not.

---

[5]From *The Wayward Pressman* (New York: Doubleday and Company, Inc., 1947). Reprinted by permission of Mr. Liebling.

Consider the following, in which jarring elements seem to have slipped in by accident:

> The physician reported that his patient had recovered from mononucleosis and that his condition was *just dandy*.

> The suggestion of intentional obfuscation in the candidate's dissertation *flabbergasted* the *profs*.

> Look, son. Try anything like that in this joint again and I'll *alter the structure of your physiognomy*.

In these sentences the contrast is too strong, the mixture too extreme. The result is amusement at the writer's expense.

42c/Colloquial English

Colloquial is the range of Standard English most remote from Formal. Although, as we have seen, colloquialisms (expressions characteristic of speech) often find their way into informal writing, Colloquial English is essentially the language of speech — as the *American College Dictionary* describes it, "the informal but polite conversation of educated people." Colloquial would use "lost out in the race," "stay put," and "in a fix," where formal usage would prefer "defeated in the campaign," "remained stationary," and "in a dilemma." Colloquial would say "We stopped for a coke. Then we drove on for a couple of hours more." Formal usage would be "After stopping for a Coca-Cola, we drove several hours longer." Colloquial English seldom uses the more formal connectives, such as *nonetheless*, *whereas*, and *notwithstanding*. Colloquial is full of contractions: *don't*, *shan't*, *it's*, etc.; it prefers the impersonal *you* to *one* or *he*; it is full of words like *enthuse*, *exam*, *lab*, *prof*, *get up*, *stay put*, *date*, and *hot rod*. Here is an extreme example:

When you take your jalopy to a garage to have it fixed, you'll find that you have to hang around while some fellow takes his own good time in getting around to looking at it. Then when he does fix it, you're floored because his price is just too steep for your pocketbook.

While the language of this passage is appropriate to the subject, and the diction is all of a piece, neither the language nor the subject is particularly suitable for college writing.

Perhaps the best advice is to avoid all extremes. Overformal and stilted language is affected, pretentious, and, at its worst, unintentionally funny. Excessively colloquial expressions and slang (see pages 210–211) always run the chance of being offensive, at least to some people. The middle range is broad enough for most if not all college needs.

EXERCISES

A

Rewrite the passage about the jalopy above. Change the diction from Colloquial to Informal English.

B

Rewrite the same passage in Formal English. You may have to imagine that you are a member of a governmental agency making a report.

C

In the story "Spotted Horses," William Faulkner has a backwoodsman describe how a Texan rides a wild horse as follows:

Then it was all dust again, and we couldn't see nothing but spotted hide and mane, and that ere Texas man's bootheels like a couple of walnuts on two strings, and after a while that two-gallon hat come sailing out like a fat old hen crossing a fence.[6]

Point out the Nonstandard words, phrases, and usages in this passage.

D

Later Mr. Faulkner revised this story and retold it himself in the novel The Hamlet, *in which he used a different kind of diction:*

They were moving now — a kaleidoscope of inextricable and incredible violence on the periphery of which the metal clasps of the Texan's suspenders sun-glinted in ceaseless orbit, with terrific slowness across the lot. Then the broad clay-colored hat soared deliberately outward. . . .[7]

What range of diction is used in this passage? Point out the words which most clearly indicate the range.

E

Using this same subject matter, write a Colloquial or Informal paragraph and indicate which it is.

F

Many of the following expressions can be Standard, Nonstandard, or either, depending on context. Suggest one or more contexts for each and label the expression in each context as Formal, Informal, Colloquial, Slang, etc.

on the cuff   the glim
off the cuff   sunglasses

---

[6]From the story originally published in *Scribner's Magazine.* Reprinted by permission of Random House, Inc.

[7]Copyright, 1940, by Random House, Inc. Reprinted by permission.

in any event
in the pink
in the red
turn over
overturn
capsize
turn turtle
indignant
angry
mad
burned
I don't like it, not one bit.
the fourth dimension
It's me.
idiomatic expressions
five smackers a slice
a date
a drag
a drag race
Gimme a drag.
work up a storm
to get pinned
to become engaged
to go steady
a Chinese puzzle
a Scotch mist
an Irish pennant
a German police dog
shipshape
College Boards
hour exam
o.k.
the human condition

shades
in this case
under the circumstances
in a state
a pretty state of affairs
in a fix
as stated above
as I said before
as we have said
as in the former case
recall that
it will be clear
don't forget
a pain in the neck
a pain in the arm
a headache
a bother
a severe annoyance
nausea
an upset stomach
a virus infection
the flu
laid up
temporarily indisposed
moving picture
movie
show
a flick
dead as a doornail
out to lunch
   (= missed the point)
faux pas (= mistake)
off the beam

Something is rotten in the state of Denmark.	He goofed.
The sky's the limit.	He made a mistake.
Ontogeny recapitulates phylogeny.	neat
	It's real gone.
peanuts	get the picture
It ain't peanuts.	(= understand the situation)
the day before yesterday	understand
in former times	comprehend
way back when	missed the boat
however	out in left field
moreover	off the beaten path
but	off the track
and so	fail to perceive
as a matter of fact	misinterpret
indubitably	all at sea
sure	confused
believe me	sadly mistaken
without a doubt	quote
incandescent bulb	quotation
electric light	loser
	winner

G

The diction in the following passage varies from Colloquial to Formal. Rewrite the passage and make the diction consistently Formal or Informal. In writing the first sentence formally, for example, you might express it thus: "What a student learns in college will depend not only upon his teachers but also upon his efforts."

What a guy gets out of college will depend not only upon the pedagogues who instruct him but also upon what he puts into it. To do high-grade work, he must apportion his time so that he studies every subject every day. Procrastinating so that he is compelled to cram for his exams is to be censured. He must develop the knack of licking many academic problems, and he must bone up on his studies conscientiously and consistently. If he will follow this line, he can become a bigwig in all his undertakings.

Appropriateness and Special Problems

Language should be appropriate to the subject, the situation, and the speaker or writer and his audience. Formal English in an informal situation is likely to sound bookish, affected, and stilted. If anyone watched a brilliant end run and said, "Observe! He is perceptibly outdistancing his would-be tacklers!" he would immediately be pronounced a "square." Likewise, anyone who wrote in a letter applying for a job, "I did real well last summer shagging ads and I could do neat work writing them, so I hope you hire me," would be likely to spend his summer warming a park bench. We are judged by our success or failure in saying the right thing at the right place and time.

43/Technical English and Gobbledygook

Every specialty, from cooking to chemistry, develops a **technical** vocabulary. Some technical words come into general use, but most remain unknown except to the specialist. Thus everyone knows *penicillin*, but few are acquainted with *penicillium notatum*, the mold from which the drug is made. And we know the plastic *lucite*, but not its chemical name, the acrylic resin *polymethyl methacrylate*. Trouble comes when the specialist either cannot or does not see the need to express technical ideas in nontechnical language for the general reader. We must assume that the following passage, for instance, is addressed to a limited group, for it can be understood only by the person who knows the technical terms used:

Whenever an effector activity (R) is closely associated with a stimulus afferent impulse or trace (s) and the conjunction is closely associated with the rapid diminution in the motivational stimulus (S_D or s_G), there will result an increment (Δ) to a tendency for that stimulus to evoke that response.

Clark L. Hull, *A Behavior System*[8]

Contrast the foregoing passage with the following, in which technical terms are held to a minimum and the needs of the general reader are kept in mind:

Investigators began to look more than 50 years ago for the dreaded invader of the central nervous system now identified as the polio virus. Once they had isolated the virus and learned to work with it in the laboratory, they made an unexpected discovery. The virus turns up much more often in the intestinal tract than it does in the spinal cord and brain. In human beings the infection usually goes unnoticed, causing no harm and conferring a lasting immunity; only occasionally does it involve the nervous system and bring on serious illness. The tracing of the polio virus to its habitat in the gut has led more recently to the discovery that it is a member of a large family of viruses. They all produce the same sort of benign infection in the alimentary tract, and exhibit the same tendency to invade other tissues, especially the nervous system, with more serious consequences. The so-called enteroviruses now number more than 50. Some have proved to be agents of hitherto mysterious diseases. Although other members of the family have not yet been incriminated, they remain under close surveillance, for there are a number of diseases that have no known cause, and the enteroviruses have not been eliminated as suspects.

Joseph L. Melnick, "Enteroviruses"[9]

---

[8]*A Behavior System: An Introduction to Behavior Theory Concerning the Individual Organism* (New Haven: Yale University Press, 1952). Reprinted by permission.

[9]From *Scientific American*, February 1959. Reprinted by permission.

Except for the terms *polio* and *virus*, generally well known, the only technical term in the passage is *enteroviruses* (intestinal viruses), whose meaning can in part be deduced from the context.

Closely related to technical writing is governmentese or **gobbledygook,** which generally makes use of many inflated and obscure words instead of plain language. Thus A. P. Herbert has suggested that Lord Nelson's famous Trafalgar message ("England expects every man to do his duty") would be written in modern gobbledygook as follows: "England anticipates that as regards the current emergency personnel will face up to the issues and exercise appropriately the functions allocated to their respective occupation groups."[10]

In writing on specialized subjects for the general reader, it is not always easy to avoid technical terms and gobbledygook, but every effort should be made to keep the language clear and plain.

44/Slang

Another body of highly specialized terms is **slang,** the private language of a social or professional group. The writer Carl Sandburg described slang as "language that takes off its coat, spits on its hands, and gets to work."[11] Slang is often vivid, vigorous, and amusing. It has, however, three great weaknesses. First, much slang is not widely known. Often it is the language of a special group — of teen-agers, college students, soldiers, workers in a particular

---

[10]Quoted in H. L. Mencken, *The American Language*, Supplement I (New York: Alfred A. Knopf, 1945), p. 413.

[11]Quoted in Mencken, *The American Language*, 4th ed. (Knopf, 1936), p. 556, n.3.

craft or trade. Hence to those not in the group, it may be incomprehensible. Second, slang is often short-lived. It may quickly become stale, meaningless, or old-fashioned. Third, it is too often an easy, popular rubber-stamp which only approximates one's idea, a lazy way of avoiding the effort to find an exact word or phrase.

Slang which is vivid and which conveys a new idea sometimes becomes standard. *Skyscraper*, *bus*, and *mob* were once slang but are now appropriate at any level.

Looked at from different viewpoints, the following selection may illustrate either the humor or the misunderstanding likely to arise from the use of slang.

Read

I DON'T DIG MY FOLKS

I think it's the least the way people aren't hip to the English language these days. Ever since I blew in from college, I can't seem to make anyone dig my sounds. Like for instance last night I was bombing downstairs on my way to the flick with a chick, and the folks hung me up in the hall.

"I'm cutting out," I told them. "Gonna hit the pit, then stop for a couple of looseners."

"You're what and then what and then what?" dad asked.

"Have to book the screens, daddio. Catch a few swinging shadows, then we're gonna fall by a little session and pick up some sounds." Dad looked bewildered. "Popperoony, you're flipping. Don't gas out. I'll be cool."

"Maybe you'd better bring your overcoat," mom said nervously.

"No, mom, not cool. I mean cool. You know, mellow. Roonio. Vouté. Don't worry, I won't come back smashed."

"You get so much as a dent in that car!" dad threatened.

"You don't dig, daddio," I laughed. "I mean that I won't get blasted. Plowed. Stoned."

Mom was stirring her coffee with her fork. Dad lit the wrong end of a filter-tip cigarette.

"For Pete's sake, tell us what you're trying to say," he choked, "and don't call me daddio!"

"O.K., father bear, O.K. I gotta move now. Have to blow this old cellar. I'll clue you tomorrow."

"Are you dating Ellen tonight, dear?" mom asked. "She's going to look simply stunning when she gets those braces off her teeth."

"Come on, mom," I said, "you're goofing the goof. She's a square. She's a three-dimensional miracle you can see without glasses. I mean, she's nowhere."

Dad was chewing up the end of the cigarette; his eyes were glazed. "It's time I paid the check," I told them. "Catch your act in the morning, folks. Got to put juice in the wheels and hit the submarine races. I mean dig the whale fights. I mean check the blimps on the boondoks! Gas!"

Dad jumped to his feet and picked mom up in his arms. "Come on, flapper," he yelled, "let's drop over to the speak and sip a few orange blossoms. We'll do the black bottom and then some necking. I'll bring my uke. Hot diggety!"

Sometimes I just don't dig my folks at all.

Art Zich[12]

EXERCISES

A

Rewrite the first and fourth paragraphs of "I Don't Dig My Folks" in the slang current on your campus.

B

Rewrite these same paragraphs in dignified Informal English.

45/Dialect

Except when attempting to give the flavor of local or regional speech, Standard English avoids **dialect,** usages

―――――――――

[12]From *The Saturday Evening Post*, April 16, 1955. Reprinted with the author's permission.

peculiar to one section of the country and uncommon or unknown in others. Here are a few examples: An onion without a bulb, according to the dictionaries, is a "scallion"; in parts of the Middle West it is a "spring onion" or a "little green onion"; and in northern New York state it is a "rare-ripe." The New Englander goes to a "spa" to get a "tonic," but most Americans go to a "soda fountain" or a "soft drink parlor" to get "pop" or "soda pop." With it they may have a "dog," a "hot dog," a "frank," a "weenie," or a "red hot." The New Englander asks for a "frappé" (pronounced *frap*) when he wants a milk shake with ice cream in it; and his mother buys a "fowl" instead of a "stewing chicken" or an "old hen." The Southerner carries water in a "bucket" while a Northerner prefers a "pail." A Southerner may ask to "carry" a girl home when he only wants to escort her there.

A Midwesterner brings home groceries in a "sack," while a Bostonian uses a "bag." Some Southerners eat "ground peas" or "goobers" when others eat peanuts. The Westerner may ride a "cayuse" (small horse) down the "coulee" (valley) after a "dogie" (motherless calf). A great American pastime is sitting on the "piazza" or the "porch," though to a Southerner it may be the "gallery," to a New Yorker or Pennsylvanian the "stoop," and to a Californian the "patio." An Englishman generally sits on the "veranda."

There is no reason to erase all regional characteristics from language. Many of them add richness, flavor, and variety which it would be a pity to lose. But it is wise to avoid expressions which are not widely understood or which seem naive or out of place in reasonably formal speech or writing.

EXERCISES

A

Beside each of the capitalized words below are synonyms which are used in various parts of the country. Point out the terms which you have used or heard. Add others if you know any.

BALTIMORE ORIOLE   firebird, hangbird, hangnest, English robin, golden robin, golden oriole

SCHOOL ENDS   lets out, gets out, turns out, leaves out, goes out, closes, breaks, breaks up

DOUGHNUT   olicook, cookie, fat-cake, nut cake, fried-cake, ring, cruller

PEANUT   goober, goober pea, ground pea, pinda, pinder

DRAGON FLY   snake doctor, snake feeder, snake waiter, mosquito hawk, spindle, darning needle

B

List and define five dialect words used by the people in the area where you were reared or in some other area.

46/Archaic and Obsolete Words

Archaisms are old-fashioned words and expressions often encountered in dialect and in poetry. *Oft*, *yon*, and *holp* (past tense of *help*) are examples. They are seldom appropriate in modern speech or writing. Obsolete words, such as *jump* for "exactly," *ropery* for "roguery," and *shrewd* in the sense of "bad" or "evil," are not used in modern English.

47/Improprieties

An **impropriety** is Nonstandard use of a word in function or in meaning. Check your dictionary when in doubt.

A functional impropriety is the use of a word in one part of speech when in Standard English it is used in a different part of speech. Most nouns, for example, do not also serve as adjectives or verbs. Thus it is not standard to write *orchestra selection* for *selection by the orchestra* or *orchestral selection*. In the statement "The reporter SATIRED the President's daughter," *satired* is an impropriety. *Satire* is a noun; the verb is *satirize*. Other examples are *region championship* for *regional championship*, and *suicide* used as a verb.

An impropriety in meaning is often ridiculous:

A few *extractions* from the book will prove my point. (The word is *extracts*.)

Some of the stories my mother told me were quite exciting, although as I look back now I suspect her of a little *prefabrication*. (*prevarication* or *fabrication*)

As the sun beams down upon the swamp, no different varieties of color are reflected, only the unreal grayish color of dead *vegetarian*. (*vegetation*)

Other examples are *climatic* for *climactic*, *statue* for *stature* (or vice versa), and *dialectical* for *dialectal*.

Finally, non-words or approximations should not be used in the mistaken belief that they are standard terms. Examples are *interpretate* for *interpret*, and *predominately* for *predominantly*.

EXERCISE

Point out and correct the improprieties in the following paragraph.

When the class in sociology attended court last week, the judge had to deal with numerous kinds of cases and charges. Several of those arranged were charged with being drunkard drivers. An attractive young woman had attempted to suicide by emerging herself in the swimming pool in the city park. Two men were held over for psychiatry examination because they had attempted to do acrobats on a wire hanging from the roof of the Candler Building. When arrested, they had tried to fist fight with the officers, who had to defense themselves from being pushed off the building edge. The most pathetic case was that of an adolescence who was suspicioned of smuggling narcotics on a charted boat which he had not returned at the proper time. These and other cases made our class more aware of legal profession problems.

48/Idioms

Idioms, sometimes called "cast-iron expressions," are essential to Standard English. Rigid word patterns fixed by long usage, they are phrases which for the most part do not mean what they literally say. Such expressions as *how do you do, a man in his shirt sleeves, with the naked eye, step into a job, run for office,* and *every other day* are perfectly clear to all of us, yet could not be translated literally into a foreign language and mean the same things. How, for example, would you explain *every other day* to an Italian, who expresses the same idea in the words *un giórno sì un giórno no,* which means literally "one day yes, one day no"?

There are no rules for idioms. We learn them only by listening, reading, and consulting a dictionary. The most common failure in idiom is use of an unaccepted preposition. An unabridged dictionary will give more help than a desk dictionary on the idiomatic use of prepositions.

Study the following list of common idioms.

UNIDIOMATIC	IDIOMATIC
all the farther	as far as
angry at a person	angry with a person
between all of us	among all of us
blame it on him	blame him for it
cannot help but	cannot help
comply to	comply with
different than	different from
doubt if	doubt that, whether
ever now and then	every now and then
identical to	identical with
in back of	behind
in search for	in search of
inside of a week	within a week
intend on doing	intend to do
in the year of 1956	in the year 1956
kind of a	kind of
might of	might have
off of	off
plan on	plan to
stay to home	stay at home
superior than	superior to
take sick	get sick
try and see	try to see
type of a	type of

EXERCISE

Point out and correct the unidiomatic expressions in the following.

Since I was the city boss, the leader of Ward 15 called me off to

the side and made his position quite clear. He said that he had gone

all the farther he would go until the matter of Gallagher's candidacy was clarified up. He doubted if Gallagher would be acceptable by the voters of Ward 15. And knowing as he did who was in back of Gallagher, he did not intend on working any more for the fund-raising project or giving any further thought of getting votes lined up. He also felt that we must gain more insight to the kind of a program the opposition was likely to put forward. He believed that if it was identical to the one they had last year it might actually conform better than our own with the general interests of his ward. He hated to admit that our opponents' political acumen might be in any way equal with ours, and he would try and say little as regards to these private opinions of his. But until he had enough evidence that would clear off his doubts, he would refrain to take any further direct action. I could not help but conclude that we would have to find another leader to Ward 15.

49/Triteness

The language is filled with **clichés,** stock phrases and figures of speech which were once strikingly original but which have been used so often that they have lost their suggestive value. Thus *a bull in a china shop* was once vivid and funny, but it has been used so many times that we no longer visualize the snorting bull and the flying fragments of china. Examples of triteness are innumerable:

flat as a flounder, pandemonium broke loose, true blue, apple of his eye, tired but happy, all in all, quick as lightning, quick as a wink, quick as a flash, and so forth. Trite phrases, like much slang, provide ready-made substitutes for original thought and expression, and so rob one's language of freshness and force. A writer or a speaker should strive for fresh and original expression.

EXERCISE

Point out and replace with more original phrasing the trite expressions in the following passage.

Honest politicans in the campaign for the state legislature were as scarce as hen's teeth. Every candidate was a snake in the grass who pretended that he was as honest as the day is long but who was really hoping to be elected so that he could make hay while the sun shone and sell the people out lock, stock, and barrel. The oratory flowed like water and smelled to high heaven. When election day rolled around, the people, who had not kept abreast of the times, made a beeline for the polls and voted the straight ticket because they had swallowed the poppycock hook, line, and sinker. All in all, this state will be in a bad way until the people come down to earth and quit voting for politicians who use tactics that ought to be dead as a doornail.

Vocabulary

The English language has a vocabulary of some 600,000 words, and few people learn more than a few thousand of them. Individual vocabularies vary greatly in size and in nature, depending on personal interests, jobs, avocations, acquaintanceship, and reading habits. Most people have a recognition vocabulary much larger than their active vocabulary. That is, when reading or listening, they can understand many words which they do not use in their own speech or writing. In college one learns large numbers of new words — a new range, in fact, for every subject studied. But enlarging one's vocabulary is not merely a process of learning words; it is also a matter of learning new concepts, processes, and information. New words mean new thoughts. It is impossible to acquire either without thinking; mere memorizing is not enough. Nor is it necessary to use every big word one knows. The complexity of diction should reflect the complexity of thought, and often even very complex ideas can be stated in simple words.

50/Vocabulary Building

Study the following suggestions for improving your vocabulary.

Add words to your vocabulary.

Building a vocabulary takes work. Deduce the meanings of new words from context, and when in doubt consult a dictionary. You will seldom find it helpful merely to memorize new words. A grasp of the ideas connected with a word helps to make it yours.

Make yourself word-conscious.

Watch for new words and new meanings as you read; use your dictionary; listen to others, especially to people with a vocabulary which is notably large, varied, and effective. When possible, jot down for later study words you do not understand. These words at first become part of your recognition vocabulary.

Transfer words from your recognition vocabulary to your active vocabulary.

Words learned through reading and listening are gradually transferred from the recognition vocabulary to the active vocabulary as they are needed. Papers which deal with ideas and information met in reading, in lectures, and in conversation naturally demand the use of many terms necessary to the discussion of special subjects. It is hard, for instance, to go far in college without hearing such words as *referendum, osmosis, hard money, due process, syllogism, preterite, existentialism,* and *new criticism.* As you learn the meanings of these and many other new words and the ideas associated with them, you will almost certainly introduce some of them into your writing. When you do, you begin to transfer these words into your active vocabulary.

VOCABULARY TEST[13]

Printed below is a brief vocabulary test. It has been found that the average major executive will make from two to four mistakes on this test; the average college graduate, five or six; the average high-school graduate will get about half of the answers right.

Read each sentence below and underline the one of the five words or word groups following it which most nearly corresponds in meaning to the italicized word in the sentence.

1. They play with *abandon.*
   enthusiasm   skill   loss   unrestraint   listlessness

---

[13]*The Inglis Tests of English Vocabulary,* Form B, as reprinted in *An Outline for Dictionary Study* (G. & C. Merriam Company); by permission of Ginn and Company.

2. He was *absolved*.
   acquitted   bankrupt   discovered   anointed   impressed
3. He *accosted* the officer.
   reviled   hated   addressed   liked   deceived
4. I am *actuated* by friendship.
   encouraged   aided   impelled   betrayed   supported
5. He is in his *adolescence*.
   old-age   youth   prime-of-life   office   apprenticeship
6. An *agglomeration* of roots.
   examination   fertilization   exhibition   loss   mass
7. He *alleges* insanity.
   suspects   studies   claims   fears   denies
8. *Amenable* to kindness.
   responsive   opposed   pledged   disposed   devoted
9. I ignored the *animadversion*.
   interruption   remark   question   criticism   opposition
10. *Apathetic* listeners.
    attentive   courteous   pitiful   sympathetic   unresponsive
11. He seems *apprehensive*.
    angry   guilty   anxious   generous   arrested
12. *Arson* is a crime.
    theft   murder   assault   incendiarism   perjury
13. It *assuages* thirst.
    satisfies   arouses   increases   prevents   prolongs
14. I attended an *auction*.
    card-game   town-meeting   public-sale   trial   opera
15. We demanded an *autopsy*.
    automobile-cover   apology   hearing   refund   examination
16. That is a *bagatelle*.
    suit-case   trifle   riddle   sea-shell   insult
17. A *batch* of bread.
    loaf   sale   quantity   kind   pan
18. He *bestows* favors.
    receives   requests   collects   despises   confers
19. A *blend* of coffee.
    brand   shipment   drink   mixture   imitation

20. A *bosky* path.
    narrow bushy dangerous slippery precipitous
21. He is a *bravo*.
    hero escaped-convict soldier villain conqueror
22. The *buckram* was sold.
    coarse-cloth pirate-ship carriage shield stag
23. I heard of the *cabal*.
    horse hut celebration marriage plot
24. Do you like *cameos*?
    paintings shell-fish puns dry-etchings carved-gems
25. The enemy *capitulated*.
    lost-his-head surrendered retreated attacked escaped

A good score on this test does not mean that there remains
no room for improvement. A poor score indicates the need
for redoubled efforts to improve your knowledge of words.

EXERCISES

A

*Reading of the right kind is one of the chief ways to build your
vocabulary. The context of words, their setting or "surroundings" in
a particular passage, can often help you to figure out their meanings.
Test your ability to define words through context in the following sentences. At the end of each sentence is a list of four words or phrases.
Indicate the one which most nearly expresses the meaning of the
italicized word.*

1. He had tried hard, and we felt that he really did not deserve
the *stricture*. (watch, reprimand, compliment, penalty)
2. All the younger neighbors were delighted when she moved
away, for she had often *maligned* them to some of her older friends.
(ignored, slandered, praised, discussed)
3. The dealer sold Becky the table as a genuine antique, but it
later turned out to be *spurious*. (maple, counterfeit, authentic,
damaged)

4. The *apposite* illustrations used by the speaker made his talk very effective. (opposite, impertinent, vague, appropriate)

5. When transported to this new habitat, the little creatures died before they were sufficiently *acclimatized*. (put in a cage, fed and watered, adjusted, inoculated)

6. Before the robbery, the gangsters had made a thorough examination of the store through frequent visits to it with the *ostensible* purpose of pricing diamond rings. (pretended, showy, frank, secret)

7. He always tried to guide the discussions and was forever offering his services. He was, in fact, the most *officious* member of the committee. (diplomatic, meddlesome, official, tactful)

8. He used such an excessive number of synonyms, repetitions, and round-about expressions that his style was *copious* and hence deadening. (a copy of someone else's, succinct, bountiful, wordy)

9. Had he been less *desultory* in his reading and study, he would have made better grades last term. (aimless, deliberate, intent, procrastinating)

10. If the sergeant's voice had been somewhat less *strident*, he might have got along better with the men. (mild, hoarse, harsh-sounding, pleading)

B

Certain pairs of words are often misused because they are similar in form or in meaning. Select the correct word in each of the sentences below.

1. While our graduating class was in Washington, we went through the (capitol, capital) building.

2. My teacher yanked us both out of our seats and rushed us to the (principle's, principal's) office.

3. The candidate did not say it openly, but he (inferred, implied) that his opponent was a fool.

4. He threw the rock with all his might and it (scintillated, ricocheted) across the water.

5. We lived for a while in a poorer part of the city, and some of our neighbors were not among the most (elect, select) people I have ever met.

6. The beautiful coloring caused the critics to praise the (sensuousness, sensualness) of the artist's work.

7. Naturally, the boys were not (adverse, averse) to having Marge go with them to the dance.

8. Like a true (epicure, glutton), she daintily tasted each bite of food with obvious pleasure.

9. The professor showed his class an (exotic, esoteric) flowering plant which he had found on a trip to Brazil.

10. Self-gratification was his sole end, and he did nothing he did not consider from an (eccentric, egocentric) point of view.

C

Perhaps you need to express your ideas more briefly than you now do. For the italicized wordy expressions in the following sentences substitute one of the words or phrases listed at the end of the exercise. Notice how many words you have saved. This principle should be applied to your own writing — strive for the exact word or phrase which expresses your thought.

1. The poor fellow *didn't know how to read or write.*

2. She *wouldn't pay any attention to anything anybody told her.*

3. Although she was *a woman who had lived in a city all her life,* she quickly adjusted herself to small-town ways.

4. He is *the kind of person who thinks of everything as it relates to himself.*

5. His father was *always inclined to think things would end unhappily.*

6. He is *the kind of student who always puts things off until tomorrow.*

7. *Getting to their engagements on time* is a characteristic of but few people.

8. This particular tribe *spent its whole time wandering about all over the country.*

9. After final examinations he *felt as if it wouldn't do any good to put out any further efforts.*

10. He took *something to put him to sleep.*

of urban background	a procrastinator
pessimistic	was despondent
punctuality	a soporific
was nomadic	was illiterate
egocentric	was intractable

D

Choose any two of the ideas listed below and write down as many ways of expressing each as you can think of. When you have exhausted your stock of words and phrases, turn to your dictionary and add others. For example, if you start with walk, *you may add* saunter, stroll, stride, amble, stagger, meander, breeze along, *etc.*

1. Place of habitation for human beings
2. Child
3. To express ideas
4. Money
5. To look at

E

Read the following passage. Then, from the antonyms (words of opposite meaning) listed at the end, select the ten which may be most meaningfully substituted for the italicized words.

Ladies and gentlemen, we are gathered here this evening to discuss the *ignorant* condition of the voters in this state. Their attitude toward matters of great public interest is most *reprehensible*. This fact, I am thoroughly convinced, was concretely demonstrated by the large number of votes recently cast for Mrs. Annah Tilburn, a *crude*, *egotistic* woman whose *unconcern* for the public welfare is equaled only by the *rashness* of her fiscal policies. Her answer to every question asked her during the campaign was *ambiguous* and *discursive*. The *inflexible* quality of her mind was most clearly demonstrated when she spoke on the matter of taxes for our public schools. It will be a *bleak* day for this grand old state of ours when she finally becomes governor — as I am sure she will.

muscular	silent	prudence
bright	exact	comprehensible
courage	zeal	taciturnity
understandable	commendable	enlightened
altruistic	impetuosity	slovenly
elastic	brilliance	cultivated
neat	ardor	concise

TERM PROJECTS

A

*An article by Johnson O'Connor entitled "Vocabulary and Success"
is very readable and stimulating. Since its first appearance in the*
Atlantic Monthly *in February 1934, it has been reprinted in numerous
collections of essays. Find it and read it. You will enjoy it.*

B

*In your English notebook reserve a special section which is to be
headed* VOCABULARY. *List in this section all the unfamiliar
words which you encounter in reading and listening. Begin today by
listing five to ten such words. Add to these regularly during the term.*

C

*Keep a list of those words in your recognition vocabulary which
you would like to add to your active vocabulary. Practice using them
in writing and speaking.*

D

*Keep your vocabulary eyes and ears alert when reading or attending
lectures. Write down each new word and perhaps also the phrase or
the sentence in which it occurs.*

E

*Look up each new word in your dictionary. Study its origin or
etymology, its parts of speech, its various meanings, its synonyms, its
antonyms.*

GENERAL EXERCISES

A

In the following list, label words that are colloquial, slang, dialectal, poetic, archaic, or technical. (See §40h and your dictionary.)

blockhead
bunk (to occupy a bed)
bunk (nonsense)
clove
  (past part. of *cleave*, "split")
edifice
Erin
erstwhile (adv.)
fardel
feist
fresh (presumptuous)
gobbledygook
hen (a woman)

high-hat
hunky
hunky-dory
hussy (a small case for sewing
  equipment)
kine
octane
rattle (to confuse)
sidle
set
steed
traumatic
y-clept

B

A. Name the range of diction in each of the statements below (formal, informal, nonstandard, dialectal, etc.).

B. Upon what occasion or in what situation do you think that each would be appropriate?

1. The answer is simply not correct. The facts behind it will not bear it out, and the reasoning is wrong.

2. That pitch don't hold no water with me. It don't figure, and the guy what dreamed it up is a sure enough screwball.

3. That conclusion appears unsatisfactory. The supposed facts upon which it is based would seem to be inaccurate, and the reasoning strikes the present writer as being unsound.

4. That ere answer ain't so, I reckon. It just don't make no sense in some ways, and I don't see how the guy who figgered it out got that way.

5. That conclusion is untrue and is based on an invalid inference. The empirical data reveal a neglect of negative instances, and the implication is fallacious since it involves a petitio principii.

6. That answer is incorrect. The facts are wrong, and the reasoning is illogical.

C

Read the following passage carefully and then answer the questions given below.

JACK CARSON'S PLEA

Jack Carson, or his press agent, has dreamed up the CPA (Cowboy-Parents Association), which would be analogous to the PTA. Purpose of the association is to improve the language and behavior patterns of cowboy-indoctrinated youngsters. Carson prefers that his children call him "Dad" — not "podner" or "you ole critter."

He would encourage the cayuse cavaliers to substitute the precise enunciation of Ronald Colman for their slurred drawls and twangs. In addition to their use of proper English spoken in pear-shaped tones, Carson would have the cowhands work arithmetic problems beside the campfire. This, he believes, would inspire little Rodlow to do his homework, since the tiny Hopalongs emulate their range heroes.

What Carson is suggesting may bring about a new cycle in Westerns. For instance, instead of some one exclaiming, "He went thet-away!" — the posse informant would declare: "The fugitive, bestride a handsome mount, galloped in a northerly direction." No more would "them varmints" be so designated. They'd be called "those varmints." The hero would not vow, "Ah aims tuh git them cattle rustlers." He'd say, "I fully intend to bring to justice those felons who have purloined members of my bovine herd."

The standard oat-opera dialogue employs this cliché:
"Y'all a stranger in these parts?"
"Yup."
"Wall, we don't like strangers, stranger."
If Carson, no relation to Kit, has his way, this stock gambit
would be replaced by:
"Have you recently arrived in our community?"
"Yes, sir. I arrived aboard the 5:15 stage."
"I regret to inform you that the natives are afflicted with xeno-
phobia."
These plans of Carson to rearrange range repartee, would have
one unfortunate result. The running time of the pictures would be
lengthened considerably. As it is, too many contemporary Westerns
have discarded the notion that actions speak louder than words.
Extending the words would diminish the action. And since the
Western, basically, is action fare, use of proper English or American might completely destroy the horse opera. If so, parents
would be forced to care for and train their youngsters instead of
relying on the lariat lotharios.

David Steinberg[14]

QUESTIONS

1. If this selection has a serious purpose, state it.
2. List the dialectal words in this passage.
3. List the words which you consider technical or learned.
4. What is the level of diction in the last paragraph? How is it
appropriate or inappropriate to the author's purpose?
5. Is there anything unusual in the linking of such word groups
as "cowboy-indoctrinated," "Hopalongs emulate," "those varmints," "rearrange range repartee"?
6. Why does the author use the term "oat-opera"?
7. What does Mr. Steinberg mean by "proper English or American" in the next to last sentence? Do you agree with him? Is his
"proper" the same as Standard English? Are his revisions of
Western English intended to be serious or comic?

[14]From *The Newark Sunday News*, December 17, 1950. Reprinted
by permission.

Style

STYLE IS THE MANNER of writing, the way the writer expresses his thoughts in language. Effective writing always involves the choice of words and expressions, the arrangement of words within sentences, and variety in the patterns of sentences. We can see style or manner in the way a writer expresses himself. Different writers, trying to achieve different effects, might say, "Flip the switch," or "Provide us with illumination," or "Turn on the light." All three of these instructions "say" the same thing. It is the style or manner which makes all the difference.

Various kinds of writing may be characterized as dull, poetic, terse, flippant, monotonous, pompous, and so on. You should notice the effects achieved in the works of good writers and in your own sentences. The pattern and rhythm of your sentences should be varied, pleasing, and appropriate to your subject matter and your own personality.

Effective Use of Words

Begin your study of effectiveness by concentrating on such basic problems in the use of words as wordiness and repetition. In solving these problems, you may need to review the section on "Diction" (pages 196–231).

51/Wordiness

Do not waste words. Be concise rather than wordy so that you may save time and increase the forcefulness of your writing. Although you should not omit words necessary to the thought and the desired emotional effect, you should express your ideas in as few words as possible.

51a/Omit needless words and ideas.

Please repeat the sentence again. (5 words)
Please repeat the sentence. (4 words)

Drive a nail in the place where the two boards join together. (12 words)
Drive a nail where the two boards join. (8 words)

You will like the new style and will be very much pleased with it. (14 words)
You will be very much pleased with the new style. (10 words)

Accidents due to excessive speed often end fatally for those involved. (11 words)
Accidents due to excessive speed often end fatally. (8 words)

You should not take out the sill, because that step in the procedure is unnecessary and the house might fall. (20 words)
You should not take out the sill, because the house might fall. (12 words)

51b/Use one word for many.

She never did become a good dancer because she always had her mind too much on what other people were thinking about her. (23 words)
She was always too self-conscious to become a good dancer. (10 words)

> The love letter was written by somebody who did not sign his
> name. (13 words)
> The love letter was anonymous (*or*, was not signed). (5 or 6
> words)

51c/Use the active voice for conciseness. (See §9.)

> The truck was overloaded by the workmen with watermelons
> and cantaloupes. (11 words)
> The workmen overloaded the truck with watermelons and
> cantaloupes. (9 words)

51d/Revise sentence structure for conciseness.

> Another element which adds to the effectiveness of a speech
> is its emotional content. (14 words)
> Emotional content also makes a speech more effective.
> (8 words)

> The fact that Carl was always inattentive caused the teacher
> to send him to the dean. (16 words)
> Carl's constant inattentiveness caused the teacher to send him
> to the dean. (12 words)
> The teacher sent Carl to the dean because he was constantly
> inattentive. (12 words)

> A good home library is very useful. It also affords its owner a
> great deal of pleasure. (17 words)
> A good home library is very useful and pleasurable. (9 words)

Study your sentences carefully and make them concise
by using all the methods discussed above. The following
sentences illustrate wordiness and ways of correcting the
error.

> 1. There were two reasons why he did not get there right on
>   time. (13 words)
> 2. There were two reasons for his failure to arrive on time.
>   (11 words)

3. There were two reasons for his late arrival. (8 words)
4. There were two reasons for his lateness. (7 words)
5. He was late for two reasons. (6 words)

1. He was the kind of person who always bowed and scraped before his superiors. (14 words)
2. He always bowed and scraped before his superiors. (8 words)
3. He was always obsequious. (4 words)

1. In order to become an outstanding tennis player, a person who really loves tennis will master the four absolutely fundamental strokes. These methods of hitting the ball are, first, the serve. Next, there is the forehand. Third comes the backhand. And finally we have the overhead smash. (47 words)
2. To become an outstanding tennis player, an enthusiast will master four strokes: the serve, the forehand, the backhand, and the overhead smash. (22 words)

EXERCISE

Express the following sentences succinctly. Do not omit important ideas.

1. For many years the country was under the totalitarian rule of a dictator. The dictator was self-appointed.

2. It is very important for a speaker to have the gift of being able to give his speeches emotional content.

3. Although the Kentucky rifle played an important and significant part in getting food for the frontiersmen who settled the American West, its function as a means of protection was in no degree any less significant in their lives.

4. He wants a place for his vacation where he can be quiet. It must also be inexpensive. And there must be plenty of fishing.

5. The distant explosion was audible to the ear.

6. The journey to California was made by two of us in an English-built Ford.

7. My father first saw the light of day in the year of 1910.

8. He tried without any success to bring the other students around to thinking that his decision was correct.

9. In modern warfare every nation which is engaged in the war broadcasts over the radio information which is intended to convince the people in the enemy country that their cause is wrong.

10. It is not true that he is guilty.

52/Repetition

Repetition, when used carefully, may be effective in achieving emphasis. Avoid careless repetition of words, phrases, and sounds.

52a/Repeat a word or a phrase for emphasis or for clarity

A writer striving for a special effect often gains emphasis by repeating a word or a phrase. In the following passage the italicized words show how Melville uses repetition to create a gloomy atmosphere.

The morning was one peculiar to that coast. *Everything* was mute and calm; *everything gray*. The sea, though undulated into long roods of swells, *seemed* fixed, and was sleeked at the surface like waved lead that has cooled and set in the smelter's mould. The sky *seemed* a *gray* surtout. *Flights of troubled gray* fowl, kith and kin with *flights of troubled gray* vapors among which they were mixed, skimmed low and fitfully over the waters, as swallows over meadows before storms. *Shadows* present, fore*shadow*ing deeper *shadows* to come.

Herman Melville, "Benito Cereno"

52b/Avoid ineffective repetition.

A beginning writer often repeats a word unintentionally, or he may repeat because he believes that the idea cannot be expressed without repetition. Avoid this error by (1) using synonyms, (2) using pronouns, and (3) condensing sentences and omitting words.

Study the following repetitious sentences and the ways of improving them:

REPETITIOUS   Most campus politicians campaign with home-made *posters and signs*. These *signs and posters* are usually quite large and conspicuous.

CORRECTION BY   Most campus politicians campaign with large, CONDENSATION   conspicuous, home-made posters and signs.

CORRECTION BY   Most campus politicians campaign with home-USE OF PRONOUN   made posters and signs which are large and conspicuous.

REPETITIOUS   *My first job*, that is *my first* full-time *job*, was a somewhat *unusual job*. It was *unusual* both as a *first job* and as a *job* for a fourteen-year-old boy. My new *job* was in a sandwich bar in an army Post Exchange.

CORRECTION BY CONDENSATION AND SYNONYM	My first full-time job was somewhat unusual employment for a fourteen-year-old boy. I worked in a sandwich bar in an army Post Exchange.
REPETITIOUS	The *following* statements advise the agent what procedure to *follow*.
CORRECTION BY OMISSION	The following statements advise the agent about procedure.
REPETITIOUS	Consideration of others is really the main *quality* of a gentleman. This *quality* comes from within the man himself.
CORRECTION BY CONDENSATION AND USE OF PRONOUN	Consideration of others, which is really the main quality of a gentleman, comes from the heart.

52c/Do not use vague and awkward synonyms to avoid repetition.

When several words which mean the same thing are used within a few sentences, the passage usually needs condensation.

EXCESSIVE SYNONYMS	*Consideration of others* is really the main *quality* of a *gentleman*. A *man* who has this *trait* is sincere.
CORRECTION	Sincere consideration of others is really the main quality of a gentleman.

52d/Avoid bad repetition of sounds.

Devices like rhyme, meter, and repetition of consonants and vowel sounds are a vital part of poetry and of some kinds of creative prose, but they are generally to be avoided in expository writing.

RHYME	Professor Pennypacker sat down in the *chair*, and during the exciting lecture he remained *there*.
CORRECTION	Professor Pennypacker sat down in the chair, and during the exciting lecture he remained seated.
METER	She boúght thĕ pérfumĕ whích hĕr roómmătĕ tóld hĕr thăt thĕ mén woŭld áll ădórĕ.
CORRECTION	She selected the perfume which, according to her roommate, was appealing to men.
REPETITION OF CONSONANTS	The *des*perate *de*pression of that *de*cade *do*omed many men.
CORRECTION	The great depression of the thirties ruined many men.
REPETITION OF VOWEL SOUNDS	The ren*ow*ned c*ou*ntess fl*ou*nced out of the room after the ann*ou*ncement.
CORRECTION	The famous countess stalked out of the room after the announcement.

EXERCISES

A

Rewrite the following sentences to avoid unpleasant repetition.

1. A person should go to bed early enough to get at least eight hours of sleep. Eight hours of sleep is about the average number of hours of sleep which a person should have.

2. My first date seems insignificant to me now, but I was very much excited on the night of my first date.

3. After the game my teammates told me that I had broken the scoring record of my school by scoring that last goal.

4. Highways should be built so that they can handle present traffic, and they should also be built so that they can handle the greater traffic loads of the future.

5. By studying catalogues, I learned what each school was like and what I liked and disliked about each school described in each catalogue.

6. It was the most beautiful scene I had ever seen.

7. The quality of a painting is not only determined by considering the subject of the painting, but is also determined by considering the techniques used to represent the subject.

8. The truck contained peaches. They were large, ripe Elberta peaches, and they filled the truck completely.

9. The saucer-shaped spaceship spun crazily as the pilot sought to shake off his pursuers.

10. One who fails to pay his income tax often serves a sentence in a federal prison. Many such income-tax evaders serve their sentences in the Atlanta federal prison.

B

Rewrite the following passage. Avoid wordiness and undesirable repetition.

The collector of insects needs only a small amount of equipment to begin an insect collection. He can begin by finding many apparently useless articles around his house and converting them into efficient equipment for collecting. A light net, made of cheese cloth, is sufficient for terrestrial collecting. For aquatic collecting he should have a heavy-duty net or a net especially designed for use in collecting in the water. Before he begins to collect insects, the good amateur entomologist inspects his net and corrects all defects.

Learning the use of these nets is easy. The air net is used by simply sweeping the net over the grass and over high weeds and bushes. It is also used by simply sweeping the net through the air to catch insects which the collector sees in flight. When using the water net in still water, the collector places it on the surface of the water and moves it back and forth over the weeds and grass which are growing in the water. The net may also be used by placing it in a swiftly flowing stream, and thus when one moves a rock upstream from the net, the insects which live in the stream are frightened into the net.

The good amateur entomologist carries with him a jar in which to kill the insects after he has caught them. He can easily find an old fruit jar or a similar kind of jar lying around the house. The jar should have a tightly fitting cap. After placing the insect in the jar, the collector also places in the jar a small piece of cotton with a few drops of carbon tetrachloride on it. The insects are now collected, and the collector is now ready to take his insects home and mount them in his collection.

53/Specific and Concrete Words

Language should always be specific enough to convey the intended meaning and no other. Consider the following sentence:

Most persons entering school are not well educated.

It could mean —

Most first graders cannot read and write.

Many college freshmen have studied little or no poetry.

Few people entering dental school know how to prepare a porcelain filling.

— or any number of things.

Any statement which can have many different meanings needs to be made more specific. If your roommate struggles out of bed, stretches, and says, "Gee, I feel awful this morning," he is being specific enough for the occasion. But if, later in the day, the college doctor asks him whether he has a headache or a pain in the back and all he can say is "Gee, I feel awful," it may be hard to tell whether he needs glasses or has a slipped spinal disc. The doctor, however, can examine and diagnose his patient; most readers and listeners don't have a similar chance.

A prime cause of vagueness is the use of words which are too abstract to convey the specific meaning intended. To understand this fact, it is necessary to know something about the mental process of **abstraction.** *To abstract* means "to draw from," in particular, to draw general concepts from specific instances. The following is a simple illustration:

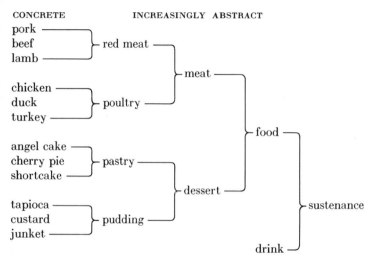

CONCRETE   INCREASINGLY ABSTRACT

In this diagram each step to the right represents a further abstraction. At the level of "food," the word "drink" represents a parallel range of abstracting, and both lead to the still broader concept, "sustenance."

Without the power to abstract, we would be bound to the immediate object or experience. We could never talk about "a meal," but only "roast beef and a baked potato." Increasingly abstract concepts like *meat*, *food*, *meal*, and *sustenance* allow us to group large numbers of objects and experiences and to combine abstractions in order to discover still more relationships — in short, to think.

But we do not independently arrive at all the abstractions we use. Rather, we borrow most of them ready-made. Consider a few high-level abstractions like *integrity*, *morality*,

243

freedom, goodness, love, justice, democracy. It is easy to trace back abstractions like *food, drink,* and *sustenance* to concrete experience; and it will be experience on which most people can agree. But *democracy* means something very different in Russia and in the U.S.A.; *love* means something a little different to almost everyone who uses the word; and so on. Such abstractions are not simple sums of concrete facts, but are built on such a complex of other abstractions that it is hard to say without thought just what we mean by them. Because high-level abstractions are hard to define and because they can mean all things to all men, we should not use them until we know what we mean and unless we can explain our meaning in concrete terms.

Notice how the following passage improves as it becomes more specific and concrete.

GENERAL

Mankind needs to recognize the geographical limitations of communities and the advantages of changes in environment. This is a principle which is evident in the movements and migrations of the creatures of nature.

MORE SPECIFIC

For the improvement of one's health, a change of environment is advisable. It is fortunate that no one place encompasses the world. The vegetation and birds of one place do not exist in another. Migratory birds are more cosmopolitan than man; they eat their meals each day in a different part of the country. Even some animals follow the seasons.

VERY SPECIFIC

To the sick the doctors wisely recommend a change of air and scenery. Thank Heaven, here is not all the world. The buckeye does not grow in New England, and the mockingbird is rarely heard here. The wild goose is more of a cosmopolite than we; he breaks his fast in Canada, takes a luncheon in the Ohio, and plumes himself for the night in a southern bayou. Even the bison, to some extent, keeps pace with the seasons, cropping the pastures of the Colorado only till a greener and sweeter grass awaits him by the Yellowstone.

Henry David Thoreau, *Walden*

EXERCISES

A

Rank each of the following groups of words by listing the most concrete first and proceeding to the most abstract.

theft, robbing a bank, offense, crime
bracelet, adornment, jewel, opal
men's clothing, coat, clothing, topcoat
alderman, government, democracy, agency
humor, joke, pun, a comedy
literature, poem, epic, *Paradise Lost*
Indian, animal, man, vertebrate

B

Write a paragraph of about 150–200 words in which you make the following general and abstract passage more specific.

The view from my window is interesting. When I look up from studying, my eyes naturally turn to all the activity outside. It is a pleasant change from the interior.

C

Change words and details in the following sentences so that they become exact, concrete, specific.

1. He consumed the food.

2. She went across the street.

3. The sunset was colorful.

4. The vegetation was thick.

5. The furniture was damaged.

D

Using concrete examples, define one of the following abstract terms in a paragraph of 200 words.

virtue   courage   imagination   humor

54/Connotation

In addition to their dictionary or **denotative meanings,** many words also carry special associations or suggestions, known as **connotative meanings.** The denotation of a word is its precise, literal, scientific, factual meaning. It is the exact definition given in a dictionary, and it is factually related to the object, thing, or idea for which the word stands. Denotatively, a dog is a four-legged carnivorous domesticated mammal. Coldly and literally viewed, in its denotative meaning, the word *dog* arouses no emotional response of any kind, no hatred, no affection.

When emotional responses are added and considered, we arrive at a connotation. What *dog* suggests to the reader or writer, what it is in addition to being a four-legged carnivorous animal, is its connotation. This may vary from reader to reader and be pleasant or unpleasant. When a dog is mentioned to a boy, he may think connotatively of "man's best friend." But to his little sister, who has been bitten by a dog, the word may connote pain and fright.

A good writer must be aware of connotations, and often he evokes certain ones by deliberately using particular words to arouse a predetermined emotional reaction. If he wishes to suggest the sophisticated, he may mention a lap dog; if he wishes to evoke the amusing or the rural, he may use a hound dog. If he wishes to connote a social distinction, he may use a more derogatory term, *cur.* Even this word may have different connotations: a social worker may react sympathetically to *cur;* a snob, contemptuously. Most dictionary terms for dogs have definitions which indicate that connotations have even become denotations. Notice, for example, the associations aroused as you think of *canine*, *pooch*, *mutt*, *mongrel*, *puppy*, and *watchdog*. Even names of breeds of dogs may arouse different kinds of responses: *bloodhound*, *shepherd*, *St. Bernard*, and *poodle*.

In the following pairs of sentences, the italicized word is used denotatively in the first sentence, and connotatively in the second.

> The *dog* is a domesticated animal.
> Lord Chesterfield has often been considered a gay *dog*.
>
> The general sat his *horse* well.
> The general was a *horse*.

Words that denotatively are synonyms may have different connotative overtones. Consider, for example, the following:

> body — corpse — remains; woman — lady — female; janitor — custodian — building superintendent;   drummer — salesman — field representative; slip — petticoat — underskirt; underwear — lingerie; bedroom — boudoir; slender — thin — skinny; resolute — strong-willed — stubborn

The careful writer will choose words whose connotations are appropriate to the tone he wishes to establish. It is often tactful to avoid a word with unpleasant associations and to choose instead a synonym which connotes greater dignity, propriety, respectability, or formality, provided this can be done without setting up equally unpleasant connotations of false elegance.

Scientific, factual writing usually avoids connotations, for it directs its appeal to the intellect rather than to the emotions. It is almost entirely denotative, as in the following description taken from the *Encyclopaedia Britannica:*

DAFFODIL, the common name of a group of plants of the genus *Narcissus*, of the family Amaryllidaceae (*see* **Narcissus**). The common daffodil, *N. pseudo-narcissus*, is frequent in woods and thickets in most parts of northern Europe, but is rare in Scotland. It is sparingly naturalized in the eastern United States as an escape from cultivation. Its leaves are five or six in number, are about a foot in length and an inch in breadth, and have a blunt keel and flat edges. The flower stalk is about 18 in. long, the spathe single-flowered. . . .

The poet, on the contrary, wishes to communicate and arouse emotion, not to furnish information. Note the emotional quality, the connotations, centered in the daffodil in the following stanzas from Wordsworth's famous poem:

> I wandered lonely as a cloud
> That floats on high o'er vales and hills,
> When all at once I saw a crowd,
> A host, of golden daffodils;
> Beside the lake, beneath the trees,
> Fluttering and dancing in the breeze.
>
> Continuous as the stars that shine
> And twinkle on the Milky Way,
> They stretched in never-ending line
> Along the margin of a bay:
> Ten thousand saw I at a glance,
> Tossing their heads in sprightly dance.

Advertising makes liberal use of words with pleasant connotations. Note the use of connotation in the following description taken from a Sears, Roebuck catalogue:

Florentine Bowl
and
4 Narcissus Bulbs

A gift suggestion of special appeal and loveliness. An offering of spring flowers long before their natural season. The delicate odor and gay greenery of these beautiful paper white narcissus add charm and grace to any room. Four bulbs in a handsome pottery bowl richly embossed in bold relief. Diameter of bowl, 7 in. Packed complete in attractive gift box.

Be sure that the words you choose give the suggestions or connotations you wish to convey. One word with the wrong connotation can easily spoil a paragraph:

> I have always admired old Professor Wilson. He is kind, witty, thoughtful, and learned. In fact, he is a grand *egg-head.*

EXERCISES

A

For each of the following words, list three synonyms with pleasant connotations and three with unpleasant connotations. Compare and discuss your lists with those of your fellow students; notice especially any disagreements about the pleasantness or unpleasantness of words.

house, liquid, garment, speech, landscape, book, stream

B

Comment on the connotations — pleasant or unpleasant, comic or poetic, etc. — of the words in each of the following groups.

stomach, belly, abdomen, middle
sip, swill, drink, imbibe
pony, horse, steed, nag
common, lowbrow, vulgar, democratic
stream, brook, creek, branch

C

Read the following paragraph carefully, and comment on the connotations of the italicized words. Notice especially whether the context may suggest connotations that would not occur to you if you saw the words by themselves.

Claribel grew up in Tennessee, an *orphan* under the roof of an aunt and uncle who fought like *cats and dogs*. We need not dwell on these unhappy years except to say that Claribel at twenty came to *New York*, began — somehow — her bookshop, was admired all up and down *Park Avenue*, seemed wistful to *authors*, and strove earnestly to forget her entire beginnings, which I suppose was natural.

Of late years, however, she has had a great number of *rich* friends who are buying *plantations* in *South Carolina* and *Virginia*, or living like *lords* (on the *Riviera*) in *Florida*, and they have often invited her down to these splendid demonstrations of estates and one-generation *patriarchy*. Furthermore she has heard of much biography, of fiction and of other matters in travel magazines, all dealing with the Southern material (every early fan window in Massachusetts having already been photographed). Going *South* has become very *smart*. How et cetera, et cetera, it all is! And how *cheap* it is! Restore the plantation great houses! C——, of the well-known *soups*, has opened up Belle Chasse, in the tidewater country. Claribel hears this at dinner parties.

"I'm all for the South," she has begun to say.

Stark Young, "Encaustics for Southerners"[1]

55/Figurativeness

Cultivate your ability to write imaginatively, to give life and color to your writing through the use of **figures of speech.** Everyone thinks and speaks figuratively — the politician, the sports writer, the writer of advertisements, the student. Slang and dialect and conversation are often vividly figurative. In writing formal English, however, many of us simply forget or neglect the figurative language which

[1]From *The Virginia Quarterly Review*, Spring 1935. Reprinted by permission of the author.

we might use in conversation. Do not mistakenly assume (1) that formal English is always drab or solemn or (2) that to be figurative you must use slang or trite comparisons.

55a/Use figurative comparisons.

Most figures of speech are based on comparisons; and the more thoughtful, apt, and illuminating the comparison, the more telling the figure. A mastery of the following principles will enable you to develop figurativeness in your writing.

Use **personifications.** When thinking of human qualities helps you to describe a thing, characterize it in human terms.

> He was a historian who never listened to the voice of history.
> Throughout the stormy night the thunder spoke to him of untold horrors.
> He stepped from the doorway into the welcoming, embracing fog.
> Suddenly the sun burst in with a cheerful invitation to get started.

Use **stated comparisons,** which are most often expressed with *as* or *like.* Probably you will begin by making such an easy comparison as the following: "The kitten felt soft and fluffy, like cotton." Or you may say, "Rita's feet are like boats." Or, "He climbed the tree as nimbly as a squirrel." But with a little thought, you can begin to write more unusual comparisons. To what, for example, would you compare a woman's voice? long brocaded drapes? a man in a tweed overcoat? a fat woman's manner of walking? Miss Eudora Welty, in her story "Old Mr. Marblehall,"[2]

[2] In *A Curtain of Green* (New York: Harcourt, Brace and Company, Inc., 1941).

describes a character whose voice "dizzies other ladies like
an organ note, and amuses men like a halloo down the well."
The drapes are "as tall as the wicked queens in Italian tales";
the man in the overcoat is "as gratified as an animal in its
own tingling fur"; the woman "rolls back into the house
as if she had been on a little wheel all this time."

Use **implied comparisons.** In this kind of figure, *as,
like,* and other words which state the comparisons are
omitted, and one thing is said to *be* something else. You
may say that the kitten "is a tiny ball of cotton," or that
Rita's feet "are boats." Alfred Noyes calls a moonlit road
"a ribbon of moonlight" and the moon "a ghostly galleon."
In Stephen Crane's sentence, "Their eyes glanced level, and
were fastened upon the waves that swept toward them,"
the word *fastened* is figurative, because eyes cannot be
literally attached to waves. Even the common expression
to smother with attention is a figure; the person who receives
the attention is not literally smothered. The phrases *hard
light, the cold facts, prickly speech, naked moon, airy gems* all
contain figurative modifiers.

Do not force figures of speech, but be alert to use good
ones which come to you naturally, particularly when they
help you describe or characterize something in a vivid word
or two. And remember that freshness and originality —
without strain — are essential in the successful use of figurative language; avoid the stock figures that have long since
worn out their communicative force (see §49).

55b/Avoid mixed and inappropriate figures of speech.

A mixed figure is usually incongruous or absurd. You may
correct this error by avoiding the figure or by making it
consistent.

STRAINED   A bottle of ink had been tipped over and dark liquid was dripping with a steady thump like the footsteps of a giant in the distance.

IMPROVED   A bottle of ink had been tipped over and a dark liquid was dripping like water from a leaking faucet.

ABSURD   The United States is following in the same steps that the Roman Empire took toward its downfall. These steps are eating away at the very heart of our society — the younger generation.

IMPROVED   The United States is following the same road that the Roman Empire took toward its downfall. This road will lead to the ruin of our younger generation.

CONFUSED   When put to the acid test, his principles were found to be as crazy as a loon.

IMPROVED   When put to the acid test, his principles dissolved.

Not only does a good writer avoid mixed and incongruous figures, but he also is constantly aware of the appropriateness of figures, of the times when they should be used and when avoided. In descriptive writing there may be many figures. In accounts of fast and exciting action, however, figurative language may get in the way of the reader intent on finding out what happens. And in factual and scientific writing, figurative language is seldom appropriate, because it is likely to distract attention from the informational content.

In describing the construction of a modern skyscraper, for example, a writer who seeks to entertain as well as to inform might use many figures of speech, as in the following:

The foundations were finished and the first thin steel columns stretched upward. In a day they multiplied. A hundred black shoots pierced the soil; a hundred sprouting shoots, in even rows, like a well-planted garden. In ordered plan the crossbeams fell into their places, and the great lattice of the substructure shaped itself. Then, above the uproar and vibration of the street, rose the angry clatter of the pneumatic riveters, steel against steel in a shattering reverberation. Joseph Husband, *America at Work*[3]

In a factual progress report about the building of a skyscraper, on the other hand, an engineer would be unlikely to express himself in figurative language:

The framework of thirteen floors of the Warren Building has been erected at a cost to this date of $300,000. The construction proceeds on schedule. It is estimated that all the framework and the exterior will be completed by March 13.

EXERCISES

The phrases and sentences in Exercises A, B, and C are taken from the work of professional writers who have used figurative language effectively in these contexts.[4] *Try your hand at original, humorous figurative speech in these same contexts. Then discuss the relative merits of your choices and those of your classmates.*

A

Complete each of the following comparisons by a figure of speech.

1. A voice as thin as _____.

2. A voice almost as low as _____.

3. Earrings like _____. (They are large.)

---

[3]Boston: Houghton Mifflin Company, 1915.
[4]Many of these figures were quoted in the columns of the *Reader's Digest.*

4. As informal as _____.

5. To dance with Lena was like _____. (Lena was ponderous.)

B

Use figurative verbs in the following blanks.

1. She _____ like a string of firecrackers.

2. He was so bashful that his voice _____ when he used it.

3. Time, the careless laundryman, _____ many of our ideals.

4. At twelve-thirty a quartette of excited young things burst in, babbling madly. All of them had their evening wraps with them; all talked at once. One of them, a Dresden-china girl with a heart-shaped face, was the center of attention. Around her the rest _____ like monstrous butterflies. . . .

5. He _____ over his premise and sprawled on his conclusion.

C

Supply figurative terms in the blanks below.

1. He was not made for _____ the tree of knowledge.

2. Her iron will is _____ with the acid of the years.

3. He was _____ with habit. (Suggest his being covered all over.)

4. A perfect _____ of a woman, looking for whom she might sink.

5. Lakes _____ with sunset.

6. She held up her end of the conversation until it was practically _____.

7. Away she _____, over the lawn, up the path, up the steps, across the veranda, and into the porch. (A light-hearted young girl in a big hurry is your subject here.)

8. Every autumn some thousands of freshmen come thronging through the academic gates and are helplessly _____ into the vortex of an elective curriculum.

9. The fog comes _____ _____ _____ _____. (Suggest that it approaches quietly, stealthily.)

10. A face as calm as _____.

D

List five figures of speech taken from slang.

E

List five figures of speech found in your reading (from newspapers, magazines, novels, textbooks, etc.).

56/Fine Writing

Avoid **"fine writing"** — language that is excessively figurative or self-consciously colorful. Sincerity, naturalness, and simplicity achieve more than ornate, would-be-poetic writing and oratory. Blown-up phrases are pompous and artificial. *These United States* rather than *the United States* and *in the year of 1941* rather than *in 1941*, for example, seem to have more the ring of affectation than of truth. *The green lawn* is more natural than *the verdant sward*. *Spade* and *shovel* are more meaningful terms than *a simple instrument for delving in Mother Earth*.

FINE WRITING	The competitor in the pigskin sport suffered from a poignant affliction.
NATURAL	The football player had a sprained ankle.
FINE WRITING	As a young lad I delighted in laving my feet in the purling and babbling stream which flowed behind our domicile.

NATURAL   As a boy I enjoyed wading in the creek which
                 flowed behind our house.

FINE WRITING   He stretched his nether limbs on the downy couch
                 just as Old Sol first shone in all his glory through
                 the leafy foliage.

NATURAL   He lay down on the couch at dawn.

FINE WRITING   From the auspicious moment when he came into
                 this world, he had an unbounding affection for
                 Old Glory, the glorious flag of his motherland.

NATURAL   All his life he has been patriotic.

Effective Sentences

A major consideration in writing effectively is the use of
sentences which vary in structure, pattern, and length.

57/Periodic Sentences

A **periodic sentence** is one in which the main idea is
withheld until the end of the sentence has been reached. A
loose sentence, on the other hand, is one in which the
main idea is given before the end. Most sentences are loose,
and you should not hesitate to write this kind of sentence
when it is effective. When you wish especial emphasis,
however, you should sometimes write a periodic sentence.

LOOSE   He discovered a human skeleton when he entered the
                 cave, although he had doubted the rumors.

PERIODIC   Although he had doubted the rumors, when he entered
                 the cave he discovered a human skeleton.

LOOSE   The true place for a just man is a prison when he is
                 under a government which imprisons any unjustly.

PERIODIC   "Under a government which imprisons any unjustly, the
                 true place for a just man is also a prison."

                          HENRY DAVID THOREAU, "Civil Disobedience"

58/Balanced Sentences

Proper use of loose, periodic, and balanced sentences will help you to achieve variety in your style. (See **§60.**) A **balanced sentence** has parts which are similar in structure and length. There is, of course, a close relationship between balance and parallelism, since balance is simply refined and extended parallelism. Notice the perfect symmetry in the following sentence by Dr. Samuel Johnson: "Marriage has many pains, but celibacy has no pleasures."

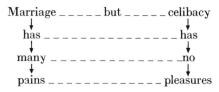

A sentence is also termed balanced if only parts of it are symmetrical, as in this sentence by Thomas Babington Macaulay: "Thus the Puritan was made up of two different men, the one all self-abasement, penitence, gratitude, passion; the other proud, calm, inflexible, sagacious."

Thus
the Puritan
was made up
of two different men,

| the one _ _ _ _ _ _ _ _ _ _ _ _ _ _ _ the other |
| all self-abasement _ _ _ _ _ _ _ _ _ _ _ _ _ _ proud |
| penitence _ _ _ _ _ _ _ _ _ _ _ _ _ _ _ _ calm |
| gratitude _ _ _ _ _ _ _ _ _ _ _ _ _ _ _ inflexible |
| passion_ _ _ _ _ _ _ _ _ _ _ _ _ _ _ _ sagacious |

59/Climactic Order

Elements are **climactic** when they are arranged in the order of increasing importance. Using an order of decreasing importance results in loss of emphasis, anticlimax, and often humor, intentional or unintentional.

UNEMPHATIC   The hurricane left thousands of people homeless, ruined the crops, and interrupted transportation.

CLIMACTIC   The hurricane interrupted transportation, ruined the
ORDER   crops, and left thousands of people homeless.

ANTICLIMAX
FOR HUMOR   Death claimed both her husband and her poodle.

EXERCISES

A

Rewrite the following sentences and make them periodic. If you consider a sentence already periodic, indicate this by a check mark.

1. A desire to learn should be the chief motivation of any student in college.

2. The frontier, according to many historians, has been the most important single element in the formation of American character.

3. Nonconformity was the center of Percival's every thought and the reason for all his actions.

4. Mr. Cobb at last decided that resignation was the only solution to his many problems.

5. The idea of total depravity was a central point of Calvinistic and Puritan theology.

B

Rewrite the following sentences to give them balanced constructions.

1. The man of action often devotes his time to manual labor, sports, and physical activity; but reading, contemplation, and mental activity are the chief interests of the thinking man.

2. Intellectuals on the frontier tried to establish an American culture, but Europe was the place to which those of the East looked for cultural patterns.

3. The coach maintains that athletic scholarships enable young men to get an education, but many athletes on scholarships are too tired to study and learn, in the dean's opinion.

4. The elder child, said the lecturer, is responsible, but dependence upon others was in his opinion a characteristic of younger children.

5. Although a college student emphasizes the monetary value of an education, his instructor believes that an education should teach the student how to live.

C

Rewrite the following sentences according to the principles of climactic order. If a sentence is correct, mark it C.

1. Persecution, abuse, and scorn must be endured by those who refuse to conform.

2. Ignatius decided to marry Clementine because of her intelligence, beauty, and agreeableness.

3. The letter stated that the applicant lacked character, a sense of humor, and ambition.

4. The fire destroyed an apartment house, a hospital, and a hot-dog stand.

5. Benjamin Franklin, one of the most versatile Americans, helped to write the Constitution, established the American postal system, and invented the lightning rod.

60/Sentence Variety

Vary your sentences in structure, length, pattern, and order. Lack of variation in these respects makes your writing dull, repetitious, and monotonous. The variety of your thoughts and feelings should be represented by the variety of your sentences.

Structure. Vary your writing by using simple, compound, complex, and compound-complex sentences. Avoid excessive repetition of any one kind of sentence structure.

Length. Write long, short, and medium-length sentences. Consistently short, choppy sentences or series of long, involved sentences create monotony and difficulty for your reader. (See §4.) Make the sentence length appropriate to the content.

Pattern. Write loose, balanced, and periodic sentences. A passage in which all sentences are loose sentences usually lacks emphasis. On the other hand, a passage consisting solely of balanced or periodic sentences seems artificial and contrived.

Order. Constantly vary the order of words within your sentences. If all your sentences follow the normal pattern of subject, verb, complement, the effect is monotonous. Invert the pattern occasionally. The inexperienced writer often tacks all dependent clauses and long phrases onto the ends of his sentences. Remember that the most emphatic

positions are the beginning and the end. You should therefore place important elements at these two places. Study
the kinds of order in the following sentences.

NORMAL ORDER

SUBJECT   VERB   OBJECT   MODIFIERS
  ↓   ↓   ↓

She attributed these *defects* in her son's character to the general
weaknesses of mankind.

SENTENCE BEGINNING WITH DIRECT OBJECT

These *defects* in her son's character she attributed to the general
weaknesses of mankind.

SENTENCE BEGINNING WITH PREPOSITIONAL PHRASE

To the general weaknesses of mankind she attributed the defects in her son's character.

SENTENCE BEGINNING WITH ADVERB

Slowly she rose to dance.

INVERTED SENTENCE BEGINNING WITH CLAUSE USED AS OBJECT

That the engineer tried to avert the catastrophe, none of them
would deny.

SENTENCE BEGINNING WITH DEPENDENT ADVERBIAL CLAUSE

"*If you wish to create a college, therefore, and are wise*, you will
seek to create a life." (Woodrow Wilson)

SENTENCE BEGINNING WITH PARTICIPIAL PHRASE

Flying for hours low over the water, the plane searched for
survivors.

Experiment with the order of sentence elements. Use the
examples above as models for varying your sentence patterns.
This kind of practice will improve your style. In the actual
writing of your papers, however, remember that too much
experimentation and too many sentences in unusual order
can give an impression of strain and be distracting to the
reader.

EXERCISES

A

Show how variety is achieved in the following paragraph.

Satan, we are told, finds work for idle hands to do. There is no mistaking the accuracy of this proverb. Millions of men have heaped up riches and made a conquest of idleness so as to discover what it is that Satan puts them up to. Not one has failed to find out. But never before has a great nation of brave and dreaming men absent-mindedly created a huge class of idle, middle-aged women. Satan himself has been taxed to dig up enterprises enough for them. But the field is so rich, so profligate, so perfectly to his taste, that his first effort, obviously, has been to make it self-enlarging and self-perpetuating. This he has done by whispering into the ears of girls that the only way they can cushion the shock destined to follow the rude disillusionment over the fact that they are not really Cinderella is to institute momworship. Since he had already infested both male and female with the love of worldly goods, a single step accomplished the entire triumph: he taught the gals to teach their men that dowry went the other way, that it was a weekly contribution, and that any male worthy of a Cinderella would have to work like a piston after getting one, so as to be worthy, also, of all the moms in the world.

Philip Wylie, *Generation of Vipers*[5]

B

Rewrite the following passage so that it is more varied in style.
Army ants abound in the tropical rain forests of Hispanic America, Africa and Asia. Army ants are classified taxonomically into more than 200 species. They are distinguished as a group chiefly by their peculiar mode of operation. They are organized in colonies 100,000 to 150,000 strong. They live off their environment by systematic plunder and pillage. They are true nomads. They have no fixed abode. Their nest is a seething cylindrical cluster of themselves. Ant is hooked to ant. Queen and brood are sequestered in a labyrinth of corridors and chambers within the ant mass. They stream forth from these bivouacs at dawn. They move in tightly organized columns and swarms to raid the surrounding terrain. Their columns often advance as much as 35 meters an hour. They may finally reach out 300 meters or more in an unbroken stream. They may keep their bivouacs fixed for days at a

[5]Reprinted by permission of Rinehart & Company, Inc., publishers.

time in a hollow tree. They often stay in some other equally pro-

tected shelter. They then for a restless period move on with every

dusk. They swarm forth in a solemn, plodding procession. Each

ant holds to its place in line. Its forward-directed antennae beat a

hypnotic rhythm. Throngs of larvae-carriers come at the rear. The

big, wingless queen is at the very last. She is buried under a melee

of frenzied workers. They hang their new bivouac under a low

branch or vine late at night.

Adapted from T. C. Schneirla and Gerard Piel, "The Army Ant"[6]

GENERAL EXERCISES

In the following passages point out repetition of words and sounds, periodic and balanced sentences, parallelism, climactic order, devices used to achieve variety in sentence structure, and figures of speech. (As an aid in analyzing these passages, read each of them aloud at least once.)

Write a brief description of the style of each passage.

A

And now was acknowledged the presence of the Red Death. He had come like a thief in the night. And one by one dropped the revelers in the blood-bedewed halls of their revel, and died each in the despairing posture of his fall. And the life of the ebony clock went out with that of the last of the gay. And the flames of the tripods expired. And Darkness and Decay and the Red Death held illimitable dominion over all.

Edgar Allan Poe, "The Masque of the Red Death"

---

[6]From *Scientific American*, June 1948. Adapted by permission.

B

The county courthouse was, in short, America — the wilderness America, the sprawling, huge, chaotic, criminal America. It was murderous America soaked with murdered blood, tortured and purposeless America, savage, blind, and mad America, exploding through its puny laws, its pitiful pretense. It was America with all its almost hopeless hopes, its almost faithless faiths — America with the huge blight on her of her own error, the broken promise of her lost dream and her unachieved desire; and it was America as well with her unspoken prophecies, her unfound language, her un-uttered song. And just for all these reasons it was for us all our own America — with all her horror, beauty, tenderness, and terror — with all we know of her that never has been proved, that has never yet been uttered — the only one we know, the only one there is.

Thomas Wolfe, *The Hills Beyond* [7]

C

The theory of books is noble. The scholar of the first age received into him the world around; brooded thereon; gave it the new ar-rangement of his own mind, and uttered it again. It came into him life; it went out from him truth. It came to him short-lived actions; it went out from him immortal thoughts. It came to him business; it went from him poetry. It was dead fact; now, it is quick thought. It can stand, and it can go. It now endures, it now flies, it now inspires. Precisely in proportion to the depth of mind from which it issued, so high does it soar, so long does it sing.

Ralph Waldo Emerson, "The American Scholar"

D

Once in camp I put a log on top of the fire and it was full of ants. As it commenced to burn, the ants swarmed out and went first toward the center where the fire was; then turned back and ran

---

[7]Reprinted by permission of Harper & Brothers, publishers.

toward the end. When there were enough on the end they fell off into the fire. Some got out, their bodies burnt and flattened, and went off not knowing where they were going. But most of them went toward the fire and then back toward the end and swarmed on the cool end and finally fell off into the fire. I remember thinking at the time that it was the end of the world and a splendid chance to be a messiah and lift the log off the fire and throw it out where the ants could get off onto the ground.

Ernest Hemingway, *A Farewell to Arms*[8]

E

Even though large tracts of Europe and many old and famous States have fallen or may fall into the grip of the Gestapo and all the odious apparatus of Nazi rule, we shall not flag or fail. We shall go on to the end, we shall fight in France, we shall fight on the seas and oceans, we shall fight with growing confidence and growing strength in the air, we shall defend our Island, whatever the cost may be, we shall fight on the beaches, we shall fight on the landing grounds, we shall fight in the fields and in the streets, we shall fight in the hills; we shall never surrender, and even if, which I do not for a moment believe, this Island or a large part of it were subjugated and starving, then our Empire beyond the seas, armed and guarded by the British Fleet, would carry on the struggle, until, in God's good time, the New World, with all its power and might, steps forth to the rescue and the liberation of the old.

Winston Churchill, *Blood, Sweat, and Tears*[9]

F

I love comedians, the highest and the lowest. I love cartoons, too. My allergy to comics, however, is complete, utter, absolute. I know there are bad comics, and I presume there are good comics.

[8]Reprinted by permission of Charles Scribner's Sons, publishers.
[9]Copyright 1941 by Winston S. Churchill. Used by permission of G. P. Putnam's Sons, publishers.

I have read a few of both — under protest. But I regret them both.
I deplore them. And, to continue the understatement, I abhor
them. So far as I am concerned, they might just as well be written
in a foreign language for which no dictionary was ever published.
I wish they had been.

John Mason Brown, "The Case Against the Comics"[10]

G

We have divided men into Red-bloods and Mollycoddles. "A
Red-blood man" is a phrase which explains itself, "Mollycoddle" is
its opposite. We have adopted it from a famous speech of Mr.
Roosevelt, and redeemed it — perverted it, if you will — to other
uses. A few examples will make the notion clear. Shakspere's
Henry V is a typical Red-blood man; so was Bismarck; so was
Palmerston; so is almost any business man. On the other hand,
typical Mollycoddles were Socrates, Voltaire, and Shelley. The
terms, you will observe, are comprehensive, and the types very
broad. Generally speaking, men of action are Red-bloods. Not
but what the Mollycoddle may act, and act efficiently. But, if so,
he acts from principle, not from the instinct of action. The Red-
blood, on the other hand, acts as the stone falls, and does indiscriminately anything that comes to hand. It is thus he that carries
on the business of the world. He steps without reflection into the
first place offered him and goes to work like a machine. The ideals
and standards of his family, his class, his city, his country, and his
age, he swallows as naturally as he swallows food and drink. He
is therefore always "in the swim"; and he is bound to "arrive,"
because he has set before himself the attainable. You will find him
everywhere, in all the prominent positions. In a military age he is a
soldier, in a commercial age a business man. He hates his enemies,
and he may love his friends; but he does not require friends to love.
A wife and children he does require, for the instinct to propagate the
race is as strong in him as all other instincts. His domestic life,

---

[10]From the *Saturday Review of Literature*, March 20, 1948. Reprinted
by permission.

however, is not always happy; for he can seldom understand his
wife. This is part of his general incapacity to understand any
point of view but his own. He is incapable of an idea and con-
temptuous of a principle. He is the Samson, the blind force, dearest
to Nature of her children. He neither looks back nor looks ahead.
He lives in present action. And when he can no longer act, he loses
his reason for existence. The Red-blood is happiest if he dies in the
prime of life; otherwise, he may easily end with suicide. For he has
no inner life; and when the outer life fails, he can only fail with it.
The instinct that animated him being dead, he dies, too. Nature,
who has blown through him, blows elsewhere. His stops are dumb;
he is dead wood on the shore.

G. Lowes Dickinson, *Appearances*[11]

[11]Reprinted by permission of George Allen & Unwin Ltd., publishers.

PART FOUR

LARGER UNITS

The Paragraph

ALL GOOD WRITING is a flow or continuum of ordered thought, and the paragraph is the way we divide that flow into coherent units. A **paragraph** may be defined as a group of sentences all relating to a central and unifying idea. For the writer, careful paragraphing is related to a clear organization and to the distinct separation of one important idea from another. For the reader, the paragraph assists comprehension by indicating thought units; it also gives him a sense of movement or progress, of "getting somewhere."

The indentation at the beginning of a paragraph, then, serves somewhat the same function as a mark of punctuation: it is a conventional means of indicating a division of thought. In handwriting, the indentation is about one-half inch; in typescript, usually five spaces.

61/Paragraph Unity

The essence of the paragraph is that it should be focused on a single unit of thought. Two or more unrelated thoughts within the same paragraph may puzzle or confuse a reader. The following paragraph is unified because every sentence illustrates the subject, which is announced in the first sentence:

Withal, Toscanini is the least "talking" of any conductor with whom I have ever played. Off stage he is most friendly and even garrulous. On the stand he tends to be severely formal, intent only on the work at hand. During a rehearsal there is little of the pedantic "explaining" or "teaching" type of procedure, usually the bane of an orchestra's existence. The orchestra does more playing than listening to "how" it should play. So much is expressed by eye, by stick, gesticulation, called-out suggestions, that little is left for words.

Samuel Antek, "Playing with the Maestro"[1]

Here the first sentence states the idea that in conducting an orchestra Toscanini talked very little. The remaining sentences explain and illustrate this point.

Many paragraphs wander. They seem to begin with a topic that holds promise for unified treatment, yet each new sentence throws the writer a little further off his course. Notice how the following paragraph starts with the subject of advertising, shifts to work and the boy next door, and concludes with a statement about parenthood. Though each of the transitions has a certain logic in itself, the cumulative effect is a complete change of subject between the first sentence and the last.

Advertisements in magazines and on television suggest that Americans spend all their time playing. The men who recommend cigarettes are pursuing a hobby, playing baseball, or fishing in a cool and shady lake. Apparently cigarette smokers desire only recreation: they never work. Children watch television advertisements and decide that they should never work around the home. The boy next door never works. He refuses even to take out the garbage. But his problem is that his parents never talk to him or discipline him. The lack of proper discipline is a major cause of juvenile delinquency. A problem of modern life is the attitudes of parents toward their children.

A paragraph, of course, may properly shift from one idea to another, so long as there is a close relationship between

---

[1]From the *Saturday Review of Literature*. Reprinted by permission.

the two ideas. The following paragraph, for example, pursues one course until the transitional word *however* indicates a change in direction. Both ideas, nevertheless, develop the topic stated in the opening sentence, that "Bret Harte seems to be a realist."

Bret Harte seems to be a realist. Many of his characters are gamblers, bearded miners, hardened prostitutes, and habitual drunkards — a motley crew of riffraff and wild Western bad men. Their appearances, however, do not reveal their true characters. In crises, their rough and dirty exteriors are proved to conceal hearts of true gold. For instance, old Mother Shipton, who has been a frontier courtesan for many years, starves herself to death while she is snowbound so that she may leave food for the young and innocent.

62/Topic Sentences

The idea which unifies a paragraph — the central idea — is usually expressed in a **topic sentence.** The main point of a paragraph should be unmistakably clear to the reader. Before developing the habit of writing good topic sentences, the beginner is likely to write a series of related sentences without clearly expressing their relationship or the point they are intended to make. Often the failure to write a good topic sentence may mean (1) that the writer does not really know what point he wants a group of sentences to develop or (2) that he knows the significance but does not see that the reader cannot know it without being told.

In the paragraph above about Toscanini, the first sentence announces clearly the subject for the entire paragraph. Without this sentence, the rest of the paragraph would be a mere description of Toscanini's mannerisms. The subject of the paragraph on Bret Harte would not even be apparent without the topic sentence. In informative and argumentative writing, topic sentences are guides to the reader. Occasionally some paragraphs are written without topic sentences; in general, however, obscurity may result from omitted or implied topic sentences, except in narrative and descriptive writing.

Study the italicized topic sentences in the four following paragraphs. These paragraphs demonstrate that the topic sentence does not have to be the opening sentence (though it often is). In the first paragraph, the first sentence should probably be regarded as the topic sentence, although the last also summarizes the central idea. The second paragraph consists of an initial topic sentence followed by examples. In the third, the opening sentence sets the direction for the first half of the paragraph, and a new and contrasting direction is established in the second italicized sentence. No one sentence in this paragraph satisfactorily covers both aspects of this topic and serves as a single topic sentence. In the fourth paragraph, the last sentence is clearly a summary and topic sentence for the preceding details.

The standard Horatio Alger hero was a fatherless boy of fifteen or thereabouts who had to earn his way, usually in New York City. Sometimes he had to help support a widowed mother with his bootblacking or peddling; sometimes his parentage was unknown and he lived with an aged and eccentric miser, or with a strange hermit who claimed to be his uncle. It might even be that his father was living, but was having trouble with the mortgage on the old farm. *Always, however, the boy had to stand on his own feet and face the practical problem of getting on.*

This problem was set before the reader in exact financial detail. On the very first page of *Do and Dare*, for example, it was disclosed that the young hero's mother, as postmistress at Wayneboro, had made during the preceding year just $398.50. Whenever "our hero" had to deal with a mortgage, the reader was told the precise amount, the rate of interest, and all other details. When our hero took a job, the reader could figure for himself exactly how much progress he was making by getting $5 a week in wages at the jewelry store and another $5 a week tutoring Mrs. Mason's son in Latin. Our hero was always a good boy, honest, abstemious (in fact, sometimes unduly disposed to preach to drinkers and smokers), prudent, well mannered (except perhaps for the preaching), and frugal. The excitement of each book lay in his progress toward wealth.

Always there were villains who stood in his way — crooks who would rob him of his earnings, sharpers who would prey upon his supposed innocence. His battles with these villains furnished plenty of melodrama. They tried to sell him worthless gold watches on railroad trains, held him up as he was buggy-driving home with his employer's funds, kidnaped him and held him a prisoner in a New York hide-out, chloroformed him in a Philadelphia hotel room, slugged him in a Chicago alley-tenement. *But always he overcame them — with the aid of their invariable cowardice.* (There must be many men now living who remember the shock of outraged surprise with which they discovered that the village bully did not, as in the Alger books, invariably run whimpering away at the first show of manly opposition, but sometimes packed a nasty right.) The end of the book found our hero well on his way toward wealth: a fortune which might reach to more than a hundred thousand dollars, which, to the average boy reader of the seventies and eighties, was an astronomical sum. . . .

Sometimes this capital was inherited: the supposed orphan, ragged though he was, proved to be the son of a man whose supposedly worthless mining stock was good for $100,000. Sometimes the capital was a gift: rich Mr. Vanderpool was so impressed with the boy's pluck that he made over to him the $50,000 that the boy had helped him to save from the robbers. Or the boy was out in Tacoma, buying lots as a real-estate agent (on his boss's inside information that the Northern Pacific was to be extended to the Coast), and in a Tacoma hotel he befriended an invalid gentleman, who out of gratitude gave him a part interest in some lots that promptly soared in value and put him on Easy Street. *The method varied; but when the time came for our hero to get into the money, it was a transaction in capital which won the day for him.*

Frederick Lewis Allen, "The Road to Riches"[2]

EXERCISES

The topic sentences have been here omitted from the following paragraphs (A–E). Read each paragraph carefully, determine the central unity of thought, and then write a good topic sentence which will make this thought immediately apparent.

A

Many signs suggest it. Books dealing with frankly religious themes appear high on the best-seller lists. Movies on biblical and religious subjects are popular box-office attractions. Gospel songs sung by crooners and swing quartets can frequently be heard on radio and television. Popular mass-circulation magazines seem to include articles on religion more frequently than they used to. Bishop Sheen, Billy Graham, and Norman Vincent Peale each number their adherents and admirers in the thousands if not the millions.   Harry C. Meserve, "The New Piety"[3]

B

Some Indian maharajas, like the Nizam of Hyderabad who has a garage of fifty Rolls-Royces of various vintage and design, run to leopard-skin upholstery and built-in wine coolers. The Maharaja

[2]From the *Saturday Review of Literature*, September 17, 1938. Reprinted by permission.
[3]From *No Peace of Mind*, © 1955, 1958, by Harry C. Meserve. Reprinted by permission of Harcourt, Brace and Company, Inc.

of Patiala has a weakness for gold-plated instrument panels with diamond-mounted blocks by Cartier and, for some vague reason, his Rolls-Royce carries a medicine chest under the rear floor boards. Englishmen of stately dimensions have the bodywork extra high to accommodate a silk or non-Gibus-type top hat. Hollywood playboys affect silverplated bonnets and concealed bars. A New York architect a few years ago had his town-car Rolls designed with a glass panel in the roof, like a sight-seeing bus, so that he could admire the skyscrapers he had designed. A recent and venerated English monarch, who shall here be nameless in the interest of international good feeling, had a chamber pot concealed in her royal limousine. Petit-point upholstery, costly fur lap robes, gold vanities and such trifles are commonplace.

Lucius Beebe, "The Regal Rolls-Royce"[4]

C

Not simply the past dug out of history books, tracked down in obscure libraries, ferreted out of the cracked pages of old letters, diaries and ships' logs, but the more personal past — the past remembered. No writer — at least no writer such as myself — ever quite escapes his own childhood. He returns to it again and again, with affection and with longing and with increasing accuracy of recollection and detail, for this is personal history that has been experienced. And this is the stuff that stories and books are made of. Nor does it much matter where or what that past was. I know this, because I was brought up in the wrong part of London, the dull part where nothing ever happened. Yet I have gone back to that part of London again and again in my books — for events, for people, for stories, for tiny details, for settings and houses and furniture — and for me, this London can never be dull.

C. S. Forester, "Hornblower's London"[5]

[4]Reprinted from *Esquire*, June 1955.
[5]From *Holiday*, August 1955. Copyright 1955 by The Curtis Publishing Co. Reprinted by permission of Harold Matson Co.

D

Actually, a shortsighted legislative policy has forbidden young people to engage in many pursuits which once afforded opportunities for wholesome employment. I have seen prosecutions under the Child Labor Law which did more harm than good. I have in mind particularly the owner of a cleansing and dyeing shop whose fifteen-year-old brother helped him after school and who was brought into my court for violating the Child Labor Law. If a young man is not as anxious to work as he might be, let us remember that laws like that have helped estrange him from habits of industry.   Judge Elijah Adlow, "Teen-Age Criminals"[6]

E

Indeed, the one word most expressive of democracy is "no." Democracy says "no" to the government that would invade natural rights of the individual or the group. It says "no" to the government that would push people around, even though this may mean that the people can push the government around. The American Constitution is more specific concerning what shall not be part of the structure of government than it is concerning what shall. The words "no" or "not" are conspicuous in every article and section. Nowhere are those two words more in evidence than in most of the clauses of the Bill of Rights. . . .

Norman Cousins, "No"[7]

F

Write five good topic sentences, all on different subjects. Bring them to class, and be prepared to develop any one of them into a paragraph of approximately 150 words in length.

[6]From *The Atlantic Monthly*, July 1955. Reprinted by permission of Judge Adlow.
[7]From the *Saturday Review of Literature*. Reprinted by permission.

63/Paragraph Development

Paragraphs should be developed adequately and at a length appropriate to the topic.

Paragraphs vary in length from a single word to several pages, depending on the subject matter and the kind of writing. Paragraphs in a newspaper are generally short, sometimes no longer than a sentence. Such short paragraphs allow the reader to grasp the leading facts quickly and easily. But in more complex material many short paragraphs tend either to separate closely related ideas or to dismiss ideas before they are properly developed.

In most student writing, paragraphs should average 100 to 150 words in length. Paragraphs in a theme of, say, 300 words will generally be shorter and more uniform in length than those in a theme of 700 words or in a term paper of 1500 to 2000 words. A long paper, on the other hand, may suitably include one or more paragraphs of only one short sentence for transition or for the concise and emphatic expression of an important idea. The same paper may also include paragraphs of 250 or 300 words which explain or illustrate major ideas in detail.

Short paragraphs are useful (1) to give emphasis, (2) to make a transition between longer paragraphs, (3) to describe dramatic, exciting action in narration, and (4) to mark changes of speakers in dialogue (see §29a). Consistently short paragraphs, however, become monotonous. A series of paragraphs consisting of only two or three brief sentences apiece should be carefully examined. If they are closely related in thought, perhaps they should be combined into a single paragraph with a unifying topic sentence. If they are not closely related, perhaps each should be expanded with pertinent and sufficient detail. A writer who will not take the trouble to organize and develop his paragraphs may fail to make his thoughts clear. Or he may be writing short paragraphs simply because he has nothing much to say, in which case he needs to think his ideas through and build up their content.

Thought should never be divided into paragraphs at regular or mechanical intervals simply because "it's time for a change." Good paragraphs are constructed around ideas; they do not just happen and they are not arbitrary divisions. The beginning writer often uses too many paragraphs, perhaps thinking that if he uses enough divisions he cannot go wrong. Consequently the reader may become so involved with paragraph divisions that he cannot focus on the logical development of the thought. The following selection is divided into an excessive number of paragraphs, and the divisions are not logical.

The adult forgets the troubles of his youth. Comparing the remembered carefree past with his immediate problems, the mature man thinks that troubles belong only to the present.

The child, the adult thinks, does not quarrel with a wife. Making the monthly check cover all the bills is only a problem of maturity. The twelve-year-old does not worry about salary or professional advancement, whether the union will succeed in getting him a raise, whether the appointment to a vice-presidency will come to him in turn.

When the roof leaks, only the parent worries about what contractor to employ or about how he will repair it himself. The child eats, but is not forced to cook the meal.

To the adult, then, childhood is a time of freedom. The child, however, wishes always to be a man. He finds freedom in the future.

The small boy quarrels with his sister and looks forward to perfect marital bliss with a wife who never nags. To him, adulthood is a time of wealth, and his father never needs to worry about saving to buy a bicycle. Childhood is a time of study; the mature never have to go to school and worry about report cards and grades on conduct. "When I get big," he thinks, "Mother won't tell me what to eat."

Happiness is too seldom found in the present. All too often it is remembered as a thing of the past or looked forward to as a part of the future.

If many of these same paragraphs are combined, the continuity seems much more logical:

The adult forgets the troubles of his youth. Comparing the remembered carefree past with his immediate problems, the mature man thinks that troubles belong only to the present. The child, the adult thinks, does not quarrel with a wife. Making the monthly check cover all the bills is only a problem of maturity. The twelve-year-old does not worry about salary or professional advancement, whether the union will succeed in getting him a raise, whether the appointment to a vice-presidency will come to him in turn. When the roof leaks, only the parent worries about what contractor to employ or about how he will repair it himself. The child eats, but is not forced to cook the meal. To the adult, then, childhood is a time of freedom.

The child, however, wishes always to be a man. He finds freedom in the future. The small boy quarrels with his sister and looks forward to perfect marital bliss with a wife who never nags. To him, adulthood is a time of wealth, and his father never needs to worry about saving to buy a bicycle. Childhood is a time of study; the mature never have to go to school and worry about report cards and grades on conduct. "When I get big," he thinks, "Mother won't tell me what to eat."

Happiness is too seldom found in the present. All too often it is remembered as a thing of the past or looked forward to as a part of the future.

Well-developed paragraphs include varied and interesting details. One major flaw of paragraphs may be that they merely suggest the bare outlines, the dull generalities of a topic. The following paragraph, for example, is a rather boring treatment of what might be made a vivid point.

The official calendar for the varied activities of a large university is very important. Every event must be included, and there should be no conflicts. Many people in the university may rely upon this calendar in order to know what is going on.

In contrast, this same idea might be more fully developed as follows:

The official calendar for the varied activities of a large university is very important. Scheduling all of the numerous activities so that there are no conflicts is a major task. Whoever handles this matter must see, for example, that the Glee Club or the University Players do not rehearse in Harris Hall, Room A, while the Six Society Syncopators are giving out with a few hot numbers. The lower athletic field may be too small to accommodate simultaneously an extra practice session of both an intramural soccer team and the cheerleaders and majorettes who must perform in the stadium on Saturday afternoon. There might be some inconvenience if the non-fraternity men held a dance in the gymnasium while a meeting of the alumni was in progress there. And finally, many people must be given official notice of the various university activities through the calendar. Those who must supply janitors to see that doors are unlocked and buildings lighted must be notified. Matrons in the girls' dormitories and housemothers in the sorority houses must know where their charges are going and at what time the university says they must return. All deans need a copy of the calendar to remind them of engagements and events they wish to attend.

Excessively long paragraphs are hard to read, and they may be overdeveloped or not properly unified. For either reason, the reader may have difficulty in grasping the writer's purpose and emphasis. Occasionally a student's paper will be all one paragraph. Such a theme is likely to be unorganized, and at best it does not emphasize or group the major thoughts. Attention to paragraphing helps greatly in putting material in order and in making it easier to read.

EXERCISE

The writer of the following brief theme was successful in placing his ideas in a logical sequence, but his paragraphs are too short. He has not grouped his ideas well. Rewrite this theme, keeping every sentence in its present place. Supply topic sentences when they are needed, and group the sentences into more effective paragraphs.

Grandfather was fond of sitting with his back to an open fire and looking out on woods, orchards, and broad fields that slanted away from a tall hill to a distant valley. For this reason my grandfather built his house so that the den faced the woods and the distant meadow which was just visible over the trees growing on the slopes of the hill.

Two large paneled windows enabled him to look out over the whole countryside.

Grandfather framed the windows with a dark green cornice board, which blended with the color of the pine paneling. Just below the broad window he placed his bookshelves. Nearby, on a reading stand, he kept his leather-bound and brass-studded family Bible.

Across the room from the windows he built a rugged granite fireplace with a mantel carved from a slab of pink marble, which he himself chose from the quarry. The smooth pink stone, in contrast with the rugged granite, was a choice that reflected the gentleness and strength of my grandfather.

He placed two large leather chairs by the fireplace and across from the windows. Over the mantel he hung his rifle.

From the first he made this room his own, and it seemed never to belong to anyone else.

Now the chairs still have an inviting, comfortable look. The shiny, worn arms and cushions indicate how children and grand-children have played on them. The rifle is somewhat rusty, but it has the look of metal which was for years oiled after every hunt.

The classics in the bookshelves were torn by children and then grandchildren before they began gathering dust. The pages of the Bible are brown and worn, and some of the print is faded.

Family portraits, now as out-of-date as the intricately carved wooden frames that hold them, still hang on the wall. A wooden pipe rack which holds all Grandfather's pipes, an Indian peace pipe, and a humidor carved from a cypress root are the only articles left on the top of the desk.

The very desk seems to guard its contents from eyes or hands, and the swivel chair, with its tattered cushion, denies comfort to any occupant. Since Grandfather died the room has been locked most of the time, and it remains almost as it was years ago.

64/Sentence Sequence

Develop a clear and logical sequence of sentences within a paragraph. In most well-developed paragraphs each sentence has its own individual position and the ideas follow each other in a planned and orderly arrangement. Usually sentences within a paragraph cannot be shuffled about and placed in several positions; disregard of sequence may lead to poor construction.

Content usually governs the organization and logical order of a paragraph. The writer should decide what arrangement is most suitable and effective for the idea. A paragraph may proceed chronologically, from cause to effect, from effect to cause, from least important item to most important item (climactic order), from generalization to specific examples, from the concrete facts to a conclusion. These are but examples; almost always some internal factor dictates order, and paragraphs may be developed in numerous ways.

Study the order of the sentences in the following paragraph. Notice that each sentence looks back to the previous sentence and also moves the thought forward. Notice that the positions of sentences are not interchangeable:

There can be no question that the improvement in the condition of the average man, with its increase in earnings, has contributed radically to the change in attitude of parents. Most of them overlook the part which strict discipline, scanty allowances, and hard work played in their moral and physical upbringing. Instead they are determined to give to their children what was denied to them. They buy them better clothes, provide them with larger allowances, enable them to participate in sports, to attend movies, to enjoy summer vacations, and to do all those things calculated to make life agreeable. They not only relieve them of the little tasks or chores which once were a part of a boy's life, but they even frown on the performance of any manual labor, particularly for hire.

The industry that was once encouraged in youth as a virtue is now regarded as an interference with the right to enjoy life.

Judge Elijah Adlow, "Teen-Age Criminals"[8]

The general progress of this paragraph is from cause to effect. Sentence 1 introduces the attitude of modern parents. Sentence 2 suggests that, in comparison with the older outlook, the present-day attitude is producing moral and physical degeneration. The remainder of the paragraph analyzes the operation of the modern attitude. It makes use of concrete details — first, on the general subject of buying; next, on the general subject of work. The last sentence again clearly suggests the effect of all this on modern youth in general.

Many paragraphs develop details which require no particular and careful order: they can be shifted about. Notice the following description of a road in Mexico:

The road leading into Toluca became thickly dotted with Indians. Some rode on burros; some led burros laden with produce in baskets. Some drove goats and turkeys before them. Some bore sacks on their backs or trays on their heads. Women, wrapped about the head with pigeon-blue rebozos, bore babies on their backs, held toddlers by one hand, and used the other to carry foodstuff or some handicraft work.

Hudson Strode, *Now in Mexico*[9]

Sentences 2, 3, 4, and 5 could be interchanged and placed in any order so long as the reference of the pronoun *some* to Indians remained clear.

---

[8]From *The Atlantic Monthly*, July 1955. Reprinted by permission of Judge Adlow.

[9]Reprinted by permission of Harcourt, Brace and Company, Inc., publishers.

EXERCISE

The sentences in each of the following groups have been placed in faulty order. Rearrange each group so that it becomes a clear and logical paragraph in correct order.

PARAGRAPH ONE

Thus everyone wanted a coonskin cap.

When, for example, Walt Disney presented a story about Davy Crockett on television in 1955, the adult thought the boom in the mythical Crockett's popularity was a new trend in history.

Often an adult is amazed by the trends in children's games and heroes.

Some adults even charged that, as the population and the number of children increased, the mass mind began to run in the same channel.

PARAGRAPH TWO

In short, all fads like these are similar.

The child in the jungle suit was followed by one who put on Superman's wings before he retrogressed to the coonskin cap.

His contemporaries admired Jesse James before they made Buffalo Bill or Tarzan their hero of the hour.

If children in earlier times did not buy coonskin caps, they made a jungle suit of their own or broke their arms swinging through trees like Tarzan.

The truth is that this puzzled adult has forgotten how he followed fads in his childhood.

PARAGRAPH THREE

These examples prove that every age follows fads.

They are a leading characteristic of American life.

He endures a do-it-yourself craze and watches the new television program which his neighbors have recommended.

Yesterday's Jesse James now fishes or watches baseball in the summer, cheers his alma mater's football team in the fall, and has a special activity for each time of the year.

His wife may follow Dior's fashions, trim her hair short like her friends', or play the current game that has replaced canasta or scrabble.

Childhood is not the only time for fads.

65/Transition

Clear **transitions** show the connections within paragraphs and the links from one paragraph to the next. Let your reader see clearly how and why you progress from one idea to another and from one sentence to another.

Transitional Words. The easiest kinds of transitions are connective words and expressions like *however, moreover, furthermore, on the other hand, nevertheless, for example, indeed, meanwhile, so, still, after all, likewise, consequently, in summary,* and so on. These show the relationship between parts of thought.

Repeated Words. Repetition of key words and phrases helps to show connections.

Pronouns and Demonstrative Adjectives. Used effectively, pronouns connect sentences and ideas. Some of the most useful are *some, many, each, either, such, this, that, these, those.*

Study the different kinds of transition indicated in the italicized words in the following two paragraphs:

Neither party expected for the war the magnitude or the duration which it has already attained. *Neither* anticipated that the cause of the *conflict* might *cease* with, or even before, the *conflict* itself should *cease*. *Each* looked for an easier triumph, and a result less fundamental and astounding. *Both* read the *same* Bible, and pray to the *same God;* and *each* invokes His aid against the other. It may seem strange that any men should dare to ask a just *God's* assistance in wringing their bread from the sweat of other men's faces; but let us *judge not*, that we be *not judged*. The prayers of *both* could not be *answered* — that of *neither* has been *answered* fully. The *Almighty* has *His* own purposes.

Abraham Lincoln, "Second Inaugural Address"

Our life is influenced in a large measure by commercial advertising. *Such publicity* is undertaken only in the interest of the advertisers and not of the consumers. *For example*, the public has been made to believe that white bread is better than brown. *Then*, flour has been bolted more and more thoroughly *and thus* deprived of *its* most useful components. *Such treatment* permits *its* preservation for longer periods and facilitates the making of bread. The millers and the bakers earn more money. The consumers eat an inferior product, believing it to be a superior one. *And* in the countries where bread is the principal food, the population degenerates. Enormous amounts of money are spent for publicity. *As a result*, large quantities of alimentary and pharmaceutical products, at the least useless, and often harmful, have become a necessity for civilized men. *In this manner* the greediness of individuals, sufficiently shrewd to create a popular demand for the goods that they have for sale, plays a leading part in the modern world.

Alexis Carrel, *Man, The Unknown*[10]

Transitional devices are used frequently in the first and last sentences of paragraphs. They help to introduce or to conclude a paragraph, and they especially help the reader to see how one paragraph logically follows another. For such transitions a good rule is to combine a little of the old idea with a little of the new as in the following end-to-beginning paragraph links:

. . . In short the English were awed at the sheer size of the approaching Armada.

---

[10]Reprinted by permission of Harper & Brothers, publishers.

But while they kept one eye on the Spanish fleet, they kept the other on the army of the Duke of Parma in the Netherlands. . . .

"But what are we going to do?" the harassed American man cries. "There aren't enough jobs now to go round. And women are getting into industries more and more."

This is nonsense and a masculine bugaboo, though merely getting a job is not what I mean. The truth is. . . .

Pearl S. Buck, "America's Medieval Women"[11]

EXERCISE

In the following paragraph underline transitional words once, repeated words and synonyms twice, and pronouns three times.

A foolish consistency is the hobgoblin of little minds, adored by little statesmen and philosophers and divines. With consistency a great soul has simply nothing to do. He may as well concern himself with his shadow on the wall. Speak what you think now in hard words, and to-morrow speak what to-morrow thinks in hard words again, though it contradict everything you said to-day. — "Ah, so you shall be sure to be misunderstood." — Is it so bad, then, to be misunderstood? Pythagoras was misunderstood, and Socrates, and Jesus, and Luther, and Copernicus, and Galileo, and Newton, and every pure and wise spirit that ever took flesh. To be great is to be misunderstood.

Ralph Waldo Emerson, "Self-Reliance"

---

[11]From *Harper's Magazine*. Reprinted by permission.

GENERAL EXERCISES

A

Divide the following selection into paragraphs. Underline once the main transitional devices that enable the reader to see connections between sentences. Underline twice those that enable him to see the connections between paragraphs. The original passage contained four paragraphs.

"At 5 p.m.," a psychologist recently told assembled colleagues, "the American family goes to pot." He meant, in older clichés, that in the late afternoon the fabric of home life splits its seams, the simmering kettle of domesticity boils over, mother, father and offsprings jump their trolleys. Discord reigns. Because he is a professor at a university in Texas, a man of standing, his words, however lightly spoken, bear weight. The impression is likely to get around that the American family does "go to pot" with regularity. This pernicious view is bound to multiply an already existing oversupply of complexes unless some expert and experienced testimony can be brought into counterbalance. All the more so since the professor blames the trouble on literal lack of sweetness. The key to his theory is a condition known medically as hypoglycemia — low blood sugar content. It leads to irritability, snappishness and a proportionate drop in sweetness of temperament. The psychologist's reasoning was based on the fact that since dinner is further away from lunch than lunch from breakfast, blood sugar content is lowest before the evening meal. After dinner, the theory claims, gentleness returns to the hearth at about the rate of digestion. The only alternative to this perpetual cycle of crisis would be a nation of paunches — an appalling theory. Fortunately, it isn't so. Piled one atop the other, the mountain of theories on what is wrong with the American family would reach the heights of the ridiculous. That, in any case, is the considered opinion of experts here.

Flora Lewis[12]

B

Follow the instructions for Exercise A. The following selection was originally divided into nine paragraphs, including several short ones at the end.

Game time! How do I, a mere assistant professor, a joy-killer, a bird conducting a recitation on Saturday afternoon, a purveyor of mathematics, a person with a desire to shove unnatural mathematical processes down the throats of real, honest-to-goodness he-men students — how can such a grub as I tell it is game time? I can tell by the look in their eyes. If I, with my mouth full of figures, should suddenly topple over in a fit and pass to the Great Beyond, those students would shed no tears. That is the look in their eyes. They are disgusted, are those young men, with me, with mathematics, with the program which has insisted that they be so engaged at such a time as this. The game begins at 2:30; until 1:20 they shall be with me, unless fits intervene. To some, persons uninspired in the presence of a great event, the day might seem singularly drab, a brooding, bitter November day. But the perpendicular face of the new stadium, which can be seen through the classroom windows, is topped and aflutter with pennants, and

---

[12]From *The New York Times Magazine*, August 7, 1955. Reprinted by permission.

the whole world of men and automobiles seems to swarm in its direction. Of these things my class is conscious, and my class is very unhappy. Out of this general depression there stand forth two exceptions — Treadwell and Stinger. Treadwell is big, equable in temper, likable. Treadwell is varsity end, and he must be dressed and on that field by 2:15. But is he downhearted? Not that you could notice. He and Stinger alone watch me write upon the board. Apparently they alone listen as I prattle about the hieroglyphics. Apparently, I say. For, as a matter of fact, Treadwell isn't listening at all. Determinedly and conscientiously Treadwell keeps his eyes fixed on my chalk, but it is quite impossible for Treadwell to keep his mind off that football field, where in a very short time he will be careering to the applause of the assembled thousands. There is in Treadwell a great strain of honesty, of decency. It wasn't gained at the university, nor developed on the football field. It was simply born in him. So in class Treadwell always keeps his eyes on the board. But Treadwell is no student, though he is no fool. He has no more real interest in mathematics than I have in the man in the moon. He desires to be a college graduate, preferably an engineer, and for some reason, concerning which Treadwell is not quite clear, Mathematics rears its scaly back between him and his ambition. Very well. Treadwell neither whines nor sneers. His job is to get a diploma. The diploma he will get, through his affability, his size, his good looks, and his just sufficient mental effort. Even I, classroom representative of the scaly one, profess a liking for Treadwell. I had him as a freshman in analytics, and I passed him then because of his size, affability, etc., as much as for any knowledge of the subject. I admire him now, so uncompromisingly eyeing the symbols of integration when the world without is so full of pennants, whisking autos, and girls. To end the unholy farce of teaching at such a time I announce, at 1:05, that class is dismissed. There is a large gasp of astonishment. It is promptly followed by a press at the classroom door, and then, like a cork from a champagne bottle, that class is gone. Excepting Stinger. "Going to see the game, Prof?" he asks. "I think I will. Are you?" "Nix."[13]

C

Follow the instructions for Exercise A. Also, put parentheses around the topic sentences. The following selection was originally divided into six paragraphs.

We have no direct proof that any planets exist beyond our solar system. Although we have deduced the presence of a few dark bodies that revolve around certain bright stars, because they eclipse a portion of the light at periodic intervals, we cannot decide whether these bodies are planets or simply small, relatively cool stars. A planet must be at least cold enough not to shine by its own light. The question whether other worlds exist is one of the most fascinating topics in astronomy as well as one of the most difficult to discuss. It is dangerous to give free play to our imaginations; and yet, if we are to come up with any sort of answer at all, we have to resort to indirect reasoning. To approach the problem about the likelihood of other planets, we may inquire into the

---

[13]From "As the Professor Sees the Game," *Scribner's Magazine*, October 1926. Reprinted by permission.

manner of their birth. If it is as natural for a sun to have planets as it is for a cat to have kittens, the majority of stars may possess planetary families. If, on the other hand, planets come into being only as a result of some unusual cosmic event, like the collision of two stars, planets may be extremely rare. Under such circumstances, our solar system might then be unique in the entire universe. Someone recently remarked that theories of the origin of the solar system are practically as numerous as astronomers. The fact that some astronomers hold no views at all on this subject is more than offset by the fact that others have proposed a number of theories. We can divide theories of creation into two broad classes: the unitary theories and the binary theories. In the unitary theory the planets appear as the result of purely natural processes during the life of a single star. The planets, after their birth, repeat the process on a smaller scale, to form the satellites. Everything necessary for the entire solar system was contained in the original matter that eventually formed the sun and planets. On the binary hypothesis, however, we start off with a sun that has no planetary retinue. The star acquires its family by capture, adoption, or catastrophe. These processes require the action of either another star or a large volume containing meteoric material and cosmic dust. The great majority of modern theories are of the binary variety. These were forced upon us because the unitary hypothesis ran into seemingly insurmountable difficulties.

Donald H. Menzel, "Other Worlds than Ours"[14]

[14]From *The Atlantic Monthly*, November 1955. Reprinted by permission of the author.

D

Write two consecutive paragraphs on a single subject, each about 150 words in length. In the first paragraph be careful to establish your subject in a clear topic sentence. Pay careful attention to transition between sentences. For the second paragraph write a topic sentence which links the two paragraphs together.

The Theme

THE WRITING of a successful theme draws on powers of thought, memory, and imagination, on a sense of order, an ability to criticize one's own work, and a feeling for what will interest the reader. Fortunately for the student, this array of skills can be developed through practice and persistence. Theme writing is a process that can be broken down into clearly definable stages through which the student may move, in a constructive, orderly way, to the finished product. The following step-by-step suggestions should aid in the writing of better themes.

66/Choosing an Interesting Subject

If a writer is not really interested in the subject he is writing about, his treatment of it is unlikely to interest his reader. The first rule of effective theme writing, then, is to choose a topic that interests you. Even if you do not have complete freedom of choice, there will be few subjects suggested or assigned during the course which cannot be related to something that arrests your attention, something you already know about or would like to know more about.

For this reason, even assigned topics can be challenging. Suppose, for example, the instructor says that the next paper will be on clocks or the allied topic of watches or time. Papers produced by the class might have such titles as the following:

Clocks
Some Clocks I Know
Clocks Have Personality
A Brief History of the Clock
How to Repair a Clock
Clock and Watch Repairing as a Profession
Late Again
Better Late Than Never
My Neighbor Reminds Me of a Clock
Tardiness
Famous Quotations on Clocks, Watches, and Time
How I Learned to Be on Time
How I Learned to Be on Time for My Eight O'Clock Class
Master Clocks
The Clock in Center Hall
Big Ben
What Time Is It?
The Characters of Clocks
Does "Water Resistant" Really Mean Anything?
Hickory Dickory Dock
Are Imported Watches Hurting American Manufacturers?
Man Is the Slave of Time
Seth Thomas
Mother's Grandfather Clock
On Getting Up Early
Clocks Are Man's Best Friend
Clocks Are Man's Worst Enemy
I Hate Clocks
My Girl Friend Needs a Clock
The Value of Being on Time
A Trip through a Novelty Shop Specializing in Clocks
An Old Swiss Watchmaker I Knew Back Home
Novelties in Timepieces
Cuckoo

A single student would not think of all these possibilities.
But he could think of *some* of them. What may at first seem

to be a dull assignment can result in varied and interesting themes.

But suppose the instructor leaves the choice of a topic entirely up to the student. It is possible to find a good subject without worrying and fretting. First, let the mind flow thoughtfully back over the past. Notice the ideas, the possible theme topics, which come floating to the top, and jot them down. Careful thought might produce a list something like this:

When Santa Claus Slipped Up
My Pet Dog
Every Child Should Have a Pet
Funeral of a Pet Dog
The Most Interesting Person I Have Known
Our Cook
Country Cousins
Visitors
Life after Death
Ant Battle
My Father
My Mother
Mother's New Easter Hat
Train Whistles
Dreams
Childhood Heroes
Early Ambitions I Have Discarded
Advantages of Living in a Small Town
Is a Small Town More Democratic Than a City?
Rabbit Hunting
The Crow Is a Smart Bird
Older Sister
How I Ruined Sister's First Date
Women!
The Disadvantages of Being the Younger Child
When I First Fell in Love

Miss Jezebel
Table Manners
The Laziest Man I Ever Knew
The Best Man I Ever Knew
White Lies
Athletics
Are Athletics Overemphasized in High School?
What Is a Good Athlete?
Our High School Play
My Most Embarrassing Moment
Handicaps I Have Had to Overcome
How I Developed Self-Confidence
How to Produce a Good School Annual
Advice I Should Like to Give High School Students
My Ten Days on the Football Squad
Cousin Jennie
Interesting Dialectal Expressions Back Home
Spring Is in the Air
Day in Autumn
Snow Man
The Graveyard at Home
Night Scene in a Graveyard
Never Again!
My Scout Camp
Our Scout Leader
What I Learned about Human Nature at Camp
A Canoe Trip
The Call of the Wild
Kites
My Workshop
When the Crops Failed
What Hard Times Meant to My Family
How I Decided on My Life's Career
Life Is a Ladder, Not an Escalator
Obligations of Children to Parents
Responsibilities of Citizenship

Honesty Is the Best Policy
Qualities of a Good Teacher
The Best Teacher I Ever Had
My Dullest Subject in High School
My Favorite Character in Literature
A Description of a Well-Known Painting
Jazz Versus Classical Music
My Favorite Composer
Hymns
The Folk Song
What the War Meant to My Home Town
My Religion
My Philosophy of Life
Types of Freshmen
From My Dormitory Window
My Library
The Ballet Russe de Monte Carlo

Reserve a page or two in your notebook for all the topics and titles which occur to you as possible theme material. To a list of topics drawn from past experience you can add other ideas from daily events, thoughts, and observations — in the bus, at the corner grill, in the cafeteria, in the dormitory, in class, on a date, at sports events, while working, while reading, and so on. Nothing should be overlooked. It is better to have an excess of ideas from which to choose when a theme must be written than to have only a blank sheet of paper staring up from the desk. Lacking a list of topics, the student all too often plunges headlong into one fruitless attempt after another, laboring for perhaps ten or fifteen minutes on each, only to crumple the sheets of paper and throw them into the wastebasket. You can avoid wasteful false starts by examining your list of possibilities and settling on one topic at the outset.

67/Limiting the Subject

The next step is to determine whether the subject is suited to the length of the paper you are to write. It is better to select a limited subject and develop it fully, through discussion, analysis, illustration, and vivid, concrete detail, than to undertake a broad subject and merely skim the surface. On the other hand, the proposed topic must give the writer enough scope to meet the minimum requirements of length without "padding."

Naturally, a 250-word paper will call for a more limited treatment than will a 500-word or a 1000-word paper; it may even demand a different subject. Generalized treatments of large topics can be successful if they are handled with intelligence, breadth of perspective, and insight; many good editorials are written on just such topics. But the best themes are usually on limited topics which allow room for substantiation of points, telling detail, vivid treatment.

Some examples will show how a subject may be limited. "Athletics," for example, is too general a subject for a short paper, but it might be gradually narrowed down as follows:

Athletics — Amateur Athletics — Athletics in High School — High School Football — Is Football Overemphasized in High School?

Again, the topic "Military Service" is too broad in scope for brief treatment. Some particular titles developed from it might include "Four (*or* Two) Things I Learned from My Military Training," "The Sergeant Meant Business," "Military Service as a Democratizing Experience," "Service Chow," "How to Goof Off — and Not Like It," "Some Job Opportunities in Air Force Training," "What Basic Training Meant to Me," "Barracks Life," and "Air Force Slang." Or a paper on the general subject of "My Older Brother" might be limited to one of the following: "The Effect of My Older Brother on My Character," "How I Learned to Take Teasing," "A Sister Needs an Older Brother," "Muscle-Building," or "Kid Sister."

Once the general subject has been settled upon, it is wise to jot down specific aspects of it — or titles suggested by them — as they come to mind. Suppose the general topic is "Qualities of a Good Teacher." The process of limitation may begin with the decision to consider a high school teacher. But an adequate analysis of the qualities of a good high school teacher might easily run to several hundred words. Simply jotting down various qualities as they flash through the mind (with no regard to selection, order, or grouping of ideas), the student might produce a list something like this:

> humane qualities
> ability to explain
> knowledge of subject
> ability to inspire
> interest in affairs of young people
> impartiality and sense of fair play
> appearance, manner, and voice
> sense of humor
> patience
> love of subject and job
> ability to get along with people
> seriousness of purpose
> interest in students
> general culture
> quickness of mind
> common sense
> mental honesty
> ability to maintain discipline

If the assignment permits only 500 words, perhaps three or four items from this list are all that should be considered.

A still shorter paper might be written about just one or two essentials of the good teacher; or a slightly different kind of theme might show how a teacher skillfully handled a serious problem in discipline or explained a difficult bit of subject matter.

68/Suitable Treatment

The next step is to decide how you want to treat your chosen topic. The subject itself, as you have limited it, will usually give you some clue. So will your own attitude toward your subject.

68a/Kinds of Themes

Most student themes are centered on **personal experience,** on **opinion,** or on **information.** Thus, "My Ten Days on the Football Squad" would develop naturally into an account of a personal experience; "Every Child Should Have a Pet," a paper based on an opinion; and "Some Job Opportunities in Air Force Training," an informative paper. This does not mean that the theme of personal experience rigidly excludes opinion or information, and so on. "My Ten Days on the Football Squad" might well develop some conclusions or opinions, just as "Every Child Should Have a Pet" or "Some Job Opportunities" might draw on personal experiences. But the student should decide to which of these three categories his theme basically belongs, because that decision will affect his treatment of the theme.

68b/Kinds of Treatment

It has been traditional to classify prose writing as expository, argumentative, narrative, and descriptive. Like all classifications, this one is of limited usefulness, for good writing uses these kinds of discourse in combination, rather than in isolation. Nevertheless, an understanding of the differences among them can help the student approach his subject with more confidence.

Exposition is explanatory writing. It provides the reader with information, facts, and objective analysis. An informative theme is expository. A theme of opinion is expository to the extent that it uses explanation and facts to support the views expressed. Such topics as the following would lend themselves to expository treatment: "Qualities of a Good Teacher," "Interesting Dialectal Expressions Back Home," "How to Produce a Good High School Annual," "Pest Control in Citrus Growing."

Argument attempts to persuade the reader to accept the writer's views. It is most successful when it attempts to convince through reasoning supported by facts, rather than through emotional appeals and generalizations. Themes of opinion often make use of argument. The following subjects would suggest an argumentative treatment: "Are Athletics Overemphasized in High School?" "Jazz Versus Classical Music," and "Is a Small Town More Democratic Than a City?"

Narrative tells of a succession of happenings arranged in chronological order. Personal experiences lend themselves to narrative treatment. A narrative theme might be suggested by any one of these titles: "Ant Battle," "Never Again!" "The Call of the Wild," "When I First Fell In Love," "How I Ruined Sister's First Date."

Description gives the reader a word picture of a scene or a person. Sharp details, imagery, and words that convey color, shape, sound, and smell are the lifeblood of good descriptive writing. All writing makes some use of description, from the factual description of informative writing to the evocative use of descriptive words in narrative and personal accounts. Subjects that could be treated mainly as description might include "Day in Autumn," "Night Scene in a Graveyard," "From My Dormitory Window," "Cousin Jennie," and "My Scout Camp."

You will want to consider which kind of treatment is most suitable for your subject and purpose. You should not feel, however, that you are bound by a classification. For instance, a character sketch combines expository, descriptive, and even narrative techniques to portray a person in terms of his most significant physical, psychological, and moral traits. A short theme, however, is likely to be more successful if the writer will establish a prevailing mode of treatment — and stick to it.

68c/Tone

While deciding on the treatment best suited to your subject and to the kind of theme you want to write, you should also decide on the prevailing **tone**. Formal, informal, humorous, serious, nostalgic — the tone or mood of a piece of writing is the quality through which the writer invites the reader to share his attitude and viewpoint. Some titles suggest a formal organization, a logical progression, and a serious approach ("Is a Small Town More Democratic Than a City?" "Responsibilities of Citizenship," "Are Athletics Overemphasized in High School?"). Other titles suggest informality and allow for a freer play of imagination and humor ("Mother's New Easter Hat," "Women!" "Dreams," "The Call of the Wild"). Some titles may be treated in different ways. "My Ten Days on the Football Squad" might suggest to one student a humorous account of his athletic misadventures; to another, a serious theme on his disenchantment with organized sports. Tone, as determined both by the subject and the writer's attitude toward it, is an important aspect of treatment.

69/Planning and Organizing

A good theme requires both planning and extemporizing. Detailed planning can yield effective results. Yet some of the best material, the most successful management of the large parts in the outline, and the finest introductions and conclusions may come from ideas which flash through the mind during the writing process.

Begin with careful planning. If your next theme is to be 500 words on the subject of tardiness, you might start jotting down the miscellaneous ideas which flow through your mind:

Uncle John always late
8 o'clock classes
no parking place
staying up too late at night
failure of alarm clock
makes even best friends mad
need to think more of other people's feelings
budget time better
dates often late
some people late just to be stylish — "So sorry, but —"
received last-minute telephone call
some people always late
some late only sometimes
laziness
can generally be overcome — takes will power
effect on person who is always late
bad habit
just putting things off

important matter of business came up
shows weakness of character
sometimes excusable, sometimes not
missed all traffic lights or got in traffic jam
watch slow
need to start for appointments earlier
my roommate

At this point there is already enough to begin on; other ideas and details will undoubtedly come to mind. But there is no *order* in these notes. In other words, a first step in planning has been taken: the listing of possible material. But the list gives no clue to what should come first, what second, and so on. There is no principle of organization.

The various jottings in the list above naturally fall into larger groups:

Reasons and excuses
    failure of alarm clock
    missed all traffic lights
    watch slow
    fashionable lateness — dates
    laziness
    just putting things off
    staying up late at night
    no parking place
    received last-minute telephone call
    important matter of business came up

Kinds
    habitual — some people always late — Uncle John
    occasional — some people sometimes late

Curable
    can be overcome
    will power
    budgeting time better

need to start for appointments, etc., earlier
how my roommate learned to make 8 o'clock classes on time
think more of others' feelings

General and miscellaneous comments
bad habit
shows weakness of character
sometimes excusable, sometimes not

Effects
on the one who is always late
on others
makes even best friends angry

The group headed "Kinds" is closely related to "General and miscellaneous comments," since it may be considered part of the overview of the whole subject of tardiness. So the "Kinds" may be put in with the "General."

But what about the *order* of the groups? Should the paper begin with a paragraph on the various reasons and excuses for lateness? Should the positions of "Curable" and "Effects" be reversed, thus ending the paper with the idea that the habit of being late can be overcome? Wouldn't this be a more climactic ending? The following **sketchy outline** of the primary ideas for the paper could be one arrangement of the chief points:

General comments — kinds of tardiness
Reasons and excuses
Effects
Curable

Now, what is the best way to *arrange the details* under each major point? For example, which "Effects" should be treated first: the effects on the individual who is habitually tardy, or the effects on others? For a longer paper such issues would have to be settled before writing, but in this short paper of 500 words such problems can be handled as each paragraph is written. Tentatively, the effects on others may come first, and the effects on the tardy individual may come second.

Next arises the question of *proportion*, the relative space to give each major point. More details are listed under "Reasons and Excuses" than under any other heading. But though this proposed paragraph might add humor and interest, this part of the paper is perhaps ultimately less important than "Effects" and "Curable." Thus some of the details under "Excuses" may be omitted and the other two paragraphs may be expanded by the use of fuller details.

The process just described shows the way many good themes are produced. Following it will be of considerable help, especially during the earlier stages of writing.

69a/Topic Outline

An instructor may require a formal outline with the paper. Such an outline for the theme on tardiness might be developed as follows:

LATENESS

I. Introduction
 . A. Brief anecdote about typical instance of tardiness
   B. The general causes of lateness
     1. Bad habit due to weak character
     2. Unavoidable conflicts
   C. Kinds
     1. Habitual lateness
     2. Occasional lateness
 II. Reasons and Excuses

III. Effects

IV. Conclusion — A curable weakness

This is called a **topic outline,** and certain established conventions should be followed:

1. Number the main topics with Roman numerals, the large subheadings under these with capital letters, the next subheadings with Arabic numerals. If further subheadings are necessary — though they seldom are for short papers — use *a*, *b*, *c*, and (1), (2), (3).

    I. ....
        A. ....
            1. ....
                a. ....
                    (1) ....
                    (2) ....
                b. ....
            2. ....
        B. ....
    II. ....

2. Use parallel grammatical structures.

3. Use topics, not sentences. Do not place periods after the topics. Punctuate as in the outline above for "Lateness."

4. Check to see that your outline covers the subject completely.

5. Use specific topics and subheadings arranged in a logical, meaningful order.

69b/Sentence Outline

A **sentence outline** is made by expanding each topic into a complete sentence that contains a statement about the topic. Place periods after sentences in a sentence outline.

LATENESS

I. Introduction

A. Mr. and Mrs. Jones are inexcusably late to the bridge party.

B. The causes of lateness fall under two general headings.

1. Lateness is often a bad habit reflecting weakness of character.

2. Lateness is sometimes due to unavoidable conflicts.

C. There are two general kinds of lateness.

1. One is habitual.

2. The other is but occasional.

II. People offer many reasons and excuses for their lateness.

III. Lateness has a harmful effect on the tardy person and on others.

IV. Conclusion — Fortunately, the habit of being late is a curable weakness.

In a sentence outline the statements should be short and precise. When approximately the same sentences are used in the theme itself, detail and color may be added during the process of writing.

70/Detail

Use varied details for interest, illustration, explanation, proof. An abstract truth may be evident in a concrete example or action. Sometimes a writer may state the concrete fact, omit the general truth, and assume that the reader himself will arrive at the abstract conclusion about the facts. Ultimately, meaningful generalizations rest on details.

The sentences on the left below are examples of writing that is thin, vague, too highly generalized, lacking in detail. Those on the right show how the same information may be given in concrete, specific detail.

The building was beautiful.

The spacious and ordered gardens and the marble domes, arches, columns, and minarets made the palace more beautiful than any other building I had ever seen.

When we arrived at his home, our gardener was sick in bed.

After Tom and I walked through the tall weeds in the yard of the gardener's hut, we knocked on the unpainted door, which had a hole for the cat sawed out in the bottom. A voice called, "Bust on in." The gardener lay on dirty sheets in a tall, rusty iron bed in the one room of the hut. Behind his big black beard he was waxen pale. His open mouth, large protruding yellow teeth, red eyes, and labored breath showed us that he was too sick to work.

The first selection below is so brief, general, and abstract that the reader is somewhat bored. In the second selection the same generalities are made vividly specific, alive, and interesting.

One day my mother told me I would have to help her clean out the attic. We worked hard for a long time and finally had a huge pile of stuff to be thrown away. Then Mother told Father to come up and begin carrying these things out for the trash men to take off.

But Father and I did not really want to throw all these old things away. And even Mother found several things that made her change her mind and decide to keep them. All of us eventually began to move objects we wanted to keep over into a small pile, and this pile grew larger and larger. We actually wound up by discarding only a table, some picture frames, and some rubber boots.

from UP ATTIC[1]
By Walter Prichard Eaton

. . . once my mother on a rainy day decreed that the attic was to be cleared of its accumulated "rubbish," and I was to assist in the operation. We worked ruthlessly and without sentiment for a long time, dragging out trunks and boxes, fishing through cobwebs under the dusty eaves, thumbing through old books and piles of magazines, testing broken chairs, and at length accumulated a huge pile on one side of the cupola stairs marked for the discard, and on the other side a small pile of things to be saved. With a sigh of righteous satisfaction mother straightened up, adjusted the dust cloth covering her hair, and announced down the stair well that father could come up now and begin the process of removing the discards.

But before father's head appeared above the floor, I had already repented of scrapping a certain avuncular brown derby, much used in charades, and in all plays calling for a villain, and I had carried it over to the small pile. The first thing father saw, of course, was the stack of books. He immediately squatted down and began to inspect them. "What's this?" he cried. "My old geometry? — and my Latin grammar! Amo, amare, amatum — scrap this? Never!" And over to the other pile went book after book.

Meanwhile, mother was re-examining a painted chair, or fancy chair as they were sometimes called. The rush bottom had been sat through and dangled forlornly. "That was Aunt Lizzie's chair," she was saying. "I suppose it could have a new seat. These roses on the back — I guess they're roses — are kind of pretty. And who knows, it might be in style again?"

It went over to the other side.

---

[1]From *The Virginia Quarterly Review*, XXI (Spring 1945). Reprinted by permission of Mrs. Walter Prichard Eaton.

Father was sceptical about discarding a blue Staffordshire wash-bowl and pitcher and slop basin. But we had recently installed a bath room, and mother was all for getting rid of any reminders of more primitive days. As I look back on those primitive days, I don't know that I blame her. But meanwhile I had become fascinated anew by the picture in the bottom of the bowl — a romantic landscape backed by a house in the best Strawberry Hill Gothic and peopled in the foreground by languid ladies bearing parasols. My plea decided the question. Over went the blue Staffordshire to the salvage group. And then grandfather's bootjack turned up, which we had found under the eaves. It meant nothing to me, and I think mother honestly thought it was nothing but an oddly cut bit of wood. But father snatched it out angrily, proclaiming it was just what he had been searching for for years, to get his congress boots off with. In fact, he carried it downstairs and put it carefully in his closet — where it remained forgotten again.

Mother was perceptibly weakening now. Old, discarded things were telling her their stories. I saw her hand lingering on the dusty back of the little rosewood sofa, the stuffing oozed from rips in the horsehair and one leg broken. Presently she called me to push it back against the chimney. So one by one the objects in the larger pile were moved to the other pile till it became the larger, and at last little was left for father to carry downstairs but a black-walnut table with a marble top so heavy that the whole table wabbled precariously if touched, a couple of broken picture frames, and some leaky rubber boots. Even the marble table top was to go no farther than the kitchen, where it later did duty as a mixing board. And mother and I descended from the attic, dirty and defeated.

Building a Theme: A Case Study

Suppose that you have been assigned an informative paper of about 700 words on a topic of your own choosing. Sitting at your desk trying to write, you decide upon something from your list of topics and titles: college professors. You then determine to do a paper entitled "Types of College Professors." Ideas begin forming about the various kinds of professors you and your classmates have known and talked about. You jot these down hastily, something like this:

notebook lecturer
knows subject thoroughly but can't teach it
conscientious, fair, sympathetic
thinks all students smart as he is and grades accordingly
level-headed, both practical and imaginative
likes to work with people
scholar at heart, just teaches for a living
good mind
down on younger generation — everything going to dogs
egotist — likes to be looked up to and hear self talk
dry as dust
condescending — holier-than-thou
eager beaver — impossible assignments
wisdom
sense of humor
well-informed on newest information
rambler — hard to take notes on his lectures
poor speaker — uh's, ah's
lives in ivory tower
seeks truth
absent-minded
grouch
human

The list begins to look like a start, but the necessary planning is not yet complete. A little study suggests a grouping of points which would develop into a theme of contrast between "good" professors and "bad." One easy way to get a clearer notion of what each group contains is to put a check mark beside the "good" points and leave the others unmarked. Since the paper is to be relatively short and a certain amount of improvising is probably safe, it is not necessary to make such a careful outline as was done for the paper on "Tardiness" (pages 311–314). You can now carry this kind of thing in your head. Even so, it is wise to consider what will probably be the best order for the items and to number them accordingly.

notebook lecturer
knows subject thoroughly but can't teach it
8 ✓ conscientious, fair, sympathetic
thinks all students smart as he is and grades accordingly
5?✓ level-headed, both practical and imaginative
6 ✓ likes to work with people
scholar at heart, just teaches for a living
2 ✓ good mind
down on younger generation — everything going to dogs
egotist — likes to be looked up to and hear self talk
dry as dust
condescending — holier-than-thou
eager beaver — impossible assignments
3 ✓ wisdom
9 ✓ sense of humor
1 ✓ well-informed on newest information
rambler — hard to take notes on his lectures
poor speaker — uh's, ah's
lives in ivory tower
4.✓ seeks truth
absent-minded
grouch
7 ✓ human

At this point it seems safe to begin writing. You try an opening sentence: "College professors can be divided into two groups, good and bad." But this seems a bit dull; something less obvious would surely be better. To catch the reader's interest, you decide upon a question: "Did you know that college professors can be divided into two groups, good and bad?" Even worse! Perhaps a more specific and unusual touch will announce the topic and arouse interest at the same time. You write: "To go from the classes of Professor Jones to those of Professor Brown is like passing from light into darkness." This is better. But how accurately does it forecast the content of the paper? You try again: "The good professor and the bad professor are poles apart in their mental and humane qualities." This opening is the most accurate and effective yet, but still others are possible. Perhaps a brief picture of students sitting in the classes of each type of professor would catch the reader's attention and reflect the contrast which the paper is to develop. Or perhaps a striking quotation can be found to start the discussion.

If a satisfactory introduction fails to take shape, you may postpone it until after writing the body of the paper. Perhaps then you will more readily hit upon the right tone and phrasing. Many of the best introductions are written, at least in part, after rather than before the rest of the paper.

Moving on to the body of the paper, you start developing your list of items on the good professor. Write along rapidly before ideas escape like vanished dreams. On this first draft it is wise not to worry too much about matters of mechanical correctness — spelling, commas, choppy sentences, clichés, omissions, style, and so on. These can be straightened out later, in polishing and perfecting the rough draft. The important point in the first draft is to get your thoughts down on paper.

In the process of writing, a good many general ideas and specific details usually come to mind in addition to those jotted down earlier in the list of potential materials. Some of these new ideas can be incorporated immediately into the draft. Others will not belong in the paragraph being written at the time. Lest they escape, these should be noted in the margin or at the top of the draft or on an extra sheet kept for this purpose. This is very important. Fleeting thoughts not captured at once may never recur, and often some of the most telling ideas and illustrations come to mind when the writing is under way.

During the term, first drafts should improve, and many students reach the point where relatively few revisions are needed, even in themes written under pressure in class. Remember, however, that even professional writers constantly revise and perfect before they are satisfied with what they have done. Some of Keats's best details were added later; Poe's "The Raven" exists in sixteen different versions; and Gray worked on his "Elegy" for some eight years. No matter how much experience one gains, the rough draft should always be gone over carefully for improvement before being put into final form.

Let us suppose that the first draft of the proposed paper on the professor begins as shown on pages 323–326.

Although the original plan was to write on both "good" and "bad" professors, it now becomes clear that this rough draft on desirable qualities will be long enough to fulfill the assignment if it is properly revised and expanded. The paper, then, has turned out to be on "The Qualities of a Good Professor." Since part of the assignment was to choose a topic, there is no objection to this last-minute limitation of subject. Perhaps a little more care in the original planning would have shown in the first place that the "good" professor (or the "bad" one) was a sufficiently broad topic to handle in a short theme.

The next step is to perfect what you have. A careful reading of the first draft shows that there are mechanical errors — lack of agreement in number, misspellings, an incomplete sentence, improper use of *your*, wordiness, repetition, indefinite reference of pronouns, misplaced modifiers, and so on. Once spotted, these errors can easily be corrected in the next draft.

Perhaps more important at this stage, you notice that there are several possibilities for division of the material into paragraphs as you revise. Each of the proposed new paragraphs will need to be given unity and direction by some kind of governing statement or topic sentence, and the movement or transition from one point to the next within the paragraph must be made smoother and clearer than it is in the first draft.

Still other things will certainly need some revision. There are, for example, the marginal notes to be developed and incorporated into the new draft. The important thing is to examine this first draft for every possible kind of improvement. Only this kind of critical reading can make a second draft better than a first.

It is now time to begin a careful reworking of the first draft, checking points of grammar and usage in the handbook, looking up words in the dictionary, and so on. Conscientious revision yields the result shown on pages 327–330.

This paper is a marked improvement over the earlier draft, and a certain pride in it is pardonable. Consider the sentence about not being able to fool all the students all the time. Maybe the instructor will like it too. And that phrase "accentuate the positive." Of course, the paper could have been better with more time to work on it. Next time it would be wise to begin writing in the afternoon instead of late at night!

(*continued on page 334*)

The good prof. knows his stuff [inspiring makes studs int'd]

is an authority on
he ~~knows~~ his field & beside he ~~he~~ knows

other fields too just as well. But He is

never ~~thougt~~ a bookworm dealing simply

with facts. ~~He is not~~ He always shows [all knowledge his province]

the principals behind the facts ~~& how~~ & latest

the relation of facts in his field to ~~other~~ [info.]

related fields. He has a good mind &

~~he~~ is a man ~~with lots~~ of wisdom. He

always ~~looks for~~ [seeks out] looks for truth. He

doesn't ~~say he~~ claim to know it all~~y~~.

If he doesn't know something

brought up in class he says so. ~~It~~ [A]

class nearly always sees

~~is easily seen by~~ when a prof. [you can fool some studs all time etc.]

is trying to make them think he
knows something but doesn't. level headed
also etc.?
∧ Through his knowledge *& his love* of ~~truth~~ he
leads students to love ~~them~~ _it_ too.
In other words he is inspiring
along this line. You ~~partly~~ see
this _partly_ when he is ready to ~~stop~~ &
talk about ~~something~~ some new
idea or point brought up in class
that he hadn't intended to bring
~~up~~ that day but some student asks about. This also
shows he can ~~be taught by~~ _learn from_
students as well as books
& other experiences. ~~He is always~~ ?

324

He is always interested in his students as people. Every one ~~of~~ ~~them~~ is an individual to him. In his approach he ~~always tells~~ accentuates the positive ~~how they can do better~~. Which means he encourages them and emphasises more their good points and gives them hope to progress. He does not fool them along though. He shows where they are weak and where they missed the ~~boat~~. But he always shows them how to ~~get over~~ overcome their weaknesses (in a kindly manner.) He is always human and likes to work with people and is always understanding. This doesn't mean you get grades you don't deserve

never teaches just "class."

never hurts feelings

325

~~to get~~. Its just the way he does it. This is alright with you because you know he is fair. *no grouch—sense of humor*

You get exactly what you make. ~~He~~ always gets your papers back on time so you can see the things you ~~didn't do right~~ *did wrong* while you are still curious about it. And he keeps reglar office hours where you can find him when you *looks etc.* need ~~him~~ on a point or two *of English*. You know he will be there. *and glad to see you* All the way around the good prof is a valuable thing for a University to have. It helps both the ~~students~~ & the University.

326

The Qualities of a Good Professor

There are several things to be said about his mind. For one thing, he knows his stuff. He is an authority in his field. Whenever a question arises in class, he usually has the answer. He is especially careful to see that he has the latest information on any problem. In the next place, he has wide tastes and is interested also in other fields of study for he has, in the words of the poet, "taken all knowledge for his province."

The good professor is not a mere bookworm dealing simply with facts. He always shows the principles behind the facts and the relation of facts in his field to those of related studies. He has a good mind and is a man of wisdom. Furthermore, always seeking truth and knowing that truth is hard to define, he does not pretend to know it all or to have all the answers. In other words, he is mentally honest. This is good, for it is nearly always obvious to a class when a professor

1

THEME #1:   SECOND DRAFT

does not know the answers but just pretends that he does. As somebody has said, "You can fool some of the students all of the time and all of the students some of the time, but you can't fool all of the students all of the time."

The good professor is also inspiring to his students. Through the extent of his knowledge and through his love of principles, he leads students to admire these things too. He is also always willing to learn from students. He reads, studies, does research, works in his laboratory, and gathers knowledge from any possible source. If a student brings up a matter which the good professor had not known before, he is as glad to learn it from the student as if he had gotten it from a sage. Of course this doesn't happen too often, but sometimes it does.

All of these qualities help the student to appreciate and admire the mind of the good professor.

3

The good professor is also a human being. For this reason he is always interested in his students as people. Each one is an individual to him. He never teaches a "class," a mere mass of units out in front of him. He always teaches individuals. He is interested in the progress of each student. So in his approach he accentuates the positive, which means that he encourages each student and by emphasizing his good points makes him feel that he has a chance to progress in the course.

He is never sarcastic and never hurts anybody's feelings. This does not mean that he babies a student. He carefully shows him what he has missed and what his main weaknesses are. But he very kindly and in an understanding manner also shows him how to overcome his weaknesses. This does not mean that he gives grades that are not deserved. Each student gets exactly what he deserves. The good professor therefore works with his students with kindness and with a sense of humor. He is never a grouch, for he is first of all a human being.

There are some qualities about the good professor that may be called technical. He has a pleasing manner before his class, he has a good voice, and makes a good appearance. He does not have any undesirable qualities along this line, such as merely reading his notes in a deadening way, or not speaking loud enough, or talking only to two or three students during the whole hour, or with too many oh's and ah's between words, etc. He also gets your papers back early. This is a great help since a student is more interested at that time in seeing what he did wrong than he is later when the paper has gotten cold. And finally, the good professor keeps regular office hours. If a student needs help on a difficult point or two in his course, he knows that the good professor will be in his office ready to help him.

The good professor is not found too often, but when he is he is a valuable asset for both the student and the university where he teaches!

The Ideal Proffessor

Contrary to a large segment of popular campus opinion, all proffessors are not a menace. Though some may
blunt the native curiosity, scholarly potentialities,
and humane qualities of their students, most have a
decidedly beneficial effect upon the intellectual and
moral qualities of those who study under them. Among
this latter group is the teacher who combines the best
qualities of various outstanding instructors into what
we may term the ideal proffessor. What, it may be asked,
are this gentleman's qualities as a man of intellect, as
a human being, and as a teacher.

Among those qualities of the ideal proffessor which
we may term intellectual is his knowledge of his subject.
He has mastered that area of learning which he has marked
as his own. He knows all the facts and can summon them
as needed to illustrate or amplify a lecture or class

1

THEME #2:   OPENING PARAGRAPHS

discussion. Yet he is no bookworm crammed with the
dust of dry facts. He is not, as Pope expressed it,

> The bookful blockhead, ignorantly read,
> With loads of learned lumber in his head.

He knows the broad principles which underlie these
facts. He knows that one's facts are valueless unless
they lead to laws and truths. He states quite frankly
that it is the business of a university to teach, not
facts, but principles, and he busies himself to this
end. Besides his grasp of the facts and principles in
his own area of knowledge, our ideal proffessor is also
a man of culture who has a wide and vital interest in
several fields of study besides his own. His culture
may be said to resemble that of the Renaissance gentleman. Though he loves what he is doing and believes
sincerely in the value of his own area of learning,
there is no narrowness about him, no feeling that his
is the only way to truth and human values. Our ideal
proffessor is also, therefore, mentally honest--honest

not only about the unsolved problems and unknown facts in his own domain of knowledge, but honest also in his attitude toward the values inherent in the studies and intellectual interests of others. Never dead nor deadening, never without charm, warmth, graciousness, liveliness and a deep-seated sense of humor, our ideal proffessor is nevertheless a man of high seriousness. He believes in ultimate values, and he would wish his students to believe in them too. Flipness, shallowness, disinterestedness, laziness, indifference to worthwhile things have no place in his teaching. Yet his classes are never dull. For he has, finally, the wisdom not only to deal learnedly with "pure" principles and abstractions but also to bring these principles into contact with the practical, everyday affairs of life. The ideal proffessor may walk within cloistered walls, but his teaching is never obscured by thick tangles of ivy.

A few days later the instructor walks into the classroom with the bundle of graded papers under his arm. He lays them on his desk and selects several to read aloud. The theme on the good professor is one of these. The instructor follows the reading of it, however, with comments which seem rather to emphasize the negative. There are remarks about the abrupt introduction and the fact that the first sentence depends partly on the title for its meaning; the choppy sentences, especially in the first part of the paper; the fact that it was Francis Bacon, not a poet, who had "taken all knowledge for his province" and that the exact quotation is "I have taken all knowledge to be my province"; the occasional need for transitions; the general weakness of vocabulary and the use of some worn-out or slang expressions such as "knows his stuff," "have all the answers," and "along this line"; some wordiness, especially in the first part of the fifth paragraph; some repetitiousness, as in the use of "fields," "this does not mean that," and in the sentence "The good professor therefore works *with* his students *with* kindness and *with* a sense of humor." The instructor mentions that still other errors are marked in red ink on the paper.

But he does emphasize the positive to a certain extent. He points out that the paper is on a subject of general interest, far more so, for example, than the two papers entitled "When I Fell Off My Water Skis" or "Hitchhiking to Talladega." He remarks that it has more "idea content" than many freshman papers an English teacher has to read, and he says it shows an awareness of life and a willingness to observe and think upon the world. He offers encouragement because this paper shows an improvement over previous work in technical matters, such as its generally satisfactory transitions and its correct spelling. He again reads the sentence about the impossibility of fooling all the students all the time. He points out that the class responded favorably when he first read it, and he remarks that he likes it too. He calls it a "somewhat novel twist on a rather well-known phrase" and "a step in the right direction which leads toward individuality and reader interest." In short, this instructor exhibits some of the humane qualities stressed in the paper.

But he has not finished yet. He accentuates the positive still further by passing out mimeographed copies of two paragraphs from another paper on a very similar topic. (See pages 331–333.) These are the introduction and the first paragraph of the body of the paper, and they handle the same topic but in a very different way.

The instructor offers a few comments on what impressed him favorably in these paragraphs — the very readable, slightly tart lead-off sentence, the transition from the introduction to paragraph two, and the good vocabulary. He points out an error or two — the misspelling of *professor* throughout, the use of a period instead of a question mark at the end of the first paragraph. He raises a fundamental question for the class to ponder: Which is the more valuable idea in the second paragraph, the one about the teaching of principles versus the teaching of facts, or the concluding one about the practical quality of the ideal professor's teaching? The instructor favors the former and suggests that an idea so important as the teaching of principles should not be buried in the middle of the paragraph, where it may be lost upon the reader. He suggests reorganizing the paragraph to place this idea in a more emphatic position. He advises the class to think this point over both as a principle in learning and as a principle in paragraph development.

You leave the classroom resolved to show further improvement. The first step is to correct your paper as required by the instructor (see §31). Then if you make every effort to apply to your next papers what you have learned from this and earlier ones, you are sure to develop some degree of skill in theme writing.

71/Check List of Essentials

The following check list of essential matters should be a useful guide in the writing of better themes.

71a/Title

The title should properly suggest the contents of the paper.

It should attract the reader's interest without straining to be excessively novel or cute.

It should not be too long.

71b/Introduction

The introduction should be independent of the title.

It should interest the reader, catch his attention.

It should properly establish the mood of the paper as serious, fanciful, humorous, ironic, or otherwise.

It should set forth or suggest your subject and purpose.

It should not begin with material too far removed from the primary matters to be discussed in the body of the theme.

It should not be too long.

Introductory remarks may be woven into the paragraph which develops the first main point, rather than presented in a separate introductory paragraph.

71c/Body

The major divisions of the contents should be readily apparent.

The materials should be arranged in logical sequence.

Technical terms should be sufficiently defined or explained.

Paragraphs should not be choppy.

Enough space should be devoted to important ideas. Unimportant ideas should be subordinated or discarded.

Enlightening, concrete, effective details should be used when appropriate. Insignificant or irrelevant details should be omitted.

The paper should have unity and a central purpose.

The reasoning should be sound.

71d/Transitions

Good linking words should show the connections between sentences and between paragraphs. The connections between ideas should be made perfectly clear to the reader. Refer to §65.

71e/Conclusion

The conclusion should usually be a summary statement of the underlying idea developed in the theme. If a problem is discussed in the paper, the conclusion should summarize the solution and state its significance.

The conclusion should not be a mere restatement of the introduction in different words.

The paper should not end in vague and dull generalities. It should make a final and striking impression. It should not leave the reader still wondering what the point is.

The conclusion may require a separate paragraph. On the other hand, if the underlying idea is woven into each paragraph, a formal conclusion may be a waste of words.

71f/Proofreading

Allow enough time to elapse between the last draft of the paper and the final finished copy. A fresh look at the paper some time after it has been written will enable you to examine it more objectively and to spot wordiness, repetitiousness, incorrect diction, misspellings, poor punctuation, choppy sentences, vague sentences, and the like.

Never turn in a paper without giving it a careful final reading, preferably aloud. In this way you will catch any "foolish" errors, such as omitted words, mistakes in spelling due to haste, and illegibility.

71g/Final Mechanical Matters

Use the proper kind of paper.

Follow standard requirements for margins, position of title, numbering of pages, etc.

Copy pages that are sloppily written.

Endorse your paper exactly as required by your instructor.

TERM PROJECT

Keep a notebook of items which you think may be useful to you as possible subjects and materials for papers.

EXERCISES

A

For each of the topics below, suggest feasible limitations which might be made for papers of 1000 words, 600 words, and 350 words.

Vocabulary	My Life	Engines
Athletics	Pets	Leisure

Drivers	Language	Fads
Teachers	Integration	Music
Literature	Character	Causes and Results
Christmas	Life	of the Civil War

B

Make a list of four different topics for 300-word themes, four for 600-word themes, and four for 1000-word themes. Choose one topic for a 1000-word theme. Then limit it suitably for a 600-word theme and for a 300-word theme.

C

Suggest necessary changes to expand two of your 300-word topics into 1000-word topics.

D

Below is a brief summary of a paper, followed by four titles. Choose the one you consider the best. If you can think of a better one than any of the suggestions, write it down. Be prepared to defend your choice.

SUMMARY: If I were to be shipwrecked and left marooned on an island with no apparent chance to be rescued and if I were allowed only one companion, I should wish to have, in the order of preference, a strong, courageous man who knows how to live a life next to nature; a companionable and well-trained hunting dog; a pretty woman.

TITLES

Three Friends I Should Like to Have on a Desert Island
Shipwrecked
Companions in Adversity
Island Adventure

E

Supply a good title for each of the themes summarized below.

1. Some words, because of their meanings or sounds, always have pleasant associative values for me. Chief among these are *home, brother, love, lake, sunshine, cascade, destiny, prelude,* and *clandestine.*

2. Joe Sams was what the people of the neighboring villages called a "swamp rat." I met Joe and came to know him well as we chatted in his shack while at a fishing camp. He had been born with but one eye and he had a big hump on his left shoulder. His parents had deserted him in childhood. Turning from the coldness of the outside world, Joe had finally retreated into the vast world of cypress swamps. Here he had found the peace and comfort he could not discover in the busy life of men.

F

The following is a brief statement of the thesis or central idea of a formal expository paper entitled "The Greek Virtues Today." Beneath it are possible introductions. Choose the one you think best and be prepared to defend your choice. If none of the given introductions satisfies you, write one of your own.

CENTRAL IDEA: The Greeks recognized four cardinal virtues, which man might well apply as a curative to the evils existing today.

INTRODUCTIONS

1. Although a classification of virtues may be at best rather arbitrary, the Greeks recognized four cardinal virtues: prudence, fortitude, temperance, and justice. One can see how they have meaning today and how well it would be for men to develop and apply them in private conduct and group actions.

2. The Greeks recognized four of these: prudence, fortitude, temperance, and justice. A discussion of them shows how useful they would be today if we would only develop and apply them

3. The four cardinal virtues of the Greeks — prudence, fortitude, temperance, and justice — would be valuable for us today in the affairs of the world. A virtue is a moral quality on which men place a very high value. A discussion of this follows.

4. Do we of today have any need for prudence, fortitude, temperance, and justice — the four cardinal virtues of the Greeks? Indeed we do. A redevelopment and reapplication of these virtues in our private lives and our organized actions could lead mankind into a new Golden Age.

G

Write a good introduction for one of the following papers, the chief contents of which are summarized.

1. The younger generation's growing dependence upon slang is almost certain to cause a crisis in our colleges and universities. This conclusion is particularly apparent when two other fundamental trends are considered: (1) the tremendous future increase in our college population, and (2) the growing national clamor that Americans should "streamline" their vocabularies so that nothing will be expressed in any medium of linguistic exchange incomprehensible to fourteen-year-olds. How, it may be asked, can a learned college professor intelligently conduct his swollen classes with no common medium of expression except perhaps mathematical symbols, which are also not readily understood by the younger generation? How, it may further be asked, can a man with a Ph.D. degree possibly grasp the critical penetration behind the following remark about Hamlet, Prince of Denmark: "Man he ain' got no moan! He's just a plain cube. I mean he's gone. I mean — you know?" Yet, happily, there is a solution to our problem. Because of their ability to master difficult matters rapidly, our professors can begin immediately attending the new Bebop Institute, which has been established by virtue of a liberal grant from one of the wealthier philanthropic foundations of this country. The aim of both the Institute and the foundation is the improvement of education.

2. Although I find poetry stimulating, I do not read it very intelligently. Often I miss its meaning because of my enjoyment of the beauty in its images or in its rhyme, rhythm, and meter. My greatest pleasure comes from reading and rereading my favorite lines from the different poets. I hope that my study of poetry in college will deepen my understanding of the intellectual content in much of the world's greatest poetry. The type of prose fiction I read depends on my mood at the time of reading. If I am tired or simply have an idle hour to while away, I turn to short stories for entertainment. So far, I have neglected the novel. My greatest pleasure in prose writings comes from biographies. Only recently have I begun to read and to enjoy drama. This branch of literature requires, I find, all my powers of imagination in order for me to visualize the details of the action. I expect to include more drama in my future reading.

3. The old blacksmith shop offered the perfect atmosphere and backdrop for my melodramatic contrivances. Before I could commence one of my death-defying adventures, it was necessary to secure arms and a stock of ammunition — never a difficult problem since the lower floor was filled with an assortment of oddly shaped tools and parts that could serve as weapons. My grandfather was never greatly pleased when I made these confiscations of his equipment, or junk as it seemed to me. Upstairs, I always assumed an air of sobriety and earnestness. One never knew when the treacherous enemy might attack. Sometimes Indians or rustlers came up the back stairs, or maybe a group of black knights would use ladders and come right in through the windows. The fighting was always horrible. During one of my most terrible hand-to-hand combats, suddenly I looked up — and there stood Grandfather, scratching his head. "Whatcha doin'?" he asked. I turned crimson with embarrassment and mumbled an answer. "Nothin'," I said.

H

Write an introductory paragraph for the paper on "Tardiness" discussed on pages 309–314.

I

Practice organizing materials as directed below.

1. Group the following ideas and details under large headings, and arrange these headings in the order in which you think they should be treated in a theme entitled "Types of Comic Strips." (Notice how this was done for the theme on "Tardiness," pages 309–314.)

space ships, ray guns,
    disintegrators, etc.
crime solution
Little Orphan Annie
really funny or comic
Li'l Abner
Donald Duck
idealistic Pollyanna type
Blondie
Pogo
general popularity as reading material
Superman
private detectives, newspaper sleuths,
    police, G-men, etc.
science fiction
laughter at politics, greed,
    stupidity, etc.
Buck Rogers
motives
fingerprints
turning other cheek and finally winning
    over adversaries through naïveté and
    goodness
satirical plus comic

2. Suppose that your assignment demands a longer paper than the one planned in item 1. List other general categories of comic strips you might discuss, and include details under each. Also add further details under the large headings you have in item 1. Arrange the materials in suitable order for the longer theme.

3. Jot down all the ideas you can think of in connection with one of the titles below. Group these details under large headings listed according to some logical sequence. Cross out any details which prove to be of little or no value.

Skiing
Blind Dates
Selecting Christmas Presents
What I Would Do If I Were President
How to Use a Library
Should College Freshmen Be Allowed to Have Automobiles?
The Studious in College Are Not Necessarily Bookworms

J

Rewrite and expand two of the following to enrich the content by use of detail.

1. After punishment by our parents, my friend Eddie and I decided to run away. Having packed my most treasured belongings, I left home and met Eddie in a pine thicket behind our house. Here we planned to spend the rest of our lives. Our first two meals that day, the fruit of our foraging, were very skimpy. When the sun began to go down, two little Davy Crocketts returned home.

2. Travel should be more than a pleasant and happy vacation, though its most significant values are hard to define.

3. At these "Junior Activities" meetings conducted by our Sunday School teacher each Tuesday, we made many things to cheer the various sick people in our community.

4. At a football game the cheerleaders and band add to the wild, carefree enthusiasm of the crowd. The cheerleaders lead the cheers which let the team know their fans are hoping for the best. The band plays the songs which clearly denote which team it is for.

5. The most important member of my church is the minister, who is very pleasing in manner and appearance. He tactfully preaches on many different subjects which are calculated to please

all members of the congregation. After each sermon he shakes hands with everyone, being careful to show no partiality. He loves his church and his church loves him. Through him there is harmony, and the church is one.

K

Choose from among the following conclusions the one you think best for ending the theme summarized in Exercise G, paragraph 3 (page 342, above). If you can think of a better one than any of those offered, write it.

1. After such a humiliating invasion of my privacy, I found it necessary to remove to the secluded lot behind the shop, where there was an abandoned water tank. Here I could rout the Barbary pirates, polish off Captain Kidd with a deft stroke of my rusty scythe, or climb into an old barrel and sink an enemy fleet of battleships just as any well-trained submarine commander should be able to do. Nor were there any silly grownups around to disturb my peace of mind.

2. This incident indicates how little adults understand the mind of a child.

3. During one of my most terrible hand-to-hand combats, I suddenly looked up — and there stood my grandfather scratching his head in wonder. "Whatcha doin'?" he asked. "Fightin'," I said. "What's it look like I'm doin'?"

4. Was I justified in telling a lie like this? Some people say lying is never justified, but I think that in this case it was.

5. During one of my most terrible hand-to-hand combats, I suddenly looked up. There stood my grandfather scratching his head and fighting to hold back a smile. "Whatcha doin'?" he asked. I turned crimson with embarrassment and mumbled an answer. "Nothin'," I said.

L

Write a concluding paragraph for the paper on "Tardiness" discussed on pages 309–314.

M

Write a different concluding paragraph for the paper on "The Ideal Professor" on pages 327–330.

N

Write a concluding paragraph for one of the summarized papers in Exercise G, pages 341–342.

The Research Paper

THE RESEARCH PAPER, or term paper, is different in several respects from the kind of theme discussed in §§66–71. It is longer (usually running from 1500 to 5000 words); it is less personal; it is based on a systematic search for information, usually in a library; and it is a formal presentation of your studied views of the information which you have gathered. Research has been aptly compared to detective work. Each has the given problem or subject; the search for information bearing on it; the process of thinking about the information and what it means; the conclusion to be drawn or the coherent pattern to be assembled; and finally the presentation of results.

In this course you should learn the general principles of research so that you will be familiar with the basic ways of getting at material in any field. All men engaged in significant research have one thing in common: a thorough acquaintance with all that has been published about their subject. Thus, though some kinds of research are carried on in laboratories, on testing grounds, and by interviews and questionnaires, most research requires some use of a library. Here we shall be concerned with research from written (or printed) sources, and within that framework you will learn how to choose and to limit a subject, how to find source materials and to take notes, and finally how to organize, outline, write, and document a research paper.

72/Choosing a Subject

Choose a subject that will enable you to use the library extensively, to think for yourself, and to come to a conclusion which will be of some interest to a general reader. Above all, choose a subject that interests you, one that really engages your attention, that you will enjoy digging into, reading and thinking about, and writing up for others. Research and the presentation of results are fascinating and rewarding activities when you work on something that really matters to you. When you track down a significant fact or reference, you can experience the same kind of excitement that you feel when the detective in a mystery story unearths an important clue.

72a/Choosing a General Subject Area

Most students start with a general subject area and feel their way around in it before deciding what particular aspect of it to explore and develop in the research paper. If you have long had a particular interest, that may be your starting point: photography, perhaps; or boats; or painting; or Africa. If nothing comes immediately to mind, you may start with a list of broad subject areas, such as the following; decide which ones interest you most; and then move in to a close-up of some limited sector.

The Arts	Government	Industry
Literature	Sociology	Science
Philosophy	Anthropology	Technology
History	Economics	Medicine
Religion	Business	Agriculture

At this stage you are concerned primarily with relating your research to some active interest. Once you have done that, you are ready to narrow your subject down to manageable proportions.

72b/Limiting the Subject

Your subject should be limited enough in scope so that you can cover it thoroughly within the assigned length of the research paper. From your experience in choosing theme topics, you have already had some practice in limiting a subject (refer to §67). But for a research paper, the process is controlled by the central fact that you will be collecting information about your topic from library sources.

Let us suppose that you have chosen "Photography" as your general subject area. You will see at once — or you will discover after a little thought and reading and a look at the card catalogue of the library — that this is too broad a topic for one paper. You may, therefore, limit it to "Color Photography" or "Aerial Photography" or "The History of Photography." You may then discover that any of these topics could appropriately be further limited: for example, "The Effect of Color Photography on Advertising," or "The Role of Aerial Photography in World War II," or "Matthew Brady: Photographer of the Civil War." Still further limitation may be desirable, depending on the proposed length of your paper and the resources of your library.

Here is another working example of limitation:

> Painting — Italian Renaissance painting — Leonardo da Vinci — one of Leonardo's works — "The Last Supper" — the portrait of Judas.

Thus the subject arrived at is "Leonardo da Vinci's Portrait of Judas in 'The Last Supper.'"

If you are starting with one of the more abstract areas of knowledge, such as History or Science, you may move gradually toward your final subject by some such step-by-step process as the following:

History — American history — American military history — the Civil War — new weapons in the Civil War — new naval weapons in the Civil War — the submarine — Subject: "The Use of the Submarine in the Civil War."

Science — a study of science in some historical period — ancient science — ancient concepts of physics — the Greeks' knowledge of physics — the theory of the atom — Subject: "Greek Theories of the Atom."

In practice, your narrowing-down from the general to the specific subject is not likely to be quite so smooth and orderly. Perhaps by skimming an article in an encyclopedia or the subject headings in the card catalogue you will glean ideas for limiting a broad area. You may even be well into your preliminary research (see §73) before you arrive at your final subject. For example, having arrived at "Leonardo da Vinci's 'The Last Supper'" as a topic, you may find such a wealth of pertinent source material as to suggest a further limitation to a single figure in the painting, that of Judas.

Choose your subject only after careful thought and study and consultation with your instructor. Your preliminary research will then test your choice. It will suggest whether you are trying to cover too much ground, or whether, at the other extreme, you have too severely delimited yourself. If you are not satisfied with your subject after you get into your preliminary research, try with your instructor's help to work out an acceptable modification of it, rather than make an outright change of topic. This will avoid the wasted time and effort of one or more false starts.

72c/Avoiding Inappropriate Subjects

In choosing your final topic, remember that your research facility in this course will be the library. Since you will not be working in a large laboratory, on a testing ground, or in a testing center, where experimental techniques are practiced, you would do well to avoid a subject on which it is difficult to gather sufficient and up-to-date information from printed sources available to you.

Be wary of subjects that are highly technical, learned, or specialized. Only a specialist, for example, could understand and properly evaluate source materials relating to modern techniques in psychosomatic medicine or to fuels for rockets. And even such a specialist faces another difficult task in making his materials and conclusions intelligible to the general reader, as you are required to do in your research paper.

Avoid topics centered on an assertion of value-judgments, that is, matters of taste, personal opinion, or critical evaluation, to which factual information or evidence, the product of research, is irrelevant. "Why *Hamlet* Is the Greatest Play Ever Written" would be an acceptable topic for a theme of personal opinion, but it would not be a suitable subject for a research paper, because the basic assumption — that *Hamlet* is the greatest play ever written — cannot be established through the techniques of research, the assembling of evidence, and the drawing of conclusions from it. Research can yield a great deal of information on what various critics have thought of *Hamlet*, but it cannot "prove" a critical judgment of the play's merit.

Avoid topics that do not lead you to a wide range of source materials. If you find that you are using one or two sources exclusively, the fault may be with your research methods — or it may be with your topic. For example, a process topic ("how to" do something) does not lend itself adequately to library research. Instead of writing on "How to Ski," the student might harness his interest in skiing to a study of the effect of that winter sport on some industry or region of the United States.

73/Compiling a Working Bibliography

Certain guides to the knowledge stored in libraries are indispensable to research. From them you can compile a **working bibliography,** a list of publications which contain information about your subject and which you plan to read. Each entry on this list should consist simply of the author's name, the title, and the information you need in order to find the book or article in the library.

73a/The Use of the Library

The basic tool in the library is the **card catalogue.** Here you may look up books listed alphabetically by author and title. The card catalogue also provides helpful subject headings, subheadings, and cross references.

After you find the entry for the book you want in the card catalogue, the most essential information on the card is the **call number,** which will enable you to find the book if you are permitted to enter the library stacks, or the librarian to find it for you if the stacks are closed to students. Familiarize yourself also with the use of **call slips,** which in most libraries you must fill out and present to the librarian so that she can get a book for you.

The catalogue cards reproduced on the accompanying pages are typical and illustrate the kinds of information to be derived from them. A student doing research on Leonardo da Vinci would go first to the name of the painter in the card catalogue. He would find Leonardo listed as the author of some books and as the subject of others. (See cards, pages 354–355.) Usually, for convenient reference, the heading on the subject card is in red. Besides the books on Leonardo listed on the author and subject cards, the library will also contain a great number of other books which have information on Leonardo but which are not catalogued under his name. To find these, the student might first look under the subject heading *Italian Painting*, where he would find a card referring him to *Painting, Italy*. Under this heading he might find ten, twenty, or more books listed. There are, indeed, more than one hundred subheadings under *Painting* in a large library. Not all these subheadings will contain books relevant to the topic of Leonardo, but the student should carefully consider books listed under such subheadings as *Painting — Europe — History; Painting — Renaissance; Painters, Italian;* etc. Whatever your subject, be sure to consider all pertinent subject headings, subheadings, and cross references.

A good card catalogue will lead you to the books which the library contains on any subject, but finding magazine articles is a little more complicated. There are numerous **indexes to periodicals** which will tell you what articles have been written on any subject. These provide alphabetized listings of authors, articles, and subjects. The years which any given index volume covers are listed on the spine of the volume. The names of the periodicals indexed in the volume are listed inside the front cover or on the first pages. After you have chosen your subject, you should search in all the volumes of all the periodical indexes which might list articles on that subject. The following indexes are the most important ones:

Readers' Guide to Periodical Literature, 1900–.
An index to the most widely circulated American periodicals.
International Index, 1907–.
"A Quarterly Guide to Periodical Literature in the Social Sciences and Humanities."

LIBRARY CATALOGUE CARD: ENTRY BY AUTHOR

(reduced facsimile — actual size 3″ x 5″)

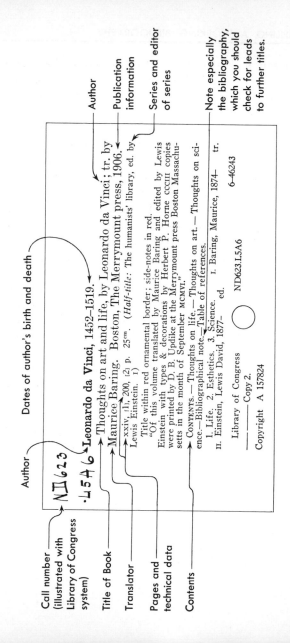

Author — Dates of author's birth and death

Call number (illustrated with Library of Congress system)

Title of Book

Translator

Pages and technical data

Contents

Author

Publication information

Series and editor of series

Note especially the bibliography, which you should check for leads to further titles.

NII623
.L54 6 Leonardo da Vinci, 1452–1519.
Thoughts on art and life, by Leonardo da Vinci; tr. by Maurice Baring. Boston, The Merrymount press, 1906.
xxiv, (1), 200, (2) p. 25ᶜᵐ. (*Half-title:* The humanists' library, ed. by Lewis Einstein. 1)

Title within red ornamental border; side-notes in red.
"Of this volume translated by Maurice Baring and edited by Lewis Einstein with types & decorations by Herbert P. Horne cccIII copies were printed by D. B. Updike at the Merrymount press Boston Massachusetts in the month of September MCMVI."

CONTENTS. — Thoughts on life. — Thoughts on art. — Thoughts on science.—Bibliographical note.—Table of references.
1. Life. 2. Esthetics. 3. Science. I. Baring, Maurice, 1874– tr.
II. Einstein, Lewis David, 1877– ed.

Library of Congress   ND623.L5A6   6-46243
—— Copy 2.
Copyright A 157824

LIBRARY CATALOGUE CARD: ENTRY BY SUBJECT

(reduced facsimile — actual size 3″ x 5″)

Library of
Congress
call number

Author

Title

Pages and
technical data

Note bibliography
to check for leads

Subject (usually in red)

Subtitle

Translator

Publication
information

ND 623
.L5 V25 — **LEONARDO da VINCI, 1452-1519**

> **Vallentin, Antonina**, 1893–
>
> Leonardo da Vinci; the tragic pursuit of perfection ₍by₎
> Antonina Vallentin, translated by E. W. Dickes. New York,
> The Viking press, 1938.
>
> xii, 561 p. front, plates (part col, 1 fold.) ports. (part col.) 24
> cm.
>
> "Translated from the German manuscript."
> "First published in November 1938."
> Bibliography : p. 547–551.
>
>   1. Leonardo da Vinci, 1452–1519.   ɪ. Dickes, Ernest Walter,
> 1876– tr.
>
>   ND623.L5V25   927.5   38—28996
>   ₍54f²₎
>   Library of Congress

Biography Index, 1946–.
"A Cumulative Index to Biographical Material in Books and Magazines."

Poole's Index to Periodical Literature, 1802–1901.
Has only subject entries; no author entries.

The Art Index, 1929–.
"A Cumulative Author and Subject Index to a Selected List of Fine Arts Periodicals and Museum Bulletins."

Annual Magazine Subject-Index, 1909–1949.
"A Subject-Index to a Selected List of American and English Periodicals and Society Publications."

The Dramatic Index, 1909–1949.
"Covering Articles and Illustrations Concerning the Stage and Its Players in the Periodicals of America and England and Including the Dramatic Books of the Year."

The New York Times Index, 1913–.
"The Master Key to the News."

The Education Index, 1929–.
"A Cumulative Author and Subject Index to a Selected List of Education Periodicals, Books and Pamphlets."

Agricultural Index, 1919–.
"Subject Index to a Selected List of Agricultural Periodicals, Books and Bulletins."

The Industrial Arts Index, 1913–.
"Subject Index to a Selected List of Engineering, Trade and Business Periodicals."

Engineering Index, 1884–.
Index to engineering, industrial, governmental, scientific, technical publications.

Suppose that you are writing your research paper on Leonardo da Vinci. Looking under *Leonardo da Vinci* in the *Readers' Guide to Periodical Literature*, volume eleven, 1937–1939, you find the following entry:

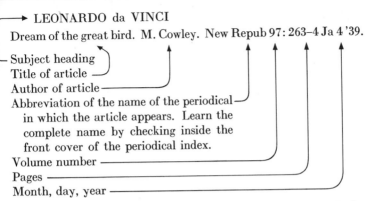

LEONARDO da VINCI
Dream of the great bird. M. Cowley. New Repub 97: 263–4 Ja 4 '39.

Subject heading
Title of article
Author of article
Abbreviation of the name of the periodical
   in which the article appears. Learn the
   complete name by checking inside the
   front cover of the periodical index.
Volume number
Pages
Month, day, year

With this information, you should be able to find the periodical which contains the article if it is in your library. Of course, you will be unable to read thoroughly all the articles ever written about a broad subject. But you will be able to exclude some articles from your working bibliography merely by studying the titles in the periodical index. If your paper deals with Leonardo's portrait of Judas in "The Last Supper," for example, you will not need to consult an article about Leonardo's flying machine.

Besides using the card catalogue and the periodical indexes, you will need to know about several **general reference aids.** Many of these will give you bibliographical listings as well as short surveys of your subject.

The Book Review Digest, 1905–.
Cambridge Histories: Ancient, 12 vols.; Medieval, 8 vols.; Modern, 13 vols.
The Cambridge History of American Literature, 1917–1921. 4 vols.
The Cambridge History of English Literature, 1907–1933. 15 vols.
The Cambridge Bibliography of English Literature, 1941–1957. 5 vols.

Current Biography, 1940–. "Who's News and Why."

Dictionary of American Biography, 1928–1958. 22 vols.

Dictionary of National Biography, 1885–1949. 63 vols. and 10 supplementary vols. Biographies of distinguished people in the British Empire.

Encyclopaedia Britannica, 1955. 24 vols. Supplemented by *Britannica Book of the Year*, 1938–.

Encyclopaedia of Religion and Ethics, 1908–1927. 13 vols.

Encyclopaedia of the Social Sciences, 1930–1935. 15 vols.

The Encyclopedia Americana, 1954. 30 vols.

Encyclopedia of the Arts, 1946.

Grove's Dictionary of Music and Musicians. Fifth edition, 1954. 9 vols.

Harper's Encyclopedia of Art, 1937. 2 vols.

Literary History of the United States, 1948. 3 vols. (Vol. III, Bibliography.) Bibliography Supplement, 1959.

The Mythology of All Races, 1916–1932. 13 vols.

The New Century Cyclopedia of Names, 1954. 3 vols.

Sarton, G. *Introduction to the History of Science*, 1927–1948. 3 vols.

Van Nostrand's Scientific Encyclopedia. Third edition, 1958.

Check your card catalogue to determine what the special tools of reference are in the area of knowledge that includes the subject of your research paper.

Your working bibliography should continue to grow as you proceed with your research. Be sure to include all the information that will help you find each item listed: along with the author and title, you will need the library call number for books, and the date, volume, and page numbers for articles.

73b/A Variant Procedure — Controlled Research

In some courses students are asked to write their first research paper from a **sourcebook of selected research**

materials assigned by the instructor. Such a book typically contains a large selection of extracts from books, periodicals, and documents, all related to some broad subject. This way of presenting the methods and techniques of research is called "controlled research" because it sets specific boundaries within which you and your instructor work toward your mastery of research procedures before you go on to independent research in the library. In other words, instead of practicing *all* the techniques of research in your first paper, you will concentrate on the final selection, organization, and synthesis of materials, and on the mechanics of documentation; and you will practice gathering your materials from the library at another time.

If you are being introduced to the writing of your first research paper by the "controlled" method, your choice of a general subject area will have been settled for you. Your instructor may further assign the limited final topic, or you may be expected to choose your specific topic yourself within the broad area covered by the given materials. You may or may not, on your first paper, be asked to supplement these materials with others that you find in the library. In any case, you should treat the materials in the assigned sourcebook just as though you had assembled them yourself, examining them for relevance to your limited topic and taking notes as directed in §75. The source of each selection will be given in the "controlled research" text, and sometimes the page numbers of the original source will be indicated also. Your instructor will tell you how he wishes you to use this information on your note cards and in your documentation.

In short, with a sourcebook in hand you will be in a position comparable to that at which you would have arrived if you had combed the card catalogue and the periodical indexes in the library, compiled your working bibliography, and assembled all your materials on the table before you. You are now ready, that is, to read, take notes on your reading, and otherwise proceed as described in the following sections.

74/Primary and Secondary Materials

Whenever you are engaged in research, you should keep in mind the difference between primary and secondary materials. **Secondary materials** consist of those things which have been written *about* your topic of research. In a study of the life of soldiers overseas during World War II, the writings of historians on this subject are secondary. The significance and accuracy of all secondary sources should be evaluated. The value of an article or a book can be estimated by a consideration of such things as the time when the work was written, the information that was available to the author at the time, the general scholarly reputation of the author, the extent of the author's research as indicated in preface or footnotes or bibliography, the thoughtfulness and logic he has used in proving his points, and even the medium of publication. A general article in a popular magazine, for example, is likely to be less accurate and valuable than a scholarly article in a learned journal.

Primary materials are such things as a painting, a poem, a novel, a motor, a stock exchange, an animal, a virus, or a poll of public opinion. In research on gasolines, for example, the gasolines tested are primary materials; the writings of engineers about gasolines are secondary. Primary materials in a study of the life of soldiers overseas would consist of published and unpublished diaries and journals and letters by the soldiers, recordings, songs, equipment, interviews of veterans, and anything which was a part of the soldier's life. In the specimen research paper on pages 379–401, the primary materials used are "The Last Supper" and the writings of Leonardo da Vinci. By using these the student was able to reach independent conclusions and was not forced to rely entirely on the conclusions of historians and critics who have written about "The Last Supper." Primary materials usually enable the research worker to arrive at conclusions on his own. A topic which has no primary materials is merely an exercise, but it can still be useful in helping to teach principles that may be used in later research.

75/Gathering and Organizing Materials

Before you begin to take notes, it is a good idea to do some broad **preliminary reading** on your subject in an encyclopedia or in other general studies which you find while compiling your working bibliography. This preliminary reading will give you an overview, a kind of map of the territory within which you will be working; it will help you to know where you are and in what direction you are going.

75a/Taking Notes

After you have compiled a working bibliography, located some of the sources which you wish to use, and done some preliminary general reading, you are ready to begin collecting information for your paper. As you use each source listed in your working bibliography, make a **bibliography card** for it, a full and exact entry of bibliographical information, using a three-by-five-inch filing card. From these cards you will compile the bibliography at the end of your paper. A sample bibliography card is shown on page 362. The

BIBLIOGRAPHY CARD

(reduced facsimile — actual size 3" x 5")

Author's name → *Clark, Kenneth*

Title → *Leonardo da Vinci: An Account of His Development as an Artist*

Place of publication → *Cambridge [England]*

Date of publication → *1939*

Call number → ND 623 .L5 C5

Bibliography ←
A label which indicates that this is a bibliography card. Keep these cards separate from those on which you take notes. They will eventually be the bibliography for your paper.

essential bibliographical information includes the name of the author, the title of the work, and the place and date of publication. If the work has an editor or a translator, is in more than one volume, or is part of a series, these facts should be included also. Finally, the library call number should be noted down.

Having made the bibliography card, you are ready to read the book and take notes from it. For **note-taking,** provide yourself with a supply of cards or slips of paper uniform in size. Cards are recommended because they are easier to use than slips of paper and withstand more handling. Most students find $3 \times 5''$ filing cards convenient, though some prefer to use the $4 \times 6''$ size for notes, reserving the $3 \times 5''$ size for the bibliography cards.

To handle the large amount of reading matter listed in your working bibliography, develop the knack of "skimming" so that you can move quickly over material that does not pertain to your subject and can concentrate on a thorough reading of relevant information. Don't overlook the help you can get from a book's table of contents, section headings, and index in finding chapters or pages of particular significance to you.

As you read and take notes, you should be deciding what subtopics you will consider under your subject. The two processes work together: your reading will give you ideas for subtopics, and the subtopics will give direction to your note-taking. Suppose you wish to make a study of the portrait of Judas in "The Last Supper." You might work up the following list of tentative topics:

Other representations of "The Last Supper" besides Leonardo's
The moment of action which Leonardo chose
Positions of the figures in the painting
Light in the painting
Other portraits of Judas done by other artists

The salt cellar
Judas's face
The moneybag
Judas's actions in the painting

These subject headings may not be the final ones chosen. You should constantly be ready to delete, supplement, and change them as you read and take notes. At this stage, too, the final ordering of the headings — the outline — may be neither possible nor necessary.

To illustrate the process of note-taking, let us suppose that you have found in A. E. Crawley's article on "Metals and Minerals" in the *Encyclopaedia of Religion and Ethics* the following useful information about salt:

Harmless superstitions about salt have lasted into modern civilization, owing to its having been a sort of symbol of food-communion and of the common meal. . . . Salt has been much used in sacrifice, indicating the analogy between sacred and ordinary meals. *Mola salsa* was offered by the Latins to the *lares*, and salt was sprinkled by Greeks and Latins on the head of the sacrificial animal. . . . Salt has been widely used in protective and curative magic. . . . Salt is a cure for many sicknesses, and procures disenchantment. Like blood and iron, it is a favourite medium for the oath; in early Teutonic custom the swearer dipped his finger in salt, and then took the oath. (VII, 591–592)[1]

There are several possible ways of taking notes on this passage: by paraphrasing, by quoting, or by combining short quotations with paraphrasing.

To paraphrase is to express the sense of the passage entirely in your own words, selecting and summarizing the most useful information and ideas in the course of restatement. The card opposite shows how the student has identified the source, given the card a subject heading, indicated

[1]From the *Encyclopaedia of Religion and Ethics*, ed. James Hastings. Reprinted by permission of Charles Scribner's Sons, publishers.

PARAPHRASED NOTES
(reduced facsimile — actual size 3" x 5")

Subject heading

Saer Cellar

Crawley –

Identification of source (Full bibliographical information will have been taken down on the bibliography card.)

Page number

591 - 592 Salt has been used to indicate fellowship, in religious ceremonies such as sacrifices, in magical rites, in curing the sick and breaking magical spells. Some ancient peoples even swore by salt.

the page number, and then taken down in his own words the information he wishes to use. It is a good note because it extracts items of information instead of merely recasting the entire passage and line of thought in different words. Notice the careful selection of details and the fact that the paraphrase is considerably shorter than the original material.

If at the time of taking his notes a student is unable to determine precisely what information he wishes to extract from a useful passage, he may of course copy it entire. For his own future reference, he must be careful to show by quotation marks that it is copied verbatim. Later, when writing his paper he may either quote directly or paraphrase. Except for four ellipses, the following note has gone directly from the book to the student's card. An ellipsis, or omission, is shown by the use of three spaced periods, in addition to the period that ends the sentence.

Salt Cellar

Crawley 591-592

"Harmless superstitions about salt have lasted into modern civilization, owing to its having been a sort of symbol of food-communion and of the common meal.... Salt has been much used in sacrifice.... Salt has been widely used in protective and curative magic.... Salt is a cure for many sicknesses, and procures disenchantment. Like blood and iron, it is a favourite medium for the oath; in early Teutonic custom the swearer dipped his finger in salt..."

Short quotations and paraphrasing may be combined on a single card, as in the following:

Salt Cellar

Crawley - 591- 592

Salt has been connected with superstition and religion. It has been "used in sacrifice, in protective and curative magic." It has been regarded by some peoples as a "cure for many sicknesses" and a "medium for the oath."

On a card of this kind it is most important to use quotation marks accurately while writing the note, to use your own words when you are not quoting, and to transfer quotations and quotation marks from card to paper with scrupulous care.

Any single card should contain notes from only one source, and all the notes on any single card should be about one single subject, such as *salt cellar* on the cards above. This will give you maximum flexibility in arranging and organizing the materials later on when the plan or outline of the paper takes shape. When you begin taking notes, you may keep them in order according to source. After a while, when you have a quantity of note cards, you will find it more practical to arrange them by topic.

The accuracy of your research paper depends to a great extent on the accuracy of the notes you take. Be sure to indicate on each note card the source and page numbers and to use an appropriate subject heading. Then just before you write the final draft of your paper, check your notes again by comparing them with the sources.

Because note-taking is not a mechanical process, but involves interpretation and evaluation, two students writing on the same subject and using the same sources would probably not take the same notes, and their papers would differ accordingly in content and organization. Study the following passage about "The Last Supper." Assume again that you are writing a paper on the portrait of Judas. Decide what notes and what kind of notes you would take.

The painters of the *quattrocento* isolated Judas, like a man stricken with plague, on the opposite side of the table, as though all knew already of his treachery. Leonardo boldly set him next to the disciple whom Jesus most loved. In this Leonardo was a better psychologist than his fellow-artists; he knew that treason dwells close to trust, and can strike with such confidence only because it is embedded in faith and loyalty, was there for all to see but was observed by none.

Leonardo knew this from his own bitter experience; and he also had his own way of making the traitor recognizable in the midst of the company. He had immersed Jesus in light; he immersed Judas in shadow. The face of the Saviour was framed in radiance; Judas was thrust away from the source of light by his instinctive recoil from Peter's forthrightness, the almost imperceptible recoil of the bad conscience. His evil, vulture-like profile, with his shifty glance, stands out, as the only dark silhouette, so plainly that his identity is clear enough even without the evidence of the hand clutching the bag.[2]

---

[2]From *Leonardo da Vinci: The Tragic Pursuit of Perfection* by Antonina Vallentin. Copyright 1938 by The Viking Press, Inc. and reprinted by their permission.

From a passage as full of information as this one, it is possible to take several kinds of notes under several kinds of subject headings. Most of this material might eventually be used in a research paper, but to a certain extent the research worker makes it his own by selecting and classifying according to his own subject headings. In and through the very process of reading and note-taking he is thinking about his subject and organizing his thoughts. This is the supreme importance of taking notes, of quoting and paraphrasing.

QUOTATION

Subject Heading: Positions of the figures

"Leonardo boldly set him [Judas] next to the disciple whom Jesus most loved. In this Leonardo was a better psychologist than his fellow-artists [who "isolated Judas"]; he knew that treason dwells close to trust, and can strike with such confidence only because it is embedded in faith and loyalty, was there for all to see but was observed by none."

QUOTATION

Subject Heading: Light

Leonardo "had immersed Jesus in light; he immersed Judas in shadow. The face of the Saviour was framed in radiance; Judas was thrust away from the source of light by his instinctive recoil from Peter's forthrightness, the almost imperceptible recoil of the bad conscience."

PARAPHRASE

Subject Heading: Light

Jesus appears in the light; Judas, in the shadow and in silhouette.

QUOTATION AND PARAPHRASE

Subject Heading: Judas's face

Judas's face is "evil, vulture-like"; his eyes are "shifty."

75b/Outlining

While you are reading and taking notes, you are thinking also about the organization or outline of the paper. You revise subject headings, plan ways to put them in order, study your notes to detect gaps in information or in supporting details, and strive to fill these in through further research.

Your cards should now be arranged by subject headings. Try to put them in a meaningful and logical order — the order in which you will present the information in your research paper. You will probably have to shuffle the cards around many times before you arrive at an order that satisfies you, a proper and final order. And it is not unlikely that you will yet make some changes in the arrangement of topics during the actual process of writing.

Your final, formal outline, the result of continual card-sorting and mental outlining, might be as follows:

OUTLINE

LEONARDO DA VINCI'S PORTRAIT OF JUDAS IN "THE LAST SUPPER"

I. Introduction — Contrast between Judas and Christ

II. Portraits of the Last Supper — the moments chosen
    A. Other artists' treatment
    B. Leonardo's treatment

III. Arrangement of Figures

IV. Light
    A. Other figures besides Judas
    B. Judas

V. Judas
    A. Other artists

    B. Leonardo
       1. Actions
       2. The moneybag
       3. Salt
       4. Judas's face
       5. Judas's hand
VI. Conclusion

For the form of the outline, refer to **§69a** (Topic Outline) and **§69b** (Sentence Outline).

76/Documentation

The integrity and intelligence of the research worker are on trial when he writes his paper. To be honest, he must acknowledge all indebtednesses to other writers and scholars, indicating in the text and in the footnotes exactly what he has taken from them.

76a/Quoting, Paraphrasing, and Footnoting

Some of the principles of quoting and paraphrasing have already been discussed under the topic of taking notes. These principles must also be kept in mind during the writing and revision of the paper. Finally, the quoting and paraphrasing should be carefully re-examined after the paper is completely written.

All direct quotations must be placed in quotation marks and footnoted. If quotation marks are used without a footnote, the documentation is inadequate because the source is not given. If a footnote is used without quotation marks, the reader assumes that you are giving someone else credit for the idea but that the words are your own. Even when you take only a phrase or a single unusual word from a passage, you should enclose it in quotation marks.

You may quote words, phrases, clauses, sentences, or even whole paragraphs. Generally you should quote a sentence or a paragraph only when the authority cited has phrased the statement more effectively than you can and when you need to give all the information which he has given. One kind of error is quoting too much. A sequence of quotations strung together with a few words of your own is not a satisfactory presentation of material. Excessive quoting indicates that you have not properly digested the sources, thought about the ideas, and learned to express them in your own words and relate them to your own ideas.

All paraphrases and citations must be footnoted. You should credit your source when you cite ideas or information from it, even though you do not quote directly from it. The fact that you have altered the wording does not make the substance your own. A footnote not only gives evidence of your honesty in research; it also supports or authorizes your statement. If while you are writing you need to consult a source or a note which you have made, you probably are paraphrasing or citing and you probably need a footnote.

When paraphrasing, you are expressing in your own words the ideas of another writer. A good paraphrase preserves the sense of the original, but not the form. That is, it does not retain the sentence patterns and merely substitute synonyms for the original words, or retain the original words and merely alter the sentence patterns. It is a genuine restatement, selecting, compressing. Invariably it should be briefer than the material paraphrased. If the source has stated the idea more concisely than you can, you should quote, not paraphrase. Do not make use of extended paraphrases. If a good many of your paragraphs are simply long paraphrases, your reader will assume that even your organization is taken from the sources cited. He will conclude that you have not assimilated your materials and thought independently about them — in short, that you have not done an acceptable piece of research.

There are only two exceptions to the rule that everything in the research paper must be documented. (1) A part of every paragraph, a major portion of your paper, and certainly the introduction and the conclusion should come from the general ideas which you have formed about the subject or problem as a whole and from your reactions to the things you have read. In any research you must interpret, and your interpretation belongs to you and therefore needs no documentation. (2) Other information may be written without a footnote only if it meets all of the four following conditions:

a. It may be found in several books on the subject.
b. It is written entirely in the words of the research worker.
c. It is not paraphrased from any particular source.
d. It belongs to common knowledge.

76b/The Mechanics of Documentation

Quotation marks, footnotes, and a bibliography are only means to an end. If they seem to be one of the chief aims of your first research paper, remember that this paper is written so that you may learn the principles and the mechanics of research and documentation. A genuine grasp of research method will be a valuable asset, not only in all your college courses, but in later life.

The mechanics of documentation vary with almost every field of subject matter, with every periodical and publisher, and indeed with every instructor. The most widely adopted style is that recommended by the Modern Language Association of America in *The MLA Style Sheet*, though many of the presses which follow it have their own adaptations. The sample footnote and bibliographical entries listed below, as well as those in the specimen paper (pages 379–401), are based on the MLA style. These entries may serve as models for your own. Your instructor, however, may suggest or require modifications. The important thing is not that you learn the forms prescribed by this handbook but that you become aware of the requirements of documentation and able to follow consistently the forms required by instructor, periodical, or publisher, as the case may be.

SAMPLE FOOTNOTES

Simplest form of reference to a book:

[1]Marie Kimball, *Jefferson: The Scene of Europe, 1784 to 1789* (New York, 1950), p. 111.

Reference to a volume in a work of several volumes:

[2]Vernon Louis Parrington, *Main Currents in American Thought* (New York, 1927–1930), I, 345.

Reference to a work previously cited:

[3]Kimball, p. 210.

Reference to a work cited in the immediately preceding footnote:

[4]Ibid., p. 211.

Reference to same work and same page as in preceding footnote:

[5]Ibid.

Reference to an essay in a volume of essays:

[6]Maude H. Woodfin, "Contemporary Opinion in Virginia of Thomas Jefferson," in *Essays in Honor of William E. Dodd*, ed. Avery Craven (Chicago, 1935), p. 39.

Reference to a signed article in a reference work:

[7]Dumas Malone, "Thomas Jefferson," *Dictionary of American Biography*, X (New York, 1933), 29. [If this were an unsigned article, the reference would read: [7]"Thomas Jefferson," *Dictionary of American Biography*, X (New York, 1933), 29.]

Reference to a book that is part of a series:

[8]Frederick C. Prescott, *Alexander Hamilton and Thomas Jefferson*, American Writers Series (New York, 1934), p. lvi.

Reference to a book by two authors:

[9]William A. Lambeth and Warren H. Manning, *Thomas Jefferson as an Architect and a Designer of Landscapes* (Boston, 1913), p. 25.

Reference to a book with an editor and a translator:

[10]Dumas Malone, ed., *Correspondence between Thomas Jefferson and Pierre Samuel du Pont de Nemours, 1798–1817*, trans. Linwood Lehman (Boston, 1930), p. 133.

Reference with the title shortened when previous footnotes have cited two or more works by the same author:

[11]Malone, "Thomas Jefferson," p. 30.
[12]Malone, *Correspondence*, p. 47.

Reference to an article in a periodical:

[13]H. M. Kallen, "The Arts and Thomas Jefferson," *Ethics*, LIII (July 1943), 271.

Reference to an article in a newspaper:

[14]"Jefferson's Rule on Gifts Is Found," *The New York Times*, Friday, July 4, 1958, p. 11, col. 1.

Reference to an unpublished dissertation:

[15]Merrill D. Peterson, "The Jefferson Image in the American Mind, 1826–1861" (unpublished doctoral dissertation, Harvard University, 1950), p. 37.

Biblical reference:

[16]I Corinthians iii.10.

SAMPLE BIBLIOGRAPHICAL ENTRIES
(*in alphabetical order*)

"Jefferson's Rule on Gifts Is Found," *The New York Times*, Friday, July 4, 1958, p. 11, col. 1.

Kallen, H. M. "The Arts and Thomas Jefferson," *Ethics*, LIII (July 1943), 269–283.

Kimball, Marie. *Jefferson: The Scene of Europe, 1784 to 1789*. New York, 1950.

Lambeth, William A., and Warren H. Manning. *Thomas Jefferson as an Architect and a Designer of Landscapes*. Boston, 1913.

Malone, Dumas. "Thomas Jefferson," *Dictionary of American Biography*, X (New York, 1933), 19–35.

————, ed. *Correspondence between Thomas Jefferson and Pierre Samuel du Pont de Nemours, 1798–1817*. Trans. Linwood Lehman. Boston, 1930.

Parrington, Vernon Louis. *Main Currents in American Thought*. 3 vols. New York, 1927–1930.

Peterson, Merrill D. "The Jefferson Image in the American Mind, 1826–1861." Unpublished doctoral dissertation. Harvard University, 1950.

Prescott, Frederick C. *Alexander Hamilton and Thomas Jefferson*. (American Writers Series.) New York, 1934.

Woodfin, Maude H. "Contemporary Opinion in Virginia of Thomas Jefferson," in *Essays in Honor of William E. Dodd*, ed. Avery Craven, pp. 30–85. Chicago, 1935.

77/Writing the Paper

Although the Check List of Essentials for the writing of themes (**§71,** pages 336–338) generally applies also to the writing of research papers, a few special considerations must be kept in mind in presenting the results of research.

Remember that the research paper is a serious, formal, systematic presentation of a subject or problem, of information or evidence pertaining to it, and of your conclusions about it, based on that information or evidence. It represents not your personal opinion, but your reasoned judgment which you support by citing sources. The tone, therefore, should be impersonal; the first-personal pronoun should be avoided. Instead, for example, of saying "I think . . . ," say or imply that "A study of the evidence shows . . . ."

The title should present the subject concisely and accurately. A "catchy" title is out of place in a research paper.

There should be a formal introductory paragraph containing the statement of purpose or "thesis." Similarly, there should be a concluding paragraph restating the thesis and summarizing the writer's judgment that the thesis has been demonstrated through the information given in the paper.

In the body of the paper, the logical progression from one topic to another, which you have worked out in your outline, should be made evident to the reader through good use of transitions (see **§65**). In beginning the discussion of a new main topic, show clearly how it relates to or builds on what has gone before.

Use quotations and other citations of authority to support your own considered views of the evidence. Make the quotations and citations work for you. Show why and how each one relates to *your* interpretation of the evidence. Do not allow your paper to become a mere patchwork of quotations and paraphrases. Comment on and interpret your source materials. Too much direct quoting and paraphrasing will suggest to the reader that you have not assimilated your research and made it a part of your own thinking.

Suggested Steps in Writing Your First Research Paper

1. Choose a subject area which interests you.
2. Limit the subject to suit the assigned length of the paper.
3. Ask your instructor to approve your subject.
4. Compile a working bibliography.
5. Start reading; decide on possible subject headings.
6. Turn in sample note cards for two quotations and two paraphrases (along with a copy of the material paraphrased) to your instructor for approval.
7. Read and take notes carefully.
8. Turn in a tentative outline and bibliography for approval.
9. Continue to read and take notes.
10. Turn in sample footnotes for approval of the form.
11. Write a rough draft of your paper four or five days before the final paper must be submitted.
12. Revise! Revise! Revise!
13. Check all paraphrases, quotations, and footnotes.
14. Start writing the final version of your paper at least forty-eight hours before it is to be submitted.
15. Reread the completed paper to catch careless errors.

A specimen student research paper, with accompanying comments, is given on the following pages for study.

LEONARDO DA VINCI'S PORTRAIT OF JUDAS

IN "THE LAST SUPPER"

By John Wainwright King

English 100
Section 3

COMMENTS ON SPECIMEN PAPER

General Appearance

Allow ample and even margins.

Type the title in capital letters and center it on the page.

Triple-space between the title and the first line of text; that is, leave two blank lines and start the text on the third line.

Double-space the text.

Indent five spaces for paragraphs.

Leave two spaces after periods and other terminal punctuation.

Leave one space after other marks of punctuation.

There is no documentation in the first paragraph of this research paper. The student has wisely composed his own introduction without help from sources.

Notice the statement of the purpose — the thesis — of the paper ("A study of how he created Judas. . . ."). The statement of pur pose is usually found in the first paragraph, sometimes even in the first sentence.

Place the page number of the first page at the bottom, centered.

LEONARDO DA VINCI'S PORTRAIT OF JUDAS

IN "THE LAST SUPPER"

When Leonardo da Vinci painted "The Last Supper,"
he had to portray the greatest good known in the
Christian religion--and the greatest evil. He has
achieved this dramatically by carefully depicting each
movement and thought of the characters, especially
those of Christ and the betrayer, Judas Iscariot. In
spite of the significance of Judas in the life of
Christ and in the painting, however, Leonardo allowed
nothing in his work to detract from the centrality of
Christ. A study of how he created Judas so forcefully
without making him the major point of emphasis will
reveal some of the qualities of Leonardo's genius.

Many artists besides Leonardo have portrayed the
Last Supper. The Cyclopedia of Painters and Paintings
describes the works of thirty-three painters dealing
with this subject and adds that it has also been treated

1

Place the page number in the upper right-hand corner, two lines above the first line of text.

Place footnote numbers slightly above the line of type and after marks of punctuation. Do not leave a space before the number. Number footnotes consecutively throughout the paper. Never repeat a number in the text even if the references are exactly the same.

The footnotes in this paper are grouped in a separate section at the end of the paper. They may be placed at the bottom of the page instead, however. (See page 396 for a more detailed discussion.) Your instructor will tell you which method of placement he wishes you to use.

Quotations which are five or more typewritten lines long are blocked. Indent five spaces, and single-space within the quotation. In the work from which this quotation is taken, "The Apostles" does not begin a new paragraph. If it had done so, the first line of this quotation would be indented three additional spaces. A blocked quotation is not enclosed in quotation marks.

by fourteen others.[1] Most of these artists have depicted a moment when Christ and the disciples were par-
taking of the bread or wine. This moment, one critic
has said, "leaves no room for the play of human passions, and gives to every countenance one and the same
expression of devotion."[2] Such uniformity violated
some of the principles of Leonardo's art: "'That figure
is most praiseworthy,' he says, 'which, by its actions,
best expresses the passions of the soul.'"[3] To reveal
the individual passions of Christ and the twelve disciples, Leonardo chose the moment of supreme conflict
between Christ and his betrayer.

In "The Last Supper," Christ has just said,
"Verily, verily, I say unto you, that one of you shall
betray me."[4] Only Christ and Judas know that this
statement points directly at Judas Iscariot:

> The Apostles are shocked by this pronouncement; in
> the midst of the abruptly recoiling disciples,
> Christ is the only one who remains calm. Thus he
> appears as the suddenly isolated Deity, alone in
> the knowledge of his fate, among his mortal fol-
> lowers who are able to grasp only the obvious im-
> plications of the utterance, and are impotent to
> change the course of destiny. Each Apostle reacts

383

A new paragraph may or may not be necessary after a blocked quotation. Here the two sentences that follow the quotation are an integral part of the paragraph beginning "In 'The Last Supper' " on the preceding page; hence there is no new paragraph.

Ellipses (three spaced periods) indicate that some of the material from the source has been omitted in quoting. Here the quotation begins in the middle of a sentence, and the first word is therefore not capitalized.

> as if the words refer to himself, in a very human
> way. Their excitement increases on both sides;
> the wave of movement flows outward--expressing
> itself equally in bodies and hands--and at once
> returns to the centre. It engulfs them all, ex-
> cept Christ--and Judas.[5]

Christ's humility and goodness are emphasized by his

failure to identify Judas as the one evil disciple.   In

Leonardo's painting, Christ's head is bowed and turned

away from Judas, although one critic has noted that

his "right hand involuntarily points slightly toward

Judas."[6]

Many scholars have commented on the position of

the figures in the painting.   Leonardo has arranged

the disciples into four interesting groups of three.

". . . the composition is so well arranged that these

smaller groups seem to belong together, and yet the

whole thirteen persons form one large harmonious

group."[7]   John, whom Christ loved most, sits immedi-

ately to His right, and Judas has been placed next to

John.   "In this Leonardo was a better psychologist than

his fellow-artists; he knew that treason dwells close

to trust, and can strike with such confidence only

A quotation should follow the source exactly for spelling, capitalization, punctuation, and italics. In the source from which reference 9 was taken, no period was used after the abbreviation "St" and so no period is used here. Material which you insert in a quotation should be enclosed in brackets.

Notice the use of four periods for the ellipsis at the end of the sentence: three for the ellipsis itself, and one for the terminal punctuation mark.

At the beginning of this paragraph, the student states his own observations and conclusions, which he has reached by looking at the picture (primary source). After stating a conclusion of his own in the topic sentence, he turns to specific comments which he has found in the secondary sources cited in footnotes 10, 11, and 12. In the last sentence of the paragraph, notice the use of short quotations in a paraphrase.

because it is embedded in faith and loyalty, and was there for all to see but was observed by none."[8] St. Peter leans behind Judas and toward John. His left hand, placed on John's shoulder, forms "a bridge between the heads of St John and Judas, [and] underlines the contrast between innocence and villainy. . . ."[9]

Leonardo uses light to reveal character in "The Last Supper." Sitting before a window, Jesus is silhouetted against a light and open sky. Peter's and John's faces are highlighted. Judas, on the other hand, sits next to them but in a shadow; his is the only "dark and gloomy profile,"[10] the "only dark silhouette."[11] Of all the disciples, Judas is the only one who faces Christ while leaning backward and away from him. The darkness surrounding Judas and his "instinctive recoil" show his "bad conscience."[12]

The presentations of Judas that have been made by other artists are interestingly different from Leonardo's. Some have shown him "with his back to the spectator" and with a "decidedly vulgar" head. Others

This entire paragraph is based on one authority. The student has paraphrased and selected from a five-page article in his source. Again, wherever the words of the original have been retained, they are presented as direct quotations within the paraphrase. Though the student has handled his material acceptably, the paragraph would have had more substance if he had consulted other sources also, both primary and secondary.

Notice that the topic sentences of three of the four paragraphs on pages 4–6 are similar; each introduces a subject which, though different from the others, is parallel to them.

have depicted him as sitting alone in front, as leaning on a table "while holding a purse in his hand,"
and as standing and protesting his innocence while
holding the purse behind him. He has also been shown
as "leaving the room." One artist completely left him
out of the scene.[13]

In Leonardo's painting, Judas's actions signifi-
cantly reveal his character, and it is interesting to
note in this respect how Leonardo has changed them from
what he first thought they would be. He wrote a brief
note on "The Last Supper" before he began the painting.
In this note, which told of his plans for the actions
of the disciples, Leonardo described how one disciple,
"in turning with a knife in his hand, has upset a glass
on the table."[14] This man, in the finished picture,
says Kenneth Clark, "has suffered a curious transforma-
tion. The motive [for this action] has been given to
Judas, only instead of a knife he holds the bag, and
instead of a glass he upsets the salt, an accident
still commemorated by the superstitious."[15]

This paragraph grows out of the last sentence of the preceding paragraph, but it would have been improved by a unifying topic sentence; as it is, the paragraph breaks in two at the end of the third sentence.

The student uses four different footnotes (18–21) to indicate the sources of his information on salt. Citing a variety of sources usually is evidence of more thorough and competent research than the citation of one source or the quotation of one long paragraph. Notice, too, that the writer has related his source materials to his own thinking, so that the paragraph is something more than a mosaic of citations.

6

The bag is used to portray Judas's mercenary character. He had been treasurer for the disciples,[16] and in this office he was dishonest.[17] And of course the moneybag foreshadows Judas's betrayal of Christ for thirty pieces of silver. Leonardo's use of the salt is also significant. Superstitions concerning salt are ancient, and some have even survived into modern times. Salt has been "used in sacrifice, indicating the analogy between sacred and ordinary meals"; it has also "been widely used in protective and curative magic" and as a medicine for many sicknesses and in breaking magic spells.[18] In "The Last Supper," Peter has accidentally jostled Judas's elbow and caused him to upset the salt on the table, and this action is most ominous. In the days of Christ salt symbolized friendship and faithfulness; in the Bible it is "an emblem of the Covenant . . . between J[ehovah] and His people. . . ."[19] Christ told his disciples that they were "the salt of the earth."[20] Judas has spilled the salt. He is to betray friendship and to be disloyal. "To spill salt,

The topic sentence of this paragraph provides a transition from the subject of Judas's actions to that of his appearance. This kind of sentence shows originality of organization and of thought.

The student has studied the picture and reached these conclusions himself.

Since the quotation begins in mid-sentence, no capital letter is used.

the Greeks believed, was a bad omen, a fact which Leonardo da Vinci depicted in 'The Last Supper' to presage Christ's fate."[21]

Leonardo probably gave more attention to Judas's face than he did to his actions. For over a year he searched for a model for Judas among the lowest riffraff in the slums of Milan.[22] It is reported that he drew over forty studies of models before he finally drew Judas.[23] In "The Last Supper" Judas has an "evil, vulture-like profile" and "a shifty glance."[24] The muscles of the neck are taut, the face and the forehead are wrinkled, the nose curves downward toward the mouth, the corners of the mouth droop, the lower lip protrudes, and the chin juts outward. Dr. Von Hefele has stated that Judas's left hand

> is stretched out in a peculiar way, as if he would grasp something. This left hand, too, follows a quite different direction from his eye; truly thievish, the eye watches whether any one sees the evil attempt of the hand. Cardinal Wiseman supposed that Judas was aiming at the best and largest piece of bread which lay near his left hand. His look, not without fear and horror, is turned toward Christ; and it is very possible that the peculiar gesture of the left hand is meant to express this fear, and no intent of grasping.[25]

The conclusion or summary restates the general theme of the paper and represents the student's best judgment after his study of the painting and of the writings of authorities used in his research.

Now compare this paper with the outline on page 370, from which it was written. Consider organization, transitions, and topic sentences and their development. Can you find any evidences of more or less emphasis on any of the topics and subtopics, in their relation to the whole, in the actual writing of the paper, than the student anticipated when he prepared his outline?

8

After "The Last Supper" was restored by Mauro Pelliccioli in 1954, a writer for _Time_ called Leonardo "perhaps the most skilled painter who ever lived. . . . he could bind many different things, men and emotions into one unchanging harmony."[26] In "The Last Supper" Leonardo showed the conflict between Christ and Judas, between good and evil. The proportion of the painting and the portrait of Christ were most brilliantly done, but the portrayal of Judas was perhaps the most difficult problem. Leonardo solved it so well that those who look at the painting can understand how the completely evil may look in the presence of divine goodness.

FOOTNOTE FORM

Footnotes may be grouped in a separate section at the end of the paper and before the bibliography, or they may be placed at the bottom of the page on which the reference occurs. Both styles are used in scholarly journals. Since placement at the bottom of the page requires a good deal of experiment and practice in planning the typed page, the separate section has some advantages for first papers. If your instructor wishes you to place your footnotes at the bottom of the page of occurrence, follow the form shown here for set-up and spacing, but separate the footnotes from the text by a short ruled line starting at the left-hand margin and placed far enough below the last line of the text so that it will not be mistaken for an underline to indicate italics.

Start a new page and head it FOOTNOTES, in capital letters, centered, just as you would a title. Triple-space beneath this heading; that is, leave two blank lines and start the first entry on the third line.

Place footnote numbers slightly above the line. Do not space after the number.

Indent the first line of every footnote five spaces (four spaces for footnote numbers of two digits); do not indent succeeding lines.

Double-space between footnotes; that is, leave one blank line. Single-space within footnotes.

The author's name appears in normal order, the given name before the surname.

Footnote 1 refers to the third volume of a four-volume work. Notice that there are two authors. Notice also that when both volume and page number are given, the abbreviations "Vol." (volume) and "p." or "pp." (page, pages) are omitted.

Footnote 2 refers to a periodical article translated from an article in a foreign journal. The given name of Von Hefele was not used by *The Eclectic Magazine.*

Footnote 3 shows how to cite a quotation taken from another source. When you are able to find the original source, you should use and cite that. This footnote also illustrates the form for a book with a subtitle.

(continued on page 398)

9

FOOTNOTES

[1]John Denison Champlin, Jr., and Charles C. Perkins, eds., Cyclopedia of Painters and Paintings (New York, 1913), III, 28-32.

[2]Von Hefele, "The 'Last Supper' of Leonardo da Vinci," trans. from the Theologische Quartalschrift, The Eclectic Magazine, New Series, VI (December 1867), 690.

[3]Leonardo da Vinci, quoted by Kenneth Clark, Leonardo da Vinci: An Account of His Development as an Artist (Cambridge [England], 1939), p. 99.

[4]John xiii.21.

[5]Ludwig H. Heydenreich, Leonardo da Vinci (New York, 1954), I, 38.

[6]Von Hefele, p. 690.

[7]Ibid., p. 691.

[8]Antonina Vallentin, Leonardo da Vinci: The Tragic Pursuit of Perfection, trans. E. W. Dickes (New York, 1938), p. 228.

[9]Clark, p. 99.

[10]Heydenreich, p. 38.

[11]Vallentin, p. 228.

[12]Ibid.

[13]Champlin and Perkins, III, 28-32.

Footnotes 4, 16, 17, 19, and 20 illustrate references to books of the Bible. Notice that the name of the book is not italicized. Biblical references of this kind are not included in the bibliography.

Footnotes 6, 9, 10, 13, 15, 22, 24, and 25 illustrate the short form of reference to a work previously cited. To distinguish between authors of the same surname, use first names or initials also. When you use two books by the same author, give the titles also in subsequent references; you may use a shortened form of the title.

Footnote 7 shows how "ibid." (meaning "in the same place") is used in a reference to the same work (but a different page) cited in the immediately preceding footnote. "Ibid." is preferably not underlined (italicized).

Footnote 8 shows how to enter the translator of a work.

Footnote 12 shows how "ibid." is used to refer to the same work and the same page cited in the immediately preceding footnote.

Footnote 14 is a reference to a volume published as part of a series.

Footnote 18 is a reference to an encyclopedia. You may find the author at the end of the article, or listed at the front or back of the volume, or in the volume containing the index. Compare footnote 1; in the work listed there, authors of individual entries or articles were not given. Multi-volume dictionaries and encyclopedias are often published over a term of years; it is sufficient to give the date of the volume you use.

Footnote 21 is the simplest possible first reference to an article in a periodical.

Footnote 23 is the simplest possible first reference to a book.

Footnote 26 refers to an article which is anonymous or written by the "staff" of a periodical.

10

[14]Leonardo da Vinci, _Thoughts on Art and Life_, trans. Maurice Baring, The Humanists' Library (Boston, 1906), p. 138.

[15]Clark, p. 100.

[16]John xiii.29.

[17]John xii.4-6.

[18]A. E. Crawley, "Metals and Minerals," _Encyclopaedia of Religion and Ethics_, ed. James Hastings, VIII (New York, 1916), 592.

[19]Edward Hull, "Salt," _A Dictionary of the Bible_, ed. James Hastings, IV (Edinburgh, 1906), 355. See also Numbers xviii.19 and II Chronicles xiii.5.

[20]Matthew v.13.

[21]Bertram Vogel, "Salt, Health, and Disease," _Tomorrow_, X (June 1951), 37.

[22]Vallentin, p. 225.

[23]Otho Pearre Fairfield, _The Italian Renaissance in Art_ (New York, 1928), p. 254.

[24]Vallentin, p. 228.

[25]Von Hefele, p. 691.

[26]"The True 'Last Supper,'" _Time_, LXIV (October 4, 1954), 74.

BIBLIOGRAPHICAL FORM

Start the bibliography on a new page, as a separate section of your paper, after the section of footnotes. Head the page BIBLIOGRAPHY, in capital letters, centered. Triple-space below the heading.

Do not indent the first line of an entry; indent succeeding lines five spaces.

Double-space between entries; single-space within an entry.

List only those sources actually used in your paper and referred to in footnotes.

Authors are listed with surname first. If a book has more than one author, however, the names of all authors after the first one are put in normal order.

List entries alphabetically. When more than one book by the same author is listed, use a one-inch line in place of the author's name in entries after the first. An entry without an author (for example, an unsigned magazine article) is listed alphabetically by the first word.

List the inclusive pages of articles.

Notice that the important divisions of entries for books are separated by periods; those for articles have a period after the author's name, commas to separate the other divisions of the entry.

A bibliographical entry should include all the information that will enable the reader to find the source readily if he wishes to do so.

Study the various kinds of entries in this bibliography and on page 376, and note especially the differences between forms for books, articles, and encyclopedias.

11

BIBLIOGRAPHY

Champlin, John Denison, Jr., and Charles C. Perkins, eds. Cyclopedia of Painters and Paintings. 4 vols. New York, 1913. Vol. III.

Clark, Kenneth. Leonardo da Vinci: An Account of His Development as an Artist. Cambridge [England], 1939.

Crawley, A. E. "Metals and Minerals," Encyclopaedia of Religion and Ethics, ed. James Hastings, VIII (New York, 1916), 588-593.

Fairfield, Otho Pearre. The Italian Renaissance in Art. New York, 1928.

Heydenreich, Ludwig H. Leonardo da Vinci. 2 vols. New York, 1954.

Hull, Edward. "Salt," A Dictionary of the Bible, ed. James Hastings, IV (Edinburgh, 1906), 355.

Leonardo da Vinci. Thoughts on Art and Life, trans. Maurice Baring. The Humanists' Library. Boston, 1906.

"The True 'Last Supper,'" Time, LXIV (October 4, 1954), 74-78.

Vallentin, Antonina. Leonardo da Vinci: The Tragic Pursuit of Perfection, trans. E. W. Dickes. New York, 1938.

Vogel, Bertram. "Salt, Health, and Disease," Tomorrow, X (June 1951), 37-40.

Von Hefele. "The 'Last Supper' of Leonardo da Vinci," trans. from the Theologische Quartalschrift, The Eclectic Magazine, New Series, VI (December 1867), 687-693.

Clear Thinking

THE QUALITY of a piece of expository or argumentative writing depends to a great extent on the range, relevancy, and value of its factual content and on the clarity, logic, and validity of the thinking which the writer brings to bear upon his materials.

78/Avoiding Common Errors in Content and Thought

In the process of writing, many errors may creep in — both of fact and of thinking. Errors of fact shake your reader's confidence in you if he detects them; they misinform and mislead him if he does not. And faulty logic may give rise to serious misunderstandings, even when both writer and reader have the best intentions. The following sections are designed to help you think logically, express facts and thoughts accurately and fully, and avoid the difficulties that result from fuzzy or erroneous thinking.

78a/Use only accurate and verified data.

All figures, dates, and other factual data should be correct. Otherwise, the information may result in a faulty conclusion. If the factual material which you present as evidence is inaccurate and unreliable, you are inviting your reader to believe what is not true. At best, you will be guilty of failure to verify your data; at worst, of deliberate deception.

Errors of fact, committed through carelessness, ignorance, or dishonesty, lead to distrust and doubt. If the reader can disprove one thing which is stated as a fact, he will be likely to doubt the accuracy of a conclusion based on it. Further, he will be suspicious of other statements presented as facts.

The following statements, for example, are immediately suspect because of errors of fact which they contain:

1. Shakespeare's language seems old-fashioned to us because he lived in the Middle Ages. (Shakespeare lived in the Renaissance, long after the Middle Ages.)

2. Arthur Smith told the committee that he had broken with the Communist Party on June 31, 1935. (Thirty days hath June.)

3. Intelligent people do not buy paperback books. (The facts will not bear out this contention.)

78b/Use only reliable authority.

The findings of someone else are authoritative — that is, acceptable as fact or evidence — only if they are true. How can you decide whether a source of information is reliable, as it is your responsibility to do when you accept and make use of its statements? This kind of evaluation is not an easy task, and you may need some help at first from your instructor. Here are some points to consider:

1. What is the reputation of the writer or the work in the given field? The opinions of other writers on the subject, the comments in annotated bibliographies, and, for more recent works, the critical reviews which you can find by using the *Book Review Digest* will give you some basis for forming your judgment.

2. Is the writer a specialist on *this* subject? A competent specialist in one field may not be an authority in other fields. A scientist whose word on nuclear energy is definitive is not necessarily an authority on foreign affairs. A sports

writer who can be cited with confidence on the history of the World Series may be highly unreliable on the history of art.

3. How objective is the source? If it strikes you as biased or prejudiced or one-sided in any way, or is so described by others, you would do well to check it against other works on the same subject. Two biographies of the same man may give two very different pictures of him.

4. Are you distinguishing fact from opinion? You may be justified in accepting the factual information of a source, but not the conclusions the writer draws. If you are presenting an opinion, moreover, be sure to label it as such and not present it as though it were a fact.

5. If up-to-dateness is important, are you using a source which gives you the latest available information? Consider the date of publication of your source with this point in mind. Sometimes the information of an earlier reliable source is superseded by later findings.

78c/Avoid sweeping generalizations.

Even when the facts are accurate, they may be numerically too insignificant to support a generalization. If a person knows that three of his friends oppose capital punishment, he should not leap to the conclusion that "Everyone wishes to have capital punishment abolished." The statement is too broad for the evidence on which it is based. Such generalizations as the following may contain some elements of truth, but certainly they also contain elements of error:

Modern teen-agers have no respect for their parents.

People who smoke cigarettes have cancer.

College professors are absent-minded.

Businessmen are not interested in the arts.

Generalizations about "everybody" or "people who" or groups (like teen-agers or professors or businessmen) are tempting and easy, but they are usually inaccurate because they are too sweeping.

78d/Use enough specific evidence to prove the point.

If the conclusions are not based upon an examination of sufficient information, the content of the entire paper may be of doubtful validity. Every scientist is careful to see that his conclusions are founded on sufficient data arrived at through careful study of the findings of others and through his own painstaking experimentation. In the same way, the writer of an expository paper should accumulate enough evidence to justify the point he is making. Naturally, he may not be able to give all the relevant supportive facts in a short paper. But he can present enough to show that his conclusions have been responsibly reached.

78e/Use typical, representative instances and examples.

Guard against basing your conclusions on the unrepresentative, the atypical. Ultimately it may be true that everything is unique, is in some way different from everything else. Yet, broadly speaking, there is the representative, the typical — a typical freshman, a typical winter, a typical executive. The type is arrived at through examining many individual instances and determining what all or most of them have in common. It is based, we say, on a wide sampling of particular cases. To cite only examples of corruption in public office and conclude from them that "A typical public official is as crooked as a rattlesnake" is to base a conclusion on the exceptional rather than the typical. To cite Professor Dalrymple's interest in feminine endings in poetry as proof that "All university professors are interested in inconsequential things" is to use the odd or unique rather than the representative instance to support your argument.

78f/Stick to the point.

Do not introduce irrelevancies or wander off the subject. Except in the most informal of personal essays, digression is a sign of inability to focus attention on the problem at hand. A discussion of the artistry of a poet, for example, might be irrelevant in a treatment of his social theories. First paragraphs of themes and research papers are sometimes irrelevant because they begin at a point too far removed from the main subject of the paper. Thus in a discussion of the morals of the Prohibition era, it is hardly necessary to begin with a historical survey of moral and political decline in the latter days of the Roman Empire.

78g/Consider conflicting facts or evidence.

You should always be aware of facts and instances which may seem to refute your own views and conclusions, and you must be prepared to deal with them. You can actually strengthen your case by taking opposing evidence into consideration and showing why it is inadequate or invalid. You may show that certain facts do not really contradict your position, because they are insignificant, irrelevant, or exceptional. You may anticipate objections and answer them in advance by showing that they are based on outmoded, disproved, or false assumptions. An argument in favor of intercollegiate athletics, for example, might admit that there are, certainly, instances of corruption, but maintain that these are exceptional and that on the whole an extramural athletic program serves a college well in terms of education and public relations.

78h/Do not beg the question or reason in a circle.

A writer begs the question when he assumes that something is true and writes as if he had proved it. Here is an example:

A large part of the taxpayer's educational dollar is spent on unnecessary items like school lunchrooms, classes for handicapped children, and instruction in art and music.

That the educational items mentioned are "unnecessary" ones is a debatable proposition which the writer does not establish but merely asserts. Suppose he defends it, when challenged, as follows:

These items are unnecessary because they are "extras," and "extras" are things that are not needed.

He is still begging the question because he is simply restating the proposition in terms of itself. To assert that Mary is not pretty because she is unattractive, or that Donald's argument is unsound because it is illogical, is to beg the question. This kind of unsupported statement leads to circular reasoning, as illustrated in the following sentences:

Anyone who watches television regularly knows that the programs are shallow and superficial, for they do nothing to stimulate the mind. I have watched for hours on end without encountering any new ideas. Technically, the medium is advanced and mature; but as far as programming is concerned, television fails to challenge the viewer's mental powers because it is not profound.

In other words, television is shallow because it does not stimulate the mind, and it does not stimulate the mind because it is shallow. The writer of these sentences has gone around in a circle and has begged the question by ending where he began.

78i/Do not omit essential steps in the thought or draw false conclusions from unstated assumptions.

The omission of basic details in a sequence of actions or events or of essential steps in a train of thought may leave the reader puzzled or confused. Some elementary or obvious steps may be skipped when a specialist is writing for specialists; but the more general the audience, the fewer the steps that may be omitted. The problem here is one of clarity, rather than logic.

A logical fallacy, however, results whenever the omission or concealment of a step in the reasoning leads to a false conclusion. If one argues, for example, that "He cannot be elected to Phi Beta Kappa because he is a football player," the argument is based on a hidden — and false — assumption: that no football player ever makes good grades, or that Phi Beta Kappa will refuse to elect someone who plays football. Similar omissions of parts of the argument occur in the following sentences. What are the unstated assumptions, and why are the conclusions false?

Since he made good grades in high school, he will undoubtedly be a good student in college.

He will not make a good judge because he was once fined for speeding.

He has a wonderful personality and will certainly be successful as a salesman.

78j/Do not attempt to substitute an appeal to the emotions for an appeal to reason.

When supported by logic, emotional appeal has its proper place, but it should never be substituted for logical thinking.

Name calling is an appeal to prejudice. Do not becloud an issue by calling an opponent a hick, an egghead, or a moron. This is argument against a man rather than against a principle or a point of view.

"Loaded" words are emotional words designedly used to shape an attitude through prejudice instead of reason. In "loaded" terms a government subsidy plan might become a "hand-out scheme that a bunch of radical do-gooders are trying to fasten on the taxpayers," or a budgetary proposal might be characterized as a "reactionary attempt to turn the clock back to the economics of the McKinley era." Colorful, emotion-arousing words have their place in good writing — but not when they are used as epithets in place of evidence or reasons.

Flattery appeals to the emotions in its attempt to persuade through excessive praise. The political candidate who tells an audience that he knows they will vote for him because of their high intelligence is attempting to convince by flattering. So, more subtly, is the writer who states that any impartial person will agree with the point he is making.

Snob appeal asserts that one should adopt a certain view because all the better people do — including, of course, the writer. "More doctors smoke El Ropo than any other cigar" is a favorite form of fallacious advertising.

Mass appeal attempts to persuade by asserting that everyone follows the pattern favored by the writer. It suggests that one should not be different from the herd: everyone ought to go to college, everyone ought to own his home, everyone ought to read the best-seller *Magnolia Hall*. The assumption is that if one does not do what everyone else does he deserves to be censured or ostracized.

78k/Do not draw unwarranted conclusions about cause and effect.

When two things happen in sequence, the second thing is not necessarily caused by the first. If a man walks under a ladder and shortly thereafter loses his wallet, he is not justified in assuming that he lost his wallet *because* he walked under the ladder. If one feels better *after* taking a pill, it is not necessarily *because* one took the pill. A student's failure in college after working as a laborer during the summer does not prove that hard physical work has an adverse effect on mental activity. To show a cause-and-effect relationship between two events, it is necessary to produce evidence in addition to the mere fact that one has preceded the other.

78l/Express ideas with moderation.

Be temperate in your judgments and in your choice of words. Overstatement, overemphasis, and dogmatic assertion not only irritate most readers but arouse doubt and disbelief. The good writer knows better than to be cocksure and brash. He is careful to state that something "usually" happens in a particular situation, that a given result occurs "in most cases," and that an outcome will "probably" be a happy one or "perhaps" a disastrous one.

78m/Allow for adequate alternatives.

On some questions it is faulty logic to assume that there are *two and only two* alternatives. Often there are a number of possibilities. If, for example, a father tells his son that he must go to college or else fail in life, he has not allowed for the possibility that the son may succeed without a college education. It is tempting, because dramatic, to present things in terms of two extremes, but a simple *either-or* proposition of this kind is not always valid.

EXERCISE

Point out the errors in content and thought in each of the following.

1. Happiness is derived only from one's dealings with other people. Thus a hermit cannot have true happiness.

2. Happiness is a state of mind which results from comfort and ease.

3. The neighbor who keeps an eye on the newly planted lawn when the folks next door are away can be sure that they will do the same for him.

4. The first real basis for moral standards was the Ten Commandments.

5. A well-written theme must be in chronological order.

6. Everyone believes that we should not kill. Capital punishment is killing. Thus capital punishment should be universally abolished.

7. Mr. Pompey took three doses of Elixir of Pine and his arthritis was gone in two days. If you really wish to get rid of your rheumatism, you will try this new wonder medicine.

8. To be a gentleman is to be a Christian.

9. During the depression of the 1930's there was some suffering, but relatively few people went bankrupt. The worker's family sometimes suffered from hunger and cold, but what he already had was his own. The situation would be otherwise if we were to have a depression now. Since the last depression, Americans have discovered installment buying, and everyone would go bankrupt if we were to have another depression.

10. European and Asian countries lack resources because they lack the money it would take to create natural resources.

11. The value of π is 3.145.

12. One hundred percent red-blooded Americanism means that I have the right to poke anyone in the nose if he criticizes what I like.

13. This mountain is God's most beautiful work of art.

14. Many leaders of schools in the United States have the idea that fraternities tend to lower the scholarship level of the school. This is absolutely wrong. Such leaders are dishonest. A boy must first prove his scholastic ability to be average or above average before he is considered eligible for membership in a fraternity. This requirement serves as an incentive for the boy to do good work.

15. Truck driving is the most fascinating job in the world.

16. Being able to drive has afforded me more real pleasure and has meant more to me than any other thing I can think of.

17. Last spring I began raising chickens. The first tiny chicks to hatch filled me with joy and sent my heart soaring to new heights of ecstasy.

18. There are so many Communists in this country that we must either revoke the right of freedom of speech or give up the fight and recognize the fact that we are being defeated from within.

19. When there is a need for civic activities, American women, who are more responsible than the men, never fail to fulfill the need.

20. Only a fool and a coward succumbs to the allurements of the enemy while he is a prisoner of war.

21. Socialized medicine has been extremely successful in England. We are stupid because we have not adopted socialized medicine in America.

22. The American Medical Association strongly opposes socialized medicine. You should therefore vote against it.

GLOSSARY

OF USAGE

Glossary of Usage

LISTED HERE in alphabetical order are a number of words and expressions that often cause difficulty. Consult this glossary frequently; it can be a great help to you, not only in giving you specific information, but in making you aware of and sensitive to levels of usage. Many items not listed here are covered in other sections of this book, especially those on diction, spelling, and style. For words found neither in this glossary nor in the index, consult an up-to-date unabridged dictionary.

79/Glossary of Usage

A, an Use *a* as an article before consonant sounds; use *an* as an article before vowel sounds.

a house	an hour
(the *h* is sounded)	(the *h* is not sounded)
a historical novel	
(though the British say *an*)	
a union	an uncle
(long *u* has the consonant	
sound of *y*)	
a nickname	an ordinary thing

Accept, except As a verb, *accept* means *to receive; except* means *to exclude. Except* as a preposition also means *but.*

Every legislator *except* Mr. Whelling refused to *accept* the bribe.

We will *except* (i.e., exclude) this novel from the list of those to be read.

Accidently A misspelling usually caused by mispronunciation. Use *accidentally*.

Ad Colloquial; a clipped form of *advertisement*.

Affect, effect *Affect* is a verb meaning *to act upon* or *to influence*. *Effect* may be a verb or a noun. *Effect* as a verb means *to cause* or *to bring about; effect* as a noun means *a result, a consequence*.

The patent medicine did not *affect* (influence) the disease.
The operation did not *effect* (bring about) an improvement in his health.
The drug had a drastic *effect* (consequence) on the speed of the patient's reactions.

Aggravate Colloquial or dialectal in the sense of *annoy*, *irritate*, or *pester*. Properly, it means *to make worse or more severe*.

Agree to, agree with *Agree to* a thing (plan, proposal). *Agree with* a person.

He *agreed to* the insertion of the plank in the platform of the party.
He *agreed with* Senator Stenner that the plank would not gain many votes.

Ain't Illiterate in most uses.

All ready, already *All ready* means *prepared, in a state of readiness; already* means *before some specified time* or *previously*, and describes an action that is completed.

The hunters were *all ready* to take horse. (Fully prepared)

Mr. Bowman had *already* bagged his limit of quail for the day. (Action completed at time of statement)

All together, altogether *All together* describes a group as a⌣ ⌐ng or existing collectively; *altogether* means *wholly, entirely.*

The sprinters managed to start *all together.*

I do not *altogether* approve the decision.

Allusion, illusion An *allusion* is a casual reference. An *illusion* is a false or misleading impression.

Alright Not considered proper for *all right.*

A.M., P.M. To be used only with figures, as in "6:00 P.M." Not to be used for *morning* or *afternoon* as in "The wreck occurred this P.M."

Among, between *Among* refers to three or more persons or things; *between* usually refers to only two.

It will be hard to choose between Terry and Jim.

It will be hard to choose among so many well-qualified candidates.

Amount, number *Amount* refers to a mass or quantity; *number* refers to things which may be counted.

That is a large *number* of turtles for a pond which has such a small *amount* of water.

An See **A.**

And etc. The *and* is unnecessary; *etc.* means *and so forth* (literally, *et cetera,* "and other things").

419

Anyplace   Prefer *anywhere*.

Anyways   Prefer *anyway*.

Anywheres   Nonstandard. Use *anywhere*.

As   Not equivalent to *that* or *whether*.

> NONSTANDARD   Mr. Snipes did not know *as* the answer was correct.
>
> STANDARD   Mr. Snipes did not know *that* (or *whether*) the answer was correct.

Awful   A trite and feeble substitute for *bad, shocking, ludicrous, ugly,* etc.

Awhile, a while   *Awhile* is an adverb; *a while* is an article and a noun.

> Stay *awhile*.
> Wait here for *a while*.

Balance   Except in a context of money and banking, colloquial for *remainder* or *rest*.

> PREFERRED   He spent the *rest* of the hour looking over his notes.
>
> COLLOQUIAL   He spent the *balance* of the hour looking over his notes.

Because   See **Reason is because.**

Being as, being that   Nonstandard for *because* or *since*.

Beside, besides   *Beside* means *by the side of, next to; besides* means *in addition to*.

> Mr. Potts was sitting *beside* the coffin.
> No one was in the room *besides* Mr. Potts.

Between   See **Among.**

Between each   Illogical; omit *each*.

>   *Between classes* (not *between each class*) the students gathered
>   in excited groups

Between you and I   Nonstandard affectation for *between
you and me*.

Bust, busted, bursted   See page 40.

But, hardly, only, scarcely   Preferably not used with another negative.

AVOID	did not have but one
	can't help but realize
	can't hardly realize
	wasn't there only two weeks
	did not have scarcely enough
PREFER	had but one, had only one
	can't help realizing
	can hardly realize
	was there only two weeks
	had scarcely enough, had hardly enough

Can, may   In formal English, *can* is used to denote ability;
may, to denote permission. Colloquially the two are interchangeable.

FORMAL   *May* (not *can*) I go?

Cannot hardly, can't hardly   Double negatives. See **But,
hardly, only, scarcely.**

Cannot help but, can't help but   Double negatives. See
But, hardly, only, scarcely.

Capital, capitol   *Capital* designates a city; *capitol* designates
a building.

Center around Illogical. Use *center in* (or *on*) or *cluster around*.

Compare to, compare with After *compare* in similes, use *to;* in analyses of similarities and differences, use *with*.

> He *compared* the wrecked train *to* strewn and broken matches.
> He *compared* this train wreck *with* the one that occurred a month ago.

Complected Dialectal or colloquial. Use *complexioned*.

Considerable Basically an adjective, though used colloquially as a noun. Illiterate when used as an adverb.

STANDARD   He had a *considerable* influence on his students.

COLLOQUIAL   He made *considerable* each week.

ILLITERATE   The horse tired *considerable* on the last lap. (Use *considerably*.)

Contact Generally considered colloquial when used as a verb meaning *to get in touch with*. In writing, prefer a verb such as *write, interview, speak with*.

Continual, continuous *Continual* refers to a prolonged and rapid succession; *continuous* refers to an uninterrupted succession.

Could of See **Of**.

Couple *A couple of* is colloquial for *a few* or *several*. Properly, *couple* designates two, a pair.

Curricula, curricular Use only *curricular* as an adjective, as in "*extracurricular* activities." *Curricula* is a noun, the plural of *curriculum*.

Cute Colloquial and overused for such expressions as *pretty, dainty, attractive*.

Data A plural form, sometimes treated as a collective noun and used as a singular form. The true singular (*datum*) is rarely used.

FORMAL   These data have been carefully analyzed.

POSSIBLE   The complete data is now being reviewed.

Date Although considered colloquial for *appointment* or *social engagement* (usually with a person of the opposite sex) or for the *young man* or *young lady* with whom the engagement is made, the word *date* has no formal equivalents which are always acceptable and appropriate in these uses.

Deal Colloquial and overused for *bargain, transaction,* or *business arrangement.*

Didn't ought, hadn't ought Nonstandard for *ought not, should not, shouldn't.*

Differ from, differ with   *Differ from* expresses unlikeness; *differ with* expresses disagreement.

The twins *differ from* each other in personality.

The twins *differ with* each other about politics.

Different than   Prefer *different from.*

Done Past participle of *do.* Illiterate when used in place of *did,* as the past tense of *do:* "He *did* it," not "He *done* it."

Don't Contraction of *do not;* not to be used for *doesn't,* the contraction of *does not.*

Due to Not to be used as part of an adverbial phrase in formal English; should be avoided at the beginning of a sentence. *Due* is adjectival in origin, and *due to* is acceptable in adjectival uses.

NOT PREFERRED   *Due to* his sore arm, he could not pitch.
PREFERRED   *Because of* (or *on account of*) his sore arm, he could not pitch.

NOT PREFERRED   He was absent *due to* his sunburn.
PREFERRED
(as adjective)   His absence was *due to* his sunburn.

Effect   See **Affect.**

Enthused   Colloquial. Use *is* (or *was*) *enthusiastic.*

Equally as   The *as* is unnecessary. Instead of "*equally as* good," use "*equally* good" (or "just as good" or "as good as").

Etc.   See **And etc.**

Ever, every   Use *every* in *every other, everybody, every now and then;* use *ever* in *ever and anon, ever so humble.* (*Every so often* is colloquial for *every now and then.*)

Every day, everyday   *Every day* is used as an adverb; *everyday*, as an adjective.

He comes to look at the same picture in the gallery *every day.*
His trip to the gallery is an *everyday* occurrence.

Exam   Colloquial. Use *examination* in formal writing.

Except   See **Accept.**

Expect   Colloquial for *believe, suspect, think, suppose*, etc.

Farther, further   Generally interchangeable, though many persons prefer *farther* in expressions of physical distance and *further* in expressions of time, quantity, and degree.

My car used less gasoline and went *farther* than his.

The second speaker went *further* into the issues than the first speaker.

Fellow   Colloquial for *young man*, *person*, or *sweetheart*.

Fewer, less   Use *fewer* to denote number; *less*, to denote amount or degree.

> Because of the late frost, *fewer* (not *less*) peaches will be shipped from the state this year.
>
> *Less* paving was done in April than in February.
>
> With *fewer* advertisers, there will be *less* income from advertising.

Fine   Often a poor substitute for a more exact word of approval or commendation.

Fix   Colloquial for the noun *predicament*. As a verb, some consider it colloquial for the verb *to repair;* the basic, formal meaning is *to fasten in position*.

Flunk   Colloquial. Prefer *fail* or *failure* in formal usage.

Folks   Colloquial for *family* or *relatives*.

Funny   Colloquial for *strange*, *remarkable*, or *peculiar*. Standard for *amusing* or *comical*.

Further   See **Farther**.

Good   Incorrect as an adverb. See page 74.

Grand   Often vaguely used in place of more exact words like *majestic*, *magnificent*, *imposing*, etc.

Guy   Colloquial or slang as a noun for *a person* or as a verb meaning *to make fun of*.

Had of　Illiterate. Use *had*.

> I wish I *had* (not *had of*) known he was going.

Had ought　Illiterate for *should*.

Hadn't ought　See **Didn't ought**.

Hang, hanged, hung　See page 41.

Hardly　See **But, hardly, only, scarcely**.

Has got, have got　Wordy. Use simply *has* or *have*.

Himself　See **Myself**.

Hisself　Illiterate for *himself*.

Humans　Prefer *human beings*.

If, whether　Alternatives are introduced by *whether* more often than by *if*. In formal usage *whether* is always preferred to *if* after verbs of asking, saying, knowing, doubting, and wondering.

> Sue is undecided *whether* it would be better to look for a job now or to wait until June.
>
> I doubt *whether* you will enjoy that book.

Illusion　See **Allusion**.

Imply, infer　*Imply* means to hint or suggest; *infer* means to draw a conclusion.

> The speaker *implied* that Mr. Falkner was guilty.
>
> The audience *inferred* that Mr. Falkner was guilty.

In, into　*Into* denotes motion from the outside to the inside; *in* denotes position (enclosure).

> The lion was *in* the cage when Mr. Funkle walked *into* the main tent.

In back of   Colloquial for *behind*.

Infer   See **Imply**.

In regards to   Unidiomatic. Use *in regard to* or *with regard to*.

Into   See **In**.

Irregardless   Nonstandard for *regardless*.

Is when, is where   Ungrammatical use of adverbial conjunction after a linking verb. Often misused in definitions and explanations.

NONSTANDARD   Combustion *is when* (or *is where*) oxygen unites with other elements.

STANDARD   Combustion occurs when oxygen unites with other elements.

STANDARD   Combustion is a union of oxygen with other elements.

Its, it's   *Its* is the possessive case of the pronoun *it; it's* is a contraction of *it is*.

It's exciting to parents when their baby cuts *its* first tooth.

Kind of, sort of   Colloquial as adverbs. Use *rather, somewhat*, etc.

COLLOQUIAL   Mr. Josephson was *sort of* disgusted.

FORMAL   Mr. Josephson was *rather* disgusted.

FORMAL (not an adverb)   What *sort of* book is that?

Kind of a, sort of a   Delete the *a*; use *kind of* and *sort of*.

What *kind of* (not *kind of a*) pipe do you smoke?

Lay, lie   See page 42.

Learn, teach *Learn* means *to acquire knowledge. Teach* means *to impart knowledge.*

> He could not *learn* how to work the problem until Mr. Smithers *taught* him the formula.

Less See **Fewer.**

Liable See **Likely.**

Lie See page 42.

Like Prefer *like* as a preposition; prefer *as, as if,* or *as though* as a conjunction.

COLLOQUIAL	She acted *like* she had never been on the stage before.
FORMAL	She acted *as if* she had never been on the stage before.
FORMAL	She acted *like* a novice.

Likely, liable Use *likely* to express probability; *liable,* to express responsibility or obligation, often with legal connotations.

> You are *likely* to have an accident if you continue to drive so recklessly.
>
> Since your father owns the car, he will be *liable* for damages.

Locate A colloquialism when used for *settle.*

Loose A frequent misspelling of *lose. Loose* is an adjective; *lose* is a verb.

> She wore a *loose* and trailing gown.
>
> Speculators often *lose* their money.

Lot of, lots of Colloquial in the sense of *much, many, a great deal.*

May See **Can.**

May of   See **Of.**

Might of   See **Of.**

Most   Do not use *most* in place of the adverb *almost*.

> He is late for class *almost* (not *most*) every day.

Must of   See **Of.**

Myself, yourself, himself   These words are reflexives or intensives, not strict equivalents of *I, me, you, he, him*.

INTENSIVE	I *myself* helped Father cut the wheat.
	I helped Father cut the wheat *myself*.
REFLEXIVE	I cut *myself*.
LOOSE	The elopement was known only to Sherry and *myself*.
	Only Kay and *myself* had access to the safe.
PREFERRED	The elopement was known only to Sherry and *me*.
	Only Kay and *I* had access to the safe.

Nice   Often a poor substitute for more exact words like *attractive, modest, pleasant, kind*, etc.

No place   Use *nowhere*.

Nowheres   Dialectal. Use *nowhere*.

Number   See **Amount.**

Of   Illiterate for *have* in verb phrases like *might of, may of, could of, would of, should of*, etc.

Off of   *Off* is sufficient.

> He fell *off* (not *off of*) the water tower.

On a whole   Confusion of two constructions, *as a whole* and *on the whole*.

Only   See **But, hardly, only, scarcely.**

Ought to of   See **Of.**

Party   Colloquial when used to mean *person*, except in legal usage.

Per cent, percent   Use after figures, as "three *per cent*," "50 *per cent*." Do not use for *percentage:*

> Only a small *percentage* (not *percent*) of the class will fail.

Phenomena   Plural. The singular is *phenomenon.*

Plenty   Colloquial when used as an adverb.

COLLOQUIAL   The pet deer was *plenty* sick.

FORMAL   The pet deer was *very* sick.

P.M.   See **A.M.**

Principal, principle   Use *principal* to mean *the chief* or *most important.* Use *principle* to mean *a rule* or *a truth.*

> The *principal* reason for her delinquency was never discussed.
> The *principal* of Brookwood High School resigned.
> To act without *principle* leads to delinquency.

Prior to   Prefer *before.*

Proposition   Overused commercially and colloquially to mean *offer, plan, project, undertaking, idea,* etc.

Quite, quite a   Colloquial in the meaning of *very* or *to a considerable extent.*

COLLOQUIAL   *quite* pretty; *quite a* distance

FORMAL   *very* pretty, *rather* pretty; *a considerable* distance

Also, do not confuse the spelling of *quite* and *quiet.*

Raise, rise   See page 42.

Real   Colloquial as an adverb meaning *really* or *very*.

> He is *really* (not *real*) clever.

Reason is (was) because   Especially in writing, do not use for *the reason is that*.

> WRONG   The *reason* Abernathy enlisted *was because* he failed in college.
> (*Because* should introduce an adverbial clause, not a noun clause used as a predicate nominative.)
>
> RIGHT   The *reason* Abernathy enlisted *was that* he failed in college.
>
> RIGHT   Abernathy enlisted *because* he failed in college.

Respectfully, respectively   *Respectfully* means *with respect; respectively* means *each in the order given*.

> He *respectfully* thanked the president for his diploma.
>
> Crossing the platform, he passed *respectively* by the speaker, the dean, and the registrar.

Right   Dialectal or colloquial for *very* or *somewhat*, as in the expression "*right* tired."

Said   Not to be used in the sense of *previously mentioned*, except in a legal context (as in "The *said* object was found in the room of the accused").

Same   Rarely used as a pronoun unless it is preceded by *the*, except in legal style (as in "Drinking by minors is illegal and *same* shall result in arrest").

Scarcely   See **But, hardly, only, scarcely.**

Set, sit   See page 42.

Shall, will In formal English, to indicate simple futurity, *shall* is conventionally preferred in the first person (I *shall*, we *shall*); *will*, in the second and third persons (you *will*, he *will*, they *will*). To indicate determination, duty, or necessity, *will* is preferred in the first person (I *will*, we *will*); *shall*, in the second and third persons (you *shall*, he *shall*, they *shall*). These distinctions, however, are weaker than they used to be, and *will* is increasingly used in all persons.

Shape Colloquial for *condition*.

Should of See **Of.**

So For the use of *so* as an intensive, see page 93. The use of *so* for *so that* to express purpose is colloquial.

Someplace Use *somewhere*.

Sometime, some time *Sometime* is used adverbially to designate an indefinite point of time. *Some time* refers to a period or duration of time.

> I will see you *sometime* next week.
>
> I have not seen him for *some time*.
>
> *Some time* ago he wrote that he expected to arrive home *sometime* in June.

Somewheres Illiterate. Use *somewhere*.

Sort of See **Kind of.**

Sort of a See **Kind of a.**

Sure Colloquial as an adverb for *surely*, *certainly*.

> COLLOQUIAL   The speaker *sure* did criticize his opponent.
> FORMAL   The speaker *surely* criticized his opponent.

Sure and, try and   Colloquial for *sure to, try to.*

COLLOQUIAL   Be *sure and* notice the costumes of the Hungarian folk dancers.

FORMAL   Be *sure to* notice the costumes of the Hungarian folk dancers.

Suspicion   Dialectal as a verb. Use *suspect.*

Swell   Slang for *good;* often vaguely used for more exact words of approval.

Teach   See **Learn.**

Terrible   Should mean *dreadful.* Often a poor substitute for a more exact word.

Their, there   Not interchangeable. *Their* is the possessive of *they; there* is either an adverb meaning *in that place* or an expletive ("There is . . . ," "There are . . . .").

Their dachshund is sick.

There is a veterinarian's office in this block. (Expletive)

There it is on the corner. (Adverb of place)

These (those) kind, these (those) sort   *These (those)* is plural; *kind (sort)* is singular. Therefore use *this (that) kind, this (that) sort; these (those) kinds, these (those) sorts.*

Till, until   Do not use for *before* or *when.*

The students had hardly stopped laughing *when* (not *until*) the professor entered the room.

Try and   See **Sure and.**

Unique   Means *one of a kind;* hence may not logically be compared. *Unique* should not be loosely used for *unusual* or *strange.*

Until   See **Till.**

Use   Sometimes carelessly written for the past tense, *used.*

> Thomas Jefferson *used* (not *use*) to bathe his feet in cold water almost every morning.

Very   Should not directly precede a past participle. Use *very much admired* or *very greatly admired*, but not *very admired.*

Wait on   Unidiomatic for *wait for.* *Wait on* correctly means *to serve.*

Ways   Colloquial when used to designate a distance.

COLLOQUIAL   A long *ways*
FORMAL   A long *way*

Where   Do not misuse for *that.*

> I read in the newspaper *that* (not *where*) you saved a child's life.

Where at   The *at* is unnecessary.

NONSTANDARD   *Where* is he *at?*
STANDARD   *Where* is he?

Whether   See **If.**

While   Do not overuse for such other conjunctions as *but, and, whereas,* and *although.*

Whose, who's   *Whose* is the possessive of *who; who's* is a contraction of *who is.*

Without   Dialectal for *unless,* as in "I cannot come *without* you pay for the ticket."

Would of   See **Of.**

You all   Used colloquially in the South for the plural *you.*

INDEX

Correction Chart

(continued from inside front cover)

48 - 60
82 - 90
60 - 80
69 - 90